Sarah Hall
Critical Essays

Gylphi Contemporary Writers: Critical Essays

Series Editor: Sarah Dillon

Gylphi Contemporary Writers: Critical Essays presents a new approach to the academic study of living authors. The titles in this series are devoted to contemporary British, Irish and American authors whose work is popularly and critically valued but on whom a significant body of academic work has yet to be established. Each of the titles in this series is developed out of the best contributions to an international conference on its author; represents the most intelligent and provocative material in current thinking about that author's work; and, suggests future avenues of thought, comparison and analysis. With each title prefaced by an author foreword, this series embraces the challenges of writing on living authors and provides the foundation stones for future critical work on significant contemporary writers.

Sarah Hall
Critical Essays

edited by
Alexander Beaumont
and Elke D'hoker

A *Gylphi Limited* Book

First published in Great Britain in 2022
by Gylphi Limited

Copyright © Gylphi Limited, 2022

All rights reserved.

No part of this publication may be reproduced, stored in a retrieval system, or transmitted, in any form or by any means, without the prior permission in writing of the publisher, nor be otherwise circulated in any form or binding or cover other than that in which it is published and without a similar condition including this condition being imposed on the subsequent purchaser.

A CIP catalogue record for this book is available from the British Library.

ISBN 978-1-78024-104-3 (pbk)
ISBN 978-1-78024-105-0 (hbk)
ISBN 978-1-78024-106-7 (Kindle)
ISBN 978-1-78024-107-4 (EPUB)

Cover image by Mj, Lake District National Park, Ambleside, United Kingdom, September 13, 2020, LEICA CAMERA AG, LEICA Q2. Free to use under the Unsplash License.

Design and typesetting by Gylphi Limited. Printed by Amazon.

Gylphi Limited
PO Box 993
Canterbury CT1 9EP, UK

Series Titles

David Mitchell: Critical Essays (2011)
Edited by Sarah Dillon. Foreword by David Mitchell.

Maggie Gee: Critical Essays (2015)
Edited by Sarah Dillon and Caroline Edwards. Foreword by Maggie Gee.

China Miéville: Critical Essays (2015)
Edited by Caroline Edwards and Tony Venezia. Foreword by China Miéville.

Adam Roberts: Critical Essays (2016)
Edited by Christos Callow Jr. and Anna McFarlane. Foreword by Adam Roberts.

Rupert Thomson: Critical Essays (2016)
Edited by Rebecca Pohl and Christopher Vardy. Foreword by Rupert Thomson.

Tom McCarthy: Critical Essays (2016)
Edited by Dennis Duncan. Foreword by Tom McCarthy.

M. John Harrison: Critical Essays (2019)
Edited by Rhys Williams and Mark Bould. Foreword by M. John Harrison.

Nicola Barker: Critical Essays (2020)
Edited by Berthold Schoene. Foreword by Nicola Barker.

Michel Faber: Critical Essays (2020)
Edited by Rebecca Langworthy, Kristin Lindfield-Ott and Jim MacPherson. Foreword by Michel Faber.

Sarah Hall: Critical Essays (2022)
Edited by Alexander Beaumont and Elke D'hoker. Foreword by Sarah Hall.

Contents

Foreword   1
Sarah Hall

Introduction   5
Alexander Beaumont and Elke D'hoker

Chapter 1   31
REAL NATURE
Melanie Ebdon

Chapter 2   55
VITAL ANIMALS IN NIETZSCHE, GARNETT AND HALL
Elke D'hoker

Chapter 3   77
HOMO SAPIENS: BEING HUMAN IN *HOW TO PAINT A DEAD MAN* AND *THE WOLF BORDER*
Natalie Riley

Chapter 4   99
REWILDING WELFARE: SARAH HALL AND THE STATE OF NATURE
Pieter Vermeulen

Chapter 5   121
POST-BRITISH POLITICS AND SARAH HALL'S *NORTH*
Chloé Ashbridge

Chapter 6   149
BORDERLANDS: SPATIALIZING FEMINIST STRUGGLE IN SARAH HALL'S FICTION
Emilie Walezak

Chapter 7   173
LA FIABA OSCURA: NARRATING ITALY IN *How TO PAINT A DEAD MAN*
Francesca Pierini

Chapter 8   195
SARAH HALL'S MATERIAL IMAGINATION
Alexander Beaumont

Notes on Contributors   221

Index   223

Foreword

Sarah Hall

I've often said that fiction is my first language. It feels to be the best, most comfortable and accurate way for me to communicate, odd though this may sound. Over the years I have learned to try to explain my fiction, or assist with explanations, as authors are invited to do. Mostly, this feels like trying to describe a river that is fundamentally being and describing itself. I believe that what I write is manifest testament. Fiction holds its dimensions in a formulation that cannot be better expressed. I always imagine most writers feel like this, but perhaps not. And it's not to say I don't believe that others, skilled in their analytical literary fields, find dimensions and discussions about and around the work that reveal and enhance its substance, track and catalogue its greater combined mass and history. It's not to say that I don't register the processes of thought, mechanics, and creative preoccupations in my own work.

I hope I am professionally ambitious, and that my life is never commensurate to my work. As a writer, I think I am intelligent and considered and provocative. I try to be original and fearless, humane and truthful. I know I am a conduit, though I cannot register all that passes through me into fiction – and why would I want to? That is surely for a reader to recognize and respond to. On some innate level, I really don't want to know what I'm doing; I just want to do it. No, I just do it. I tend to do it even under extraordinary pressure, in prohibitive climates, at times when productivity might reasonably be expected to stop, which has always been a bit of a mystery, to me, and those around me.

To be invited to participate in the conference in Leuven was both surprising and galvanizing. The invitation seemed to suggest I was there in terms of career establishment and body of work, that people might now be widely studying my writing, that it had become an entity worth studying. Maybe I don't look up much. The truth is, the invitation came at a very difficult, myopic and limiting time in my life, in the wake of tragedy and during hardship. I ended up travelling with my elderly father and my very young daughter to attend the conference, and I spent less time participating than I would have liked. I probably presented as stressed and distressed, fatigued, somewhat lost from identifying with my profile, and less than professional.

Of course, the welcome was warm, kind and inclusive. My family was beautifully hosted and to meet international scholars, to discuss forms of literature and find cross-cultural meaning, was a delight, a reminder to look up. I had been invited to speak and read to a group of discerning academics. I'd prepared to painfully dust off my higher faculties, step out of the role of practitioner and into the role of self-expert (though I am not a self-expert). But I made a different choice. I read a very new short story called Sudden Traveller. The story is based around the traumatic events I had recently undergone, including bereavement. It's probably the most personal piece of fiction I've ever written. Not a great choice for a public reading, or for someone in my current state to present. What was I doing? Raising the cultured mask maybe. Disrobing. Disembowelling. Offering up the raw, creative core of the author – the barely cooled materials. But I read it, and, like the narrator who must carry her mother's coffin across a drowned cemetery, I did it without slipping or breaking down. This, I admit, told me something shocking about myself. When it comes to fiction, I am a brutal survivalist. Some programming allows it, enables it. I have never read the story out loud publicly again; I doubt I will. But in Leuven, in a room lambent with intelligence, curiosity and literary sensitivity, I arrived at a visceral understanding of my practice, and perhaps myself.

The component parts of whatever passes through me onto the page I do not wish to catalogue or investigate. I'm hugely grateful and humbled that others will and do. For my part, it is about the coffin on the shoulder, finding the exact formulation of words to sensualize and visualize and virtualize its phenomenology. Creating a moment, a scene, a living world, that lets the reader experience and understand. That is what and all I do.

Introduction

Alexander Beaumont and Elke D'hoker

Sarah Hall has enjoyed a prolific career since her debut, *Haweswater*, appeared in 2002, authoring another five novels – *The Electric Michelangelo* (2004), *The Carhullan Army* (2007), *How to Paint a Dead Man* (2009), *The Wolf Border* (2015) and *Burntcoat* (2021) – as well as three collections of short stories: *The Beautiful Indifference* (2011), *Madame Zero* (2017) and *Sudden Traveller* (2019). She appeared on Granta's list of 'Best Young British Novelists' in 2013 and, in 2016, was elected as a Fellow of the Royal Society of Literature. Hall has won a gamut of literary prizes including the BBC Short Story Award, the Edge Hill Short Story Prize, the John Llewellyn Rhys Prize, the James Tiptree Jr. Award, the Portico Prize for Fiction (twice) and the Commonwealth Writers Prize (in two categories); she has appeared on the Booker longlist twice and its shortlist once, and was on its judging panel in 2017. Her work has been widely reviewed in the British press since the publication of *The Electric Michelangelo* and internationally since *How to Paint a Dead Man*; *The Beautiful Indifference* was published to significant fanfare and *The Wolf Border* established her as an internationally recognized author.

Yet, despite mounting acclaim and an increasingly prominent media profile, scholarly engagement with Hall's work has taken some time to develop. On one level this is surprising, given that her career is coeval with the rapid expansion of contemporary literary studies as a field of scholarly enquiry, particularly in her native UK. Unlike some near-contemporaries such as Zadie Smith, Monica Ali, Jon McGregor and Hari Kunzru, whose first novels were also published in the early years of the twenty-first century, Hall was absent from the rush of critical surveys published in the second half of the 2000s (Bentley, 2008; Bradford, 2007; Tew, 2007; Tew and Mengham, 2006). A little more surprisingly – and unlike, say, Tom McCarthy – she is not mentioned in *The 2000s: A Decade of Contemporary British Fiction* (Bentley et al., 2015) and receives only fleeting attention in the second, updated edition of Peter Childs's (2012) *Contemporary Novelists: British Fiction Since 1970*. Nor does Dominic Head's voluminous *Cambridge History of the English Short Story* (2016) pay any attention to Hall's short fiction. The reasons for this must necessarily be the subject of speculative analysis; however, attempting to understand why Hall's work has not, until now, garnered significant scholarly attention is helpful in identifying the singularity and timeliness of her work.

As we discuss in this introduction, Hall's novels and short stories can be seen to inherit some of the dominant concerns that literary critics have identified in British literature of the later twentieth century. However, in other ways her work is recognizably discontinuous with them. It fits uneasily into the critical discourse surrounding postmodernism and its afterlives and does not appear to belong straightforwardly to one of the widely mooted 'returns' in literary fiction, either to modernism or to realism. In a narrower sense, it has little in common with the 'New Puritans' (Blincoe and Thorne, 2001) who were attracting critical attention at the outset of Hall's career. Moreover, though her work might be understood as a subtle contribution to the revision of cultural identity that took place within British literature at the turn of the millennium, it is not obviously postcolonial or cosmopolitan after the kind of fashion that has attracted critical attention in recent years (Schoene, 2009; Shaw, 2017). And while it demonstrates a sustained and increasingly explicit preoccupation with the material constitution of world, body and mind, it is not readily assimilated into the 'new atheist novel' (Bradley and Tate, 2010) that flourished in the UK during the 2000s; indeed, in many ways, Hall's work is quite at odds with the muscular – and masculinist – liberalism that has contributed to this genre. Yet, at the same time, neither does it neatly fit with contemporary strands of feminist writing. Though examples of period writing, either in part or *in toto*, *Haweswater*, *The Electric Michelangelo* and *How to Paint a Dead Man* do not participate in the 'her-story' tradition of feminist retelling, nor do female characters take centre stage by themselves. Feminist concerns are at the heart of *The Carhullan Army*, which earns the novel a brief discussion in the final volume of *The History of British Women's Writing* (Eagleton and Parker, 2015). Still, as this discussion shows, even feminist readers and critics find Hall's depiction of a women's army hard to grapple with.

Nevertheless, despite the seeming waywardness of Hall's work and its refusal to abide by the trends just listed, it has begun to receive more scholarly attention in recent years. Winning the BBC short story award in 2013 for 'Mrs Fox' established Hall more clearly in the public spotlight and the publication of *The Wolf Border* in 2015 produced significant media attention in the context of a broader public conversation about rewilding. In the wake of the acclaim that greeted *The Wolf Border*, academic engagement has finally become notable, with a steady flow of essays – some of them published in leading journals (Cottrell, 2019; Mealing, 2014; Walezak, 2019; Yang, 2018) – testifying to rapidly growing scholarly interest in her work. Indeed, it is in this period that Hall's writing has, for the first time, appeared in critical surveys of recent British fiction (Acheson, 2017; Eagleton and Parker, 2015; Lea, 2016).[1] One reason why it has taken until now for this to happen can be apprehended by noting how firm a grasp turn-of-the-millennium critical sensibilities have exercised over the Academy, even in such necessarily modish fields as contemporary literary studies. As Eileen Pollard and Berthold Schoene (2018: 1) have argued, 'the final two decades of the twentieth century no longer constitute an integral part of what we call the contemporary': fittingly, this last term now seems more appropriately applied to writers such as Hall.

Though some critics (Lea, 2016; Vice, 2017) have offered substantive overviews of Hall's *oeuvre* to date, the current volume is the first book-length analysis to be offered to readers both within and outside academia. The conference out of which it grew took place at the University of Leuven in Belgium in May 2018 with the financial support of the Flemish Research Council. It attracted scholars of contemporary literature from universities in seven different countries and culminated in a public reading of the short story 'Sudden Traveller' by Hall herself. The editors of the current volume are grateful to all who contributed to this conference and are delighted that many of the short papers delivered there have been developed into fuller contributions here. The essays in this collection range across the majority of Hall's output thus far and cover topics such as human–animal relations; the representation of landscape; dissident politics; embodiment and the material constitution of the mind; north–south relations in England, the UK and Europe more broadly; ecological breakdown; and power, maternity and the regulatory state. By no means do they exhaust the interpretative possibilities where Hall's work is concerned: as befits a study of a living writer, they represent only a partial appraisal to which, it is hoped, much more scholarship will be added as Hall's reputation continues to grow.

In this introduction, we aim to offer an overview of Hall's career up to now, from *Haweswater* through to her more recent publications. (Since they were released while the collection was being developed, *Sudden Traveller* and *Burntcoat* do not, regrettably, receive much attention in this volume.) The introduction thus offers a framework for understanding Hall's writing that positions it within its formal, historical, institutional and critical contexts. One way to begin this process is to note that, notwithstanding their thematic and geographical specificity, Hall's novels range across a selection of genres which do broadly reflect dominant trends within British and wider Anglophone writing of the late twentieth and early twenty-first centuries. We will first evaluate Hall's contribution to the field of cultural production by examining her novels through the prism of genre. Thereafter, we will turn to her status as one of the most successful living British short fiction writers.

The Novels

Though Hall's work, as mentioned, does not engage in the feminist literary revisionism that has been noticeable since the 1970s, her first two novels can nonetheless be understood to have emerged from what Suzanne Keen (2006: 167) describes as the 'historical turn' in British fiction during the 1980s and 1990s. Moreover, her third was published at a time when mainstream literary fiction was beginning to reflect the influence of the science fiction 'boom' that had been underway since the early 1990s, together with the growing trend for dystopian and post-apocalyptic fiction in the English-speaking world. Yet, as one contemporary reviewer (Arditti, 2007: n.p.) pointed out in relation to *The Carhullan Army*, while '[d]ystopian fiction is in vogue [... w]hat distinguishes Hall's contribution is its local detail'. Indeed, it is this near-constant feature of Hall's work – the fact that it returns time and again to North West England, and specifically the author's home county of Cumbria – that has been remarked upon most frequently throughout its popular reception: another review of *The Carhullan Army*, for instance, began by noting that Hall was by that point already recognized as 'a strong regional voice' (Hore, 2007). Such a critical positioning runs two risks, however. First, it underestimates the ways in which Hall's early choice to work within established genres permitted experimentation with form and subject matter that is more daring than these genres traditionally allow. Second, in remarking upon the undeniable significance of locality to Hall's writing, it overestimates the importance of the fact that it *is* 'local' – though the exact meaning of this term too often remains unclear – while failing to recognize the significance of what it actually *does* with its geographical setting.

Thus reviews of *Haweswater* regularly noted the novel's lyricism and sought to position it in dialogue with a longstanding pastoral tradition associated with the English Lake District that venerates the natural landscape and celebrates the authenticity of rural life. A shortcoming of treating the novel is this way, however, is that it attributes insufficient importance to its formal architecture, which unsettles any facile identification with the plight of the Mardale farmers. Indeed, the novel's retrospective narrative voice qualifies its apparently tragic structure and produces a curiously detached relationship with its historical context. As one of the novel's more thoughtful reviewers (Falconer, 2002: n.p.) suggests, the diluvian moment around which the novel is constructed is 'the death of history: timelines rubbed out, the graveyard uprooted'. While, of all Hall's novels, *Haweswater* is the one most readily identified as an historical romance (Keen, 2006: 173), the romantic relationship between its two protagonists is less a narrative centrepiece than it is the means by which Hall makes the obscurity and indifference of the history recounted by the novel apprehensible to her readers. As her narrator tells us at the beginning of the novel's final chapter: 'In secure, rural places, small villages and insular hamlets, where grand events and theatrical schemes rarely take place, enormous human episodes, when they finally do rip apart the fabric of normal life, sometimes come away lacking clarity' (Hall, 2002: 253). Hall herself has pointed out that '[t]he flooding of Mardale was an inevitable industrial change' (cited in Lytollis, 2006: 22), something that has encouraged one critic (Vice, 2017: 71) to suggest that the novel 'avoids blame or nostalgia'. We might, in fact, go further: *Haweswater* is an historical novel that is not particularly interested in clarifying historical events that might be understood as minor or peripheral; what interests it is, precisely, the invisibility and obscurity guaranteed by their marginal status. If 'all (good) historical fiction is fundamentally historiographical' (Keen, 2006: 182), then the historiography offered in Hall's debut is a curious one organized around erasure, disappearance and illegibility.

Yet perhaps this preoccupation with diluvian erasure in Hall's debut – a traumatic account of the arrival of modernity in an isolated corner of England – alerts us to where her work does dovetail with some of the more significant concerns to emerge in literature (and literary criticism) at the end of the twentieth century. A literary historiography focused on the hidden, suppressed and even ghostly remainders of traumatic events that cannot be confronted directly but must be grasped through more complex forms of representation has been a pre-eminent concern of novelists for some time. As Cathy Caruth (1996: 11, emphasis in original) has influentially argued, '[t]hrough the notion of trauma [...] we can understand that a rethinking of reference is aimed not at eliminating history but at reinstating it in our understanding, that is, at precisely permitting *history to arise where immediate understanding may not*'. Certainly, Hall's second novel, *The Electric Michelangelo*, seems to reflect the ways in which trauma necessitates the development of new logics of referentiality, new forms of notation, for recognizing, remembering and recording viscerally algesic experiences that otherwise escape representation. As one contemporary reviewer (Poster, 2004: n.p.) pointed out, while the novel 'touches on many important themes' it is, 'above all, an analysis of pain'. Sometimes pain is occasioned by epochal events such as war and the human displacements caused by violent conflict, but the novel is at least as adamant in dwelling on its more mundane origins. Morecambe, where about half the narrative takes place, is supposedly a refuge for workers intent on spending 'their annual holiday week away from the mills, the mines and foundries of the north' (Hall, 2004: 7). But the representation of this holiday town is heavily focalized through the protagonist, Cy Parks, whose disgust as he empties the pails of blood produced by the guests at his mother's boarding home is palpable, even if it is given short shrift by Reeda. 'Cyril', she says, 'they did not ask to be stuck with this disease. They received it for a lifetime's honest toil' (Hall, 2004: 11). Here, again, Hall's preoccupation with region performs subtler work than might be apparent: the novel invokes the 'dignity of labour' while identifying it, and the system of industrial production upon which it is predicated, as the source of bloody, barely tolerable pain that has not yet been fully grasped.

Likewise, pregnancy provides a mundane trauma for the women attended to by Reeda in her illicit work as an abortionist. Hall thereby examines the way in which particularly female experiences, persecuted and marked with moral opprobrium, take on a traumatic resonance that can only be reckoned with partially, in the half-light of retrospection. Yet it is notable that the strange impedimenta of this profession, discovered by a curious teenage Cy one evening, foreshadow the equipment that he learns to use during his apprenticeship to the tattooist Eliot Riley. And it is here that Hall's novel connects with

Caruth's understanding of trauma. The battered bodies of *The Electric Michelangelo* often appear before the reader as artefacts of historical processes over which they have no control, revenants or spectres cast about by its implacably violent logic. '[D]enied the possibility of historical reference', however, the men and women who come to Cy to be marked by his needles locate a belated means through which to confront their traumatic experiences. The stab of the tattoo becomes the sublimated pain of the historical circumstances that produced them, delayed but inscribed indelibly upon their bodies:

> There were instances when Cy's needle unwittingly delved down into a soul and struck upon meaning, then confidential matter came up, unstemmable as arterial blood or gushing oil, and customers confessed the reason behind the art. He caught their stories in a bucket in the shop or booth and mixed it with ink and used the serum to paint translations of the very stories the tellers were haemorrhaging on to them [...] To tattoo was to understand that people in all their confusing mystery wanted only to claim their bodies as their own site, on which to build a beacon, or raise a rafter, or nail up a manifesto, warning, celebrating, telling of themselves [...] One day he [Cy] might go mad with the knowledge of too much brutality, the violations, the ripping up of hearts and minds and bodies. All the terrible information his needle bit into, all the secrets it lanced. All the memories of people who had come to him and bled their history, which he recorded like a photograph album or a diary of pictures on their bodies. (Hall, 2004: 260)

By these means, Hall identifies a kind of solution to the annihilation of history represented in *Haweswater*. The encounter with the titular electric michelangelo is turned into what Caruth (1996: 11) terms a 'bewildering encounter with trauma' through which these characters 'begin to recognize the possibility of a history that is no longer straightforwardly referential'.

The second of Hall's historical novels, therefore, answers one of the questions raised by the first, and, indeed, by a range of British writers over the last thirty years (foremost among them Pat Barker): how, at the end of an especially bloody century, amid the violence of modernity and in the wake of the 'end of history', are we to orientate ourselves? Yet, more explicitly than *Haweswater*, *The Electric Michelangelo* also asks what place art has in answering this question. Writing (upon) the body, in this novel, does not suggest straightforwardly that the body is scriptable; certainly, Hall does not suggest that the body *is* the text.[2] Asking Cy to cover her skin with innumerable tattoos of unblinking eyes, Grace wishes to use her body as a canvas on and from which to challenge the gaze so that she might become a subject of historical forces that have hitherto objectified her. Ultimately, however, Hall replicates a common materialist theme of her work in suggesting that we can never fully transcend the bare animality of our bodies. Assaulted with acid, Grace endures a violent return to immanence, the script upon her body replaced by welts and scars, and – after exacting satisfactory revenge upon her attacker – disappears once more into the inscrutable eddies of history. In some earlier intertexts such as Jeanette Winterson's *Written on the Body* (1992) and, long before it, Franz Kafka's 'In the Penal Colony' (1919), the physical body begins to disappear beneath the script that is marked upon it. In *The Electric Michelangelo*, however, this body represents the remainder that exceeds art and reminds us that everything returns to a common denominator.

This inference connects Hall's second novel with her third, which in other respects represents a significant departure. *The Carhullan Army* (2007, published in North American markets as *Daughters of the North*), pays homage to its most obvious intertext, Margaret Atwood's *The Handmaid's Tale* (1985/1996) in its autodiegetic narration and emphasis on the material process by which the narrator's testimony is documented. Sister, the radical who joins an all-female militia among the Cumbrian fells in order to escape the misogynistic biopolitical regime of 'the Authority', recounts her story from an interrogation chamber following the militia's failed attack on Rith, a nearby Authority outpost. She informs her interrogators of the indignities she experienced as a female subject, the complicity of her male partner and her remaking at the hands of the women of Carhullan. In what is described, late on, as her 'statement' (Hall, 2007: 207), Sister produces a singular image of Jackie, the commune's leader, who steers its transition from an egalitarian counterculture into an avenging army and converts Sister into one of its fiercest soldiers. This conversion is as corporeal as it is psychological. Sister's newly muscular, newly violent political commitment is communicated through the physical – and strikingly yonic – imagery of the 'gashes on my hands' which possess a 'grotesque attraction': 'I could put the tip of my tongue into the open red slit and taste the salt of myself there [...] We were living at the edge, and everything was amplified; it was beautiful, and it was rancid' (Hall, 2007: 203). As in *The Electric Michelangelo*, the body is as abyssal as it is scriptable, a site that simultaneously signifies and resists representation; above all, it is what is left when representation becomes impossible. Thus, having described Sister's radicalization, Hall does not even attempt to represent its bloody, kinetic apotheosis. Instead of witnessing the tragic-heroic attack on Rith, the reader encounters, in the midst of the novel's denouement, a frustrating bureaucratic note: '[data lost]' (Hall, 2007: 206).

This denial of the culminating moment of Sister's narrative hints once more at the fallibility of any attempt to capture experience within representation. The refusal of textual *jouissance* at the end of the novel is particularly notable given the shift in genre that Hall effects in *The Carhullan Army*, abandoning the trappings of historical fiction – to which she has, as of the current volume, yet to return – in preference for those of dystopian speculative fiction. As noted earlier, this transition reflects wider developments in literary fiction in the first decade of the twenty-first century: numerous influential critics remarked upon the prevalence of dystopian tropes at this point in recent literary history, with some (Fisher, 2009; Jameson, 2007) viewing the genre's popularity as an indication of the ways in which political horizons were closed down by the so-called 'End of History' during the 1990s at precisely the point that they needed to be dramatically opened up. Yet, while easily assimilated into a body of work that mobilizes dystopian elements in order to register the scale of the political challenges confronting humanity at the dawn of the new millennium, *The Carhullan Army* is notable not just for the way its generic makeup 'replicates some of the epistemological uncertainty characteristic of a time of climate crisis' (Bracke, 2017: 31). It is also quite explicitly a novel about ideological interpellation and the forms of political commitment and counter-hegemonic activity to which the latter gives rise. As Emilie Walezak (2019: 71) has argued, 'it is the dystopian aspect of her text that allows Hall to escape the nostalgic allure of retro aesthetics while recontextualizing the legacy of the women's movement in a spatialized regional milieu'.

How to Paint a Dead Man is a novel that breaks new ground in Hall's oeuvre, even as it appeals to various literary traditions; yet it too is a novel that remains firmly rooted in regional landscapes, of Italy in the South and Cumbria in the North. *How to Paint a Dead Man* also brings to the fore a theme that has existed, explicitly or implicitly, in Hall's work since her debut – that is, art and aesthetics – inspired as it is by the life and work of the Italian painter Giorgio Morandi. Moreover, in terms of form the novel participates in the tradition of the composite novel, which was particularly prominent in British literature of the first decades of the twentieth century. Like novels such as Ali Smith's *Hotel World* (2001), David Mitchell's *Cloud Atlas* (2004), John Lanchester's *Capital* (2012) and Zadie Smith's *NW* (2012), *How to Paint a Dead Man* offers a collage in which four protagonists gradually turn out to be related in various ways. In an alternating sequence that is kept up almost to the end, the chapters entitled 'The Mirror Crisis' tell the story of Susan Caldicutt, who is trying to cope with the death of her brother; the 'Translated from the Bottle Journals' sections are drawn from the diary of an Italian painter; 'The Fool on the Hill' focuses on British painter Peter Caldicutt and his near fatal accident in Cumbria; and 'The Divine Vision of Annette Tambroni', finally, relates the life of an Italian girl who is slowly going blind. Situated mid-way between the short story cycle, with its sequence of interlocking short stories, and the more conventional single-plot-based novel, the composite novel is a multiperspectival and polyphonic form that allows different voices and experiences to be staged without either the unity or the hierarchical division of protagonist and side characters, main and sub plot, that characterize the integrated novel. Yet, unlike in the postmodern experimental novel, the emphasis is less on fragmentation than on collation as the composite novel's emphasis is typically on the – often hidden or unexpected – relations that exist between people (D'hoker, 2018: 24).

In *How to Paint a Dead Man*, too, the narrative links between the stories bring out the interconnections that exist between their characters. Some of these connections are made manifest through objects: Giorgio's diaries are being translated in London by Annette's brother, Tom, who is Susan's lover; and one of Giorgio's iconic bottles, a gift to Annette, which she has placed on Giorgio's grave, is stolen by Peter and finally gifted to Susan for her exhibition of artists' memento mori. The characters, however, are twinned on symbolic levels as well: parallels are drawn between Peter and Giorgio, who are both facing death, between Susan and Annette, immobilized by trauma, but also between Susan's brother Danny and Annette, both of whom possess a childlike wonder that seems doomed in a selfish society. On a thematic level, the four narratives are connected by their investigation of the bonds between art and life, sex and death, self and other. This creates a richly layered narrative that recalls the painterly technique advocated by Cennini for painting a dead man, as quoted on the book's last page: 'laying each of these flesh colours in its place, blending them nicely into each other, both on the face and on the body' (Hall, 2009: 288; see Lea, 2016: 177). As a composite novel, *How to Paint a Dead Man* similarly construes a textual meshwork of distinct voices and characters, which rewards each re-reading with newly uncovered echoes, blended colours, and coincidences.

It might be argued that, in its formal composition as an arrangement of four distinct but tightly articulated narratives whose protagonists meet only fleetingly, *How to Paint a Dead Man* anticipates Hall's growing investment in the short story, a form that would account for more and more of her output during the second decade of her career. On one level this makes her next novel, *The Wolf Border*, more difficult to explain, the latter being, at least at a superficial level, more traditionally 'novelistic' than its predecessor. Yet any reader of the stories published between these two novels will recognize a honing of prose style – leaner sentences which simultaneously demonstrate an impressionistic quality that Hall may have inherited from the American writer James Salter, for whom she has professed admiration (Ranscombe, 2015: n.p.) – as well as a tighter, more limited narrative perspective that renders the novel of a piece with many of the stories that are collected in *The Beautiful Indifference*. Thematically, too, *The Wolf Border* is closer to Hall's short fiction than it is to her other novels. Though landscape continues to feature prominently, animals move from the relatively peripheral position they occupy in her earlier fiction and take on a conceptual, ethical – even epistemological – centrality. The preoccupation with the human *as* animal, as something that might be pared back to an animal essence, makes an earlier but equally central appearance during the hazing rituals that Sister is forced to endure at Carhullan. What connects the concerns of *The Wolf Border* with those of Hall's short fiction, however, is how these narratives look upon this animal self quite conspicuously as Other, as something that causes Hall's protagonists to reflect upon their own animality in a way that recognizes both the proximity and remoteness of 'the animal'. The result is often uncanny (as in 'Mrs Fox') or even frightening (as in 'She Murdered Mortal He'); in *The Wolf Border* it is particularly intriguing, producing a set of fundamental antinomies that the novel inserts into an alternative present rendered both strange and, at the same time, entirely recognizable. Here, Hall's place within the landscape of contemporary fiction becomes most plainly visible, since the creaturely concerns of her work during the 2010s can so easily be read in the context of a larger cultural preoccupation with the animal within the UK and global Anglophone literature more broadly. And it is fitting that this should have occurred during a decade in which she also became known as a pre-eminent writer of short stories.

The Short Fiction

With three critically acclaimed short story collections published in a span of eight years, Hall surely ranks among the most important British practitioners of this genre. When *The Beautiful Indifference* appeared to rave reviews in 2011, some of its stories had already attracted individual attention as well: 'Butcher's Perfume' had been one of five stories on the shortlist for the BBC National short story award in 2010; 'She Murdered Mortal He' had appeared in *Granta* in 2011; and 'Vutjärvi' had been long-listed for the Sunday Times EFG Private

Bank Short Story Award in the same year. Put together, the stories make for a powerful collection, which went on to win the Edge Hill University Short Story Prize in 2012. A year later, Hall attracted the spotlight with a short story once more when 'Mrs Fox', a compelling story about a woman turning into a fox, won the BBC National Short Story Award. On the occasion, Hall (2013: n.p.) wrote an essay for the *Guardian*, asking that the genre be taken more seriously by publishers, writers and readers, for short stories are 'often strong meat' even if they are not to everyone's taste. 'The greatest short stories', she concludes,

> feel almost predestined, as if they have materialised effortlessly. They reverberate magnificently, beyond their own limits; they haunt, humour, sometimes vex and occasionally enlighten. They are a bastard to write [...] Consequently, there aren't many, and only a few writers are able to produce them consistently. It's not just conservative publishers that vet short stories, nor pound-conscious booksellers, nor the appetites of readers – in the end, the form dictates its own exclusivity. (Hall, 2013: n.p.)

Hall's greater visibility as a short fiction writer earned her several commissions for short stories for anthologies or magazines. In 2012, she was commissioned by the BBC to write a story, 'Theatre Six', to commemorate the 50th anniversary of *The Feminine Mystique*; 'Luxury Hour' was written for Tracy Chevalier's anthology *Reader, I Married Him: Stories Inspired by Jane Eyre* (2016); and several more stories were published in such publications as the *Guardian*, the *New Statesman* and *Vice*. The stories were subsequently collected in *Madame Zero* (2017), which the Scottish poet Kate Clancy (2017: n.p.) praised as 'exceptional, compelling, frightening and authentic'. The story 'Goodnight Nobody' from this collection also became one of the O. Henry Prize winners in 2019 and was included in its 100th anthology, edited by Laura Ferman. In 2016, Hall also edited a short story anthology herself, together with Peter Hobbs. *Sex & Death* contains new short stories by contemporary writers on literature's 'two greatest themes': '[t]he human embrace and the cold sweat. The weight of the coffin on the shoulder, the illicit kiss or *la petite mort*;

the sting of intimately split flesh and the wonder of holding a tiny howling genetic machine in our arms' (Hall and Hobbs, 2016: 1).

These themes are also central to the story 'Sudden Traveller', with which Sarah Hall made the shortlist of the BBC National short story award for the third time in 2018. It is also the title story of Hall's third collection, which was published in September 2019, again collecting the stories that Hall previously published in a variety of prominent newspapers and magazines over the last three years. The collection suggests a shift towards the fantastic in Hall's short fiction, with magical-realist stories like 'M', 'Who Pays', and 'Orton' depicting women who have the power to end life, either their own or that of the men who harmed them. New life too features in these stories, with 'Sudden Traveller' powerfully evoking the conflicted feelings of a new mother, who has given birth while her own mother lay dying, and 'Live That You May Live', which celebrates a mother and daughter's shared delight in storytelling and the transformative imagination. A more stifling bond between mother and daughter is depicted in another story from *Sudden Traveller*, 'The Grotesques', which made headlines in October 2020 when Hall became the first writer to win the BBC National short story award twice. Jonathan Freedland, the Chair of the jury, commented:

> In perhaps the strongest field in the history of the BBC National Short Story Award, Sarah Hall's story still stood out. A timeless, unsettling story rendered in exquisite prose, 'The Grotesques' yields more with each reading, offering layer upon layer of meaning. It is the work of a writer who is not only devotedly committed to the short story genre but, has become a master of it. Sarah Hall has now won this Award twice, recognition of her standing as this country's foremost writer of short stories.[3]

Recognizing Hall's mastery of the form, Philip Hensher picked another story by Hall, 'Later, His Ghost', for his recent anthology *The Penguin Book of the Contemporary British Short Story* as one of the 30 best British stories of the twenty-first century. In his preface, he introduces Hall's story as 'perhaps the most conventional in the book, in contemporary terms' as it 'has been formed by serious engagement with creative writing courses' (Hensher, 2018/2019: xx).

Notwithstanding her MLitt in Creative Writing from the University of St. Andrews, however, Hall has remained largely outside the creative writing circuit beyond her personal initiative of the Lycian Writers retreat, which was launched in 2019. What Hensher labels 'conventional', it seems, is Hall's rejection of the postmodernist impulse towards playfulness, parody, metafiction and experiment in favour of a reliance on the techniques of the modernist short story – ellipsis and epiphany, minimalism and suggestion – in order to create maximum effect (and affect) within a relatively short frame. Following the short story's traditional focus on the moment, similarly, Hall's stories convey the shock of sudden transformations, impulsive decisions and unobtrusively momentous events. Hall (2013: n.p.) knows what great stories can do – 'provoke potent sensations in the reader – discomfort, arousal, exhilaration, fear' – and she uses both trusted techniques and her considerable literary skill so as to effectively challenge the reader.

In her 2018 study, *Contemporary Feminism and Women's Short Stories*, Emma Young notes that the short story's reliance on ambiguity, voice and open endings make it a form particularly suited to a feminist critique of patriarchal structures and oppressive gender binaries. Hall's 'Butcher's Perfume' and 'The Beautiful Indifference' are among the many stories by contemporary British female writers she analyses for their interrogation of gender norms, sexuality, marriage and motherhood. Yet, while Hall's short fiction certainly has thematic affinities with the work of writers discussed by Young (such as Jackie Kay, Ali Smith, A. L. Kennedy, Helen Simpson and Zadie Smith), she departs from these writers' critique of the social constructedness of gender in a patriarchal society through a far greater focus on the body, desire and sexuality. This materialism – for a long time anathema to third-wave feminists – brings her closer again to the stories of D. H. Lawrence, Doris Lessing, and Angela Carter. Being compared to the latter was, Hall said in an interview about *The Electric Michelangelo*, the 'best compliment' she ever received, as she admires Carter's work for being 'powerful, formidable – she writes no-holds-barred, lit-up prose. It's brilliant. It's political – I love all that stuff' (Edemariam, 2004: n.p.).

Like several other contemporary writers, finally, Hall's short fiction also manifests a growing ecological awareness that brings her work in line with current trends in animal studies and ecocriticism. The human-animal transformation in 'Mrs Fox', for instance, has been celebrated by critics for its portrayal of a post-anthropocentic 'eradication of species boundaries' and it advocacy of an 'an ethics of companionship that relies on a being-with-otherness' (Baker, 2019: 88; Ditter, 2019: 202). Stories like 'Later, His Ghost', 'Wilderness', and 'Sudden Traveller' similarly evoke human entanglement with a natural environment that is under threat, but in these stories nature has also become a threat, has turned treacherous. Such ecological concerns also align Hall's short stories with those of other British writers. Human vulnerability in the face of climate change is a preoccupation Hall shares with Jon McGregor, who depicts disasters waiting to happen in *This Isn't The Sort of Thing That Happens to Someone Like You* (2012), while the interconnectedness of human beings with nature and creaturely life is also treated in the work of a younger generation of short story writers: Eley Williams's *Attrib. and Other Stories* (2017), Daisy Johnson's *Fen* (2016) and Lucy Wood's *The Sing of the Shore* (2018). Like Johnson and Wood, moreover, Hall's engagement with creaturely life also causes her to stray from the 'conventional' psychological realism of the modernist short story into the realm of the fantastic or the magical realist, as her last collection amply demonstrates. Together with Hall's many readers, we are curious to see where this move will take her next.

Chapter Overview

Hall's growing investment in creaturely life and ecological crisis in her recent novels and short fiction once again affirms her position as both a quintessentially contemporary writer and as a prominent writer in the contemporary literary scene. The contributions to this collection all testify to her importance as a writer while demonstrating that her work richly rewards critical engagement. The eight chapters that follow all bring new critical theories to bear on Hall's work, highlighting her original take on current debates and trends. By ranging across Hall's oeuvre rather than focusing on one book only, moreover, most contributions identify recurring patterns as well as interesting new developments in her work. In what follows we briefly introduce the different chapters, drawing attention to the lines of consensus and divergence between their approaches to Hall's work.

In the first chapter Melanie Ebdon introduces several of Hall's main concerns through a survey of her five novels. Like other twenty-first-century British novelists, she argues, Hall has left postmodernist epistemological playfulness behind for an ecocritical exploration of the human condition in the Anthropocene. Ebdon shows how Hall moves beyond the binaries of human and animal, culture and nature, to foreground the embodied and embedded nature of all human beings. By extracting her characters from conventional social situations and foregrounding their bodily, animal natures, Ebdon argues, Hall reveals the 'bare essence of our species.' At the same time, however, the many non-human animal presences in her novels push against human individualism and alert us to our essential embeddedness within the ecosystem.

Hall's animal figurations are also at the centre of the next chapter, which moves from Hall's novels to a consideration of her short fiction. In an analysis of the central metamorphosis in 'Mrs Fox', Elke D'hoker first compares Hall's take on our animal natures as well as interspecies relations with David Garnett's early-twentieth-century perspective in his novella *Lady into Fox* (1922). She then discusses the animals, typically solitary animals or predators, that riddle Hall's other stories whether as metaphors, companions, and hybrids or in momentous confrontations. Unlike most scholars in animal studies or critical posthumanism, D'hoker argues, Hall's animal figurations locate the commonality between human and non-human animals not in a shared creaturely vulnerability, but rather in the vitalist power of the body, with its instincts and desires. In this, she comes close to Nietzsche's animal philosophy, which praises the 'forgetfulness' of animals over excessive human self-consciousness. Still, Hall ultimately moves beyond this shared animality to the question of human distinction, which she, like Nietzsche, locates in care, responsibility and the 'gift-giving virtue'.

The question of what makes us human is also at the heart of Natalie Riley's chapter 'Homo sapiens: Being Human in *How to Paint a Dead Man* and *The Wolf Border*'. Along with Ebdon, Riley notes that Hall shares with other contemporary British writers an interest in human embodiment, in the biological substratum of human life. Through an analysis of Hall's multi-layered representations of life and death, art and motherhood, mortality and reproduction in her most recent novels, however, Riley shows that Hall's depiction of human life cannot be reduced to biological determinism. For, while authenticity is shown to lie in the body, 'it is in a body that is situated and contextual, touched and constructed with and fixed by others in the social world'.

In 'Rewilding Welfare: Sarah Hall and the State of Nature', Pieter Vermeulen considers another dimension of this social embeddedness, namely the changing attitudes to the welfare state in Hall's oeuvre. While her first four novels relied on an opposition between an authentic and restorative nature and intrusive state institutions, *The Wolf Border* shifts, somewhat hesitantly, to an appreciation of the welfare state and its role in human happiness. This shift, Vermeulen argues, is paralleled by a revised understanding of wilderness in Hall's work, one that is in tune with new developments in the fields of environmental humanities, especially the so-called 'new conservationism'. If, in *The Wolf Border*, good nature management thus resonates with beneficial state intervention, the figure of the wolf, a central icon of both ecocriticism and neoliberalism, also serves as a 'reminder that contemporary neoliberalism has willfully reinstituted something very much like a state of nature – a carefully cultivated state of precarity and exposure to the sovereign force of the market'.

That the wolves are compelling if slippery symbols is also recognized by Chloé Ashbridge in her analysis of *The Wolf Border* as a contemporary state-of-the-nation novel engaged with the question of an independent England. Although the campaign for Scottish independence is the central political event in the novel, its reintegration project, Ashbridge claims, can be read as an allegorical exploration of the England' potential as a politically independent nation. The wolves' carefully managed rewilding, she argues, draws attention to the limits of this devolution within the institutional structures of the British state. Ashbridge also shows how the novel's exploration of 'Englishness' in relation to the North-West, instead of its traditional association with a rural idyll located in the South, is part of the post-pastoral mode that also characterizes *Haweswater* and *The Carhullan Army*.

Hall's representation of her native Cumbria in her oeuvre more generally is the focus of Emilie Walezak's chapter 'Borderlands: Spatializing Feminist Struggle in Sarah Hall's Fiction.' Drawing on Henri Lefebvre's account of the material and social construction of space as a three-part dialectic, Walezak analyses the spatialization of Cumbria as 'conceived space', 'lived space', and 'perceived space'. In each of these spatializations, she argues, Hall foregrounds the place of women, both as exploited and administered subjects and as rural labourers, whose experience of lived space through embodiment points the way to female empowerment. By personifying Cumbria and 'naturifying' its inhabitants, Walezak concludes, Hall develops a feminist environmental ethics that acknowledges embodiment and embeddedness. In doing so, Hall's post-pastoral regional writing successfully appropriates the local context to address global geo-political concerns.

If both Ashbridge and Walezak thus praise Hall for her post-pastoral depiction of the English North, Francesca Pierini's chapter raises the question of whether this is accompanied by a far more idyllic and nostalgic vision of the European South. Pointing to the longstanding British tradition of equating the South with an instinctive, sensual and anti-rational sensibility, Pierini also finds traces of this binary in *How to Paint a Dead Man*, which juxtaposes two Italian characters against two British ones. Yet, the novel's depiction of the development of human consciousness – from childhood and young adulthood over maturity to old age – also complicates this binary opposition. By combining a cyclical and linear view of human nature, Hall departs from the traditional, Hegelian plot that has the rational (Northern) subject incorporate pre-modern (Southern) wisdom to achieve a higher existential synthesis. Instead, Pierini concludes, the novel creates a narrative pattern of human ageing and development in which traditional categories are productively blurred and opened up.

In the concluding chapter of the collection, Alexander Beaumont returns to some of the themes established early on by evaluating Hall's representation of landscape and the body in the context of the material turn in academic Geography. Beaumont positions Hall's work in relation to the development of the New Nature Writing but suggests that its post-pastoral representation of the Lake District goes beyond the salvage geography that has been associated with writers working within this genre by displacing the lyrical persona and challenging the primacy of the linguistically-endowed and culturally-situated subject. In so doing, Hall's work questions some of the central precepts of late twentieth-century critical theory, celebrating 'the limits put in place by [...] our physical constitution and the material geography of the landscapes in which we live', which 'open up new forms of understanding which cannot be exhausted by conceptual, discursive or more broadly cultural ways of describing the relationship between space, body and consciousness'. The chapter brings the collection to a close by reflecting on Hall's aesthetics and arguing that her work 'exist[s] in a curiously partial, unfinished and provocative relationship with the stuff of representation itself: that is, with language'.

Notes

1 The question of canon-formation in contemporary literary studies is notoriously vexed (Eaglestone, 2013), but Daniel Lea's (2016) inclusion of Hall among the writers he examines in *Twenty-First Century Fiction: Contemporary British Voices* is arguably the most important marker of her arrival as a writer of interest within the field. This is especially so given that, of the other four, two (Ali Smith and Andrew O'Hagan) had already been appearing in critical surveys for some time and the remainder (Tom McCarthy and Jon McGregor) had until that point attracted noticeably more critical interest than Hall. (McCarthy, for instance, has already been the subject of an entry in Gylphi's 'Contemporary Writers' series: see Duncan [2016]).

2 For a different (feminist) take on the art of tattooing as represented in the novel, see Mealing (2014), Orr (2017).
3 See the official announcement on https://www.bbc.co.uk/programmes/articles/4yzcn3rXH66p2BDlXs54HsS/sarah-hall-becomes-first-writer-to-win-bbc-national-short-story-award-twice

Works Cited

Acheson, J. (2017) *The Contemporary British Novel Since 2000*. Edinburgh: Edinburgh University Press.

Arditti, M. (2007) 'Psychopath in the Community', *Telegraph*, 8 September, URL (accessed: 31 January 2020): https://www.telegraph.co.uk/culture/books/fictionreviews/3667787/Psychopath-in-the-community.html

Atwood, M. (1985/1996) *The Handmaid's Tale*. London: Vintage.

Baker, T.C. (2019) *Writing Animals: Language, Suffering and Animality in Twenty-First-Century Fiction*. Cham: Palgrave Macmillan.

Bentley, N. (2008) *Contemporary British Fiction*. Edinburgh: Edinburgh University Press.

Bentley, N., Hubble, N. and Wilson, L. (eds) (2015) *The 2000s: A Decade of Contemporary British Fiction*. London: Bloomsbury.

Blincoe, N. and Thorne, M. (eds) (2001) *All Hail the New Puritans*. London: Fourth Estate.

Bracke, A. (2017) *Climate Crisis and the 21st-Century British Novel*. London: Bloomsbury.

Bradford, R. (2007) *The Novel Now: Contemporary British Fiction*. Oxford: Wiley-Blackwell.

Bradley, A. and Tate, A. (2010) *The New Atheist Novel: Philosophy, Fiction and Polemic after 9/11*. London: Continuum.

Caruth, C. (1996) *Unclaimed Experience: Trauma, Narrative and History*. Baltimore, MD: Johns Hopkins University Press.

Chevalier, T. (ed.) (2016) *Reader, I Married Him*. London: Borough Press.

Childs, P. (2012) *Contemporary Novelists: British Fiction Since 1970*, 2nd edn. London: Palgrave Macmillan.

Clancy, K. (2017) 'Madame Zero by Sarah Hall Review: Exceptional Stories', *Guardian*, 7 July, URL (accessed 25 November 2019): https://www.theguardian.com/books/2017/jul/07/madame-zero-sarah-hall-review

Cottrell, A. (2019) 'The Power of Love: From Feminist Utopia to the Politics of Imperceptibility in Sarah Hall's Fiction', *Textual Practice* 33(4): 679–93, DOI: 10.1080/0950236X.2017.1371218

D'hoker, E. (2018) 'A Continuum of Fragmentation: Distinguishing the Short Story Cycle from the Composite Novel', in P. Gill and F. Kläger (eds) *Constructing Coherence in the British Short Story Cycle*, pp. 17–31. London: Routledge.

Ditter, J. (2019) 'Human into Animal: Post-anthropomorphic Transformations in Sarah Hall's "Mrs Fox"', in B. Korte and L. Lojo-Rodríguez (eds) *Borders and Border Crossings in the Contemporary British Short Story*, pp. 187–204. London: Palgrave Macmillan.

Duncan, Dennis (ed.) (2016) *Tom McCarthy: Critical Essays*. Canterbury: Gylphi.

Edemariam, A. (2004) 'More Than Skin Deep (Interview with Sarah Hall)', *Guardian*, 8 October, URL (accessed 10 September 2020): https://www.theguardian.com/books/2004/oct/08/bookerprize2004.bookerprize

Eaglestone, R. (2013) 'Contemporary Fiction in the Academy: Towards a Manifesto', *Textual Practice* 27(7): 1089–101, DOI: 10.1080/0950236X.2013.840113

Eagleton, M. and Parker, E. (eds) (2015) *The History of British Women's Writing, 1970–Present*. London: Palgrave Macmillan.

Falconer, H. (2002) 'Village of the Damned', *Guardian*, 15 June, URL (accessed 31 January 2020): https://www.theguardian.com/books/2002/jun/15/featuresreviews.guardianreview26

Fisher, M. (2009) *Capitalist Realism: Is There No Alternative?* London: Zero Books.

Hall, S. (2002) *Haweswater*. London: Faber and Faber.

Hall, S. (2004) *The Electric Michelangelo*. London: Faber and Faber

Hall, S. (2007) *The Carhullan Army*. London: Faber and Faber.

Hall, S. (2009) *How to Paint a Dead Man*. London: Faber and Faber.

Hall, S. (2011) *The Beautiful Indifference*. London: Faber and Faber.

Hall, S. (2013) 'Sarah Hall on Why We Should Have a Short Story Laureate', *Guardian*, 11 October, URL (accessed 25 November 2019): https://www.theguardian.com/books/2013/oct/11/sarah-hall-short-story-laureate

Hall, S. (2015) *The Wolf Border*. London: Faber and Faber.

Hall, S. (2017) *Madame Zero*. London: Faber and Faber.

Hall, S. (2019) *Sudden Traveller*. London: Faber and Faber.

Hall, S. and Hobbs, P. (eds) (2016) *Sex & Death: Stories*. London: Faber and Faber.

Head, D. (2016) 'Introduction', in D. Head (ed.) *The Cambridge History of the English Short Story*, pp. 1–15. Cambridge: Cambridge University Press.

Hensher, P. (ed.) (2018/2019) *The Penguin Book of the British Short Story Volume 2: From P.G. Wodehouse to Zadie Smith*. London: Penguin.

Hore, Rachel (2007) 'The Carhullan Army, by Sarah Hall', *Independent*, 7 October, URL (accessed 31 January 2020): https://www.independent.co.uk/arts-entertainment/books/reviews/the-carhullan-army-by-sarah-hall-395975.html

Jameson, F. (2007) *Archaeologies of the Future: The Desire Called Utopia and Other Science Fictions*. London: Verso.

Keen, S. (2006) 'The Historical Turn in British Fiction', in J. English (ed.) *A Concise Companion to Contemporary British Fiction*, pp. 167–87. Oxford: Wiley-Blackwell.

Lea, D. (2016) *Twenty-First Century Fiction: Contemporary British Voices*. Manchester: Manchester University Press.

Lytollis, R. (2006) 'How Mardale Inspired a Novel', *News and Star* (24 June): 22.

McGregor, J. (2012) *This Isn't the Sort of Thing That Happens to Someone Like You*. London: Bloomsbury.

Mealing, L. (2014) 'The Mermaid as Postmodern Muse in Sarah Hall's *The Electric Michelangelo*', *Contemporary Women's Writing* 8(2): 223–40.

Orr, A. (2017) 'Inked In: The Feminist Politics of Tattooing in Sarah Hall's The Electric Michelangelo', *Neo-Victorian Studies* 9(2): 97–125.

Pollard, E. and Schoene, B. (eds) (2018) *British Literature in Transition, 1980–2000: Accelerated Times*. Cambridge: Cambridge University Press.

Poster, J. (2004) 'Written in Skin', *Guardian*, 27 March, URL (accessed 31 January 2020): https://www.theguardian.com/books/2004/mar/27/featuresreviews.guardianreview24

Ranscombe, S. (2015) 'Sarah Hall: "I Don't Want Only Female Readers or Young Readers"', *Telegraph*, 12 June URL (accessed 31 January 2020): https://www.telegraph.co.uk/culture/books/authorinterviews/11660349/Sarah-Hall-I-dont-want-only-female-readers-or-young-readers.html

Schoene, B. (2009) *The Cosmopolitan Novel*. Edinburgh: Edinburgh University Press.

Shaw, K. (2017) *Cosmopolitanism in Twenty-First Century Fiction*. London: Palgrave Macmillan.

Snell, K. (1998) 'The Regional Novel: Themes for Interdisciplinary Research', in K. Snell (ed.) *The Regional Novel in Britain and Ireland: 1800–1990*, pp. 1–53. Cambridge: Cambridge University Press.

Tew, P. (2007) *The Contemporary British Novel*, 2nd edn. London: Continuum.
Tew, P. and Mengham, R. (2006) *British Fiction Today*. London: Continuum.
Vice, S. (2017) 'Sarah Hall: A New Kind of Storytelling', in J. Acheson (ed.) *The Contemporary British Novel Since 2000*, pp. 70–8. Edinburgh: Edinburgh University Press.
Walezak, E. (2019) 'Landscape and Identity: Utopian/Dystopian Cumbria in Sarah Hall's The Carhullan Army', *Critique: Studies in Contemporary Fiction* 60(1): 67–74, DOI: 10.1080/00111619.2018.1479242
Yang, K. (2018) 'Restoring Life: Carnivore Reintroduction and (Eco) Feminist Science in Sarah Hall's The Wolf Border', *Women's Studies* 47(8): 829–44.
Young, E. (2018) *Contemporary Feminism and Women's Short Stories*. Edinburgh: Edinburgh University Press.

1

Real Nature

Melanie Ebdon

Since her debut novel, *Haweswater*, was published in 2002, Sarah Hall's literature has been deeply engaged with nature, ecology and the questions they bring to bear on the condition of humanity at the beginning of the twenty-first century. Just what, exactly, *are* we and how do we fit into this world around us? The premise of this chapter is that Hall's writing articulates the concerns of the new millennium, chief amongst these being the now universal concern of our status as creatures trapped within and eternally dependent upon a fragile and rapidly altering ecosystem. From the impact of latter-day industrialism as exposed in *Haweswater*, to the speculative 'cli-fi' of *The Carhullan Army* and on to the short story collection *Madame Zero* (featuring 'Mrs Fox': the award-winning tale of human-to-fox metamorphosis), it is clear that our animal selves within the ecosystem is a key point of focus in Hall's body of work.[1] Although tied by the demands of history and the political sphere, Hall's human characters present the biological continuum of the human animal. This is literature in which the materiality of our human selves is explored, often in relentless detail, as bodies are inscribed as meat, bone, sinew and synapse: Hall's writing shows us bodies which respond to seasonal alterations, climatic shifts, endorphins and pheromones.

In his journal article 'The Anxieties of Authenticity in Post-2000 British Fiction', Daniel Lea (2012: 459) makes several points along these lines, stating that Hall's oeuvre is engaged with a twenty-first century 'reemergence of authenticity as an ethical marker of contemporary subjectivity', a concern which he sees in several writers of this period such as Ali Smith, Andrew O'Hagan, Tom McCarthy and Jon McGregor. Lea (2012: 464) goes on to state: 'it is notable that the return of the real in the late-twentieth and twenty-first centuries has brought with it a reengagement with the viability of the biological ideal' which explores a 'dialectic of humanity and nature'. He argues:

> For [Hall], the forces that demand a distinction between human beings and the world they inhabit are always weaker than the forces which join them. Hall's fiction may vocalise a Romantic sensibility, but it is always paired with the consciousness of environmental catastrophe that haunts the twenty-first century. (Lea, 2016: 16)

Although Hall's work shares some concerns with other Lake District writers of previous generations, a distinctly different trajectory is at work here. Romantic poetry called for a retreat to the pastoral, a withdrawing from the modern world, while the embodied, natural, human animal is revealed by Hall's writing as a potential corrective mechanism for a future course via a reassessment of the human. No reconnection is needed and there is no bridge to be built between humans and nature: the divide between humans and nature is swept away in favour of a biological imperative. In *The Carhullan Army* in particular, the iconic Lake District setting intensifies a shift from Romantic preoccupations with the reinvigoration of the soul and society through a connection to the sublime towards, instead, urgent concerns for the survival of both civilization and humanity. Hall's writing insists that humans are materially part of the world we inhabit and that '[t]he virtual dimension does not [...] fully clean the dirt from beneath our fingernails' (Lea, 2016: 20). After the surface-play of postmodernism has run aground, Hall's growing body of work is elucidating a timely perspective of the human animal that disintegrates conventional binary hierarchies such as human/animal and culture/nature and signals that humanity must revaluate itself and its place in relation to unfolding ecological disorder.

Postmodernism to Ecocentrism

The generation of novelists who were in the early stages of their career at the opening of this millennium were born in the late 1960s and through the 1970s, coming to cultural consciousness throughout the 1980s amidst an urgent sense of ecological destruction, rainforest devastation and species-extinction. In 1985, the depletion of atmospheric ozone levels was confirmed by the British Antarctic Survey in a paper in *Nature* by Farman, Gardiner and Shanklin. Thereafter, the phrases 'greenhouse effect' and 'global warming' entered the common language; such were the forces that shaped the cultural consciousness of Generation X. There is a discernible difference between the postmodernist writing, art and criticism of the post-war period and the ecocentric concerns of a younger generation of writers who are feeling all too keenly 'the shock of the real', a phrase which appears in Hall's (2017: 91) short story 'Luxury Hour'. The crisis of meaning gave way to a crisis of survival. As Lea (2016: 9) notes, Hall's writing 'unite[s] the narrative explorations of the twentieth century with a twenty-first century structure of feeling' and this persistent focus on nature is right on the pulse of contemporary concerns: 'the brute physicality of the material world reasserts itself as a reminder that stuff cannot be outmaneuvered completely; the "real" real is non-negotiable' (Lea, 2016: 20). In his introduction to the 2012 special issue on British Fiction in *Modern Fiction Studies*, Patrick O'Donnell (2012: 431) states: 'the authors of new British fiction productively make use of postmodernism's concerns [...] while developing new ways of addressing questions of genre, identity, language as well as emergent issues related to the environment, globalization, technology, literariness, and authenticity'. Hall's work is situated within this new development as an example of literature that is indicative of a step beyond postmodernism, an evolution in creative and critical thought which has been underway since the 1990s.[2] Having dismantled the metanarratives via our incredulity, humanity does not find itself in a vertiginous space, free of restrictions: as postmodernity reached its mature state, an *absolute* was emerging; wherever we placed ourselves within a complex matrix of cultural coordinates, we were also – undeniably, un-deconstructably – *animals*, within an *ecosystem*, with nowhere else to go if it became unable to support us. This particular absolute does not require our credulity.

The ecocentric turn in creative and critical writing is only one segment of a much larger picture: a brief look at the ecological philosophy (ecosophy) of two contemporary philosophers – Timothy Morton and Michel Serres – gives us further illustration regarding the 'structure of feeling' of this new millennium and its orientation towards ecological concerns. In *Hyperobjects: Philosophy and Ecology after the End of the World* (2013), Morton critiques the perceived gap between nature and culture, arguing that this dualism is ultimately a factor which prevents us from responding appropriately to ecological crisis. For Morton, postmodernism was a continuation of European patriarchal modernity with a different hat on, a view previously articulated in the 1990s by black feminist critics such as Barbara Christian and bell hooks. Morton (2013) argues:

> The globalizing sureness with which 'there is no metalanguage' and 'everything is a metaphor' are spoken in postmodernism means that postmodernism is nothing like what it takes itself to be, and is indeed just another version of the (white, Western, male) historical project. The ultimate goal of this project, it seems, was to set up a weird transit lounge outside of history in which the characters and technologies and ideas of the ages mill around in a state of mild, semiblissful confusion.
>
> Slowly, however, we discovered that the transit lounge was built on Earth, which is different from saying that it was part of Nature. (Morton, 2013: 4)

For Morton, Nature, distinguished as a proper noun, is 'over there', not us, the Other to our Self. The configuration of 'Nature' as an entity apart from us is the key hurdle that humanity must now overcome as it begins to form an awareness of itself and all matter as interconnected in an ecosphere. This problematic dualism is debated by Jos Smith and Greg Garrard in *The New Nature Writing*. With reference to Morton's ideas outlined here, they discuss the cultural impact of the Anthropocene which has brought about a 'historic reorientation' comparable to those initiated by the work of Copernicus and Darwin: 'The recognition of the Anthropocene forces us to look very carefully at our cultures of 'Nature' and ask if they too, however well intentioned, are part of the problem. Is there, enshrined within them, a belief that 'Nature' is 'eternal and separate'? (Smith and Garrard, 2017: 12). The term 'Anthropocene' also requires interrogation: although we are still officially within the Holocene period, Anthropocene as a term has gained currency in media and critical discourse. It at once signifies an anthropocentric outlook while simultaneously laying the blame for ecocide squarely on our shoulders.

Hall's writing seems to insist that the distinction between human culture and nature is false, unrealistic. Does this require, though, a dismissal of the word 'nature' or a recalibration of its meaning? I would advocate strongly for the latter option. The work of collapsing these outmoded categories and classifications has a long tradition which we can see in Arne Naess's 'Deep Green' philosophy, described by Warwick Fox (1984) as follows:

> [T]he world simply is not divided up into independently existing subjects and objects, nor is there any bifurcation in reality between the human and non-human realms. Rather all entities are constituted by their relationships. To the extent that we perceive boundaries, we fall short of a deep ecological consciousness. (Fox, 1984: 196)

This idea shows no sign of fading and was sustained in the growth of ecocritical studies through the 1990s, featuring in landmark ecocritical texts such as *What is Nature?* by Kate Soper (1995: 49–50), who argues that 'all the ways in which we differ from other species are matters of degree, which can be all the better illuminated by seeing them as gradations within an essential sameness of being'. In tracing the development of this holistic idea, it is also important to acknowledge that significant objections can be voiced, as argued by Jan Hochman (2000: 192):

> Nature and culture cannot be willed together by glibly naturalising culture, by culture simplistically proclaiming itself part of nature, or by stupidly making worldnature into an appendage of culture, worldnature into a culturally constructed product. Any substantial (reciprocal) merging of nature and culture will take generations of internal cultural struggle. (Hochman, 2000: 192)

Hall's fiction engages in just this 'internal cultural struggle', working at the conventional boundaries of human identity in order to question their limits. As Hochman notes, this process of reconceptualizing the interrelation between nature and human culture is radical and complex, but a crucial project for the Arts in the new millennium. Lea (2016: 201) closes his chapter on Hall with just this caution: 'If the way to authenticity is through returning to nature, as much contemporary pastoral writing suggests, Hall's estimation is that the journey would be quarrelsome'. The difficult work of 'merging' also takes place in the fiction of some of Hall's British contemporaries, such as Megan Hunter, Jon McGregor, David Mitchell, and Fiona Mozley. They build upon earlier novels by writers from across the Atlantic such as Cormac McCarthy's *The Road* and Margaret Atwood's *Maddaddam* trilogy, novels which also depict the condition of contemporary humanity in situations of ecological disorder in both realist and cli-fi scenarios.

For a sustained exploration of this ontological shift, I turn to the work of philosopher Michel Serres in *The Incandescent* (originally published in French in 2003). In this work, Serres discusses his idea for a 'Grand Narrative', which he terms 'genotypic memory' (Serres, 2017: 24). This concept is distinct from personal memory (the memories of an individual lifetime) and cultural memory (which extends back several millennia and rests on archeological evidence). By contrast, genotypic memory 'plunges into evolution and its billions of years':

In barking, grazing, spinning their webs, knotting their nests or mating, living things remember the last of these conservatories [genotypic memory] rigorously; their gestures flawlessly execute its dictates. Contrary to these genetic automatons, hominization made us into monsters of forgetfulness [...] The most amnesiac of living things. (Serres, 2017: 24–5)

Hall's literature works in just this vein: it is writing which works to remember 'the vast archaism of the flesh and the Earth' (Serres, 2017: 25). A deep-green monism is at work in Serres's philosophy, notably in his insistence upon the connection not just of all species (within, for example, Soper's 'essential sameness of being'), but also of all *matter* – organic and inorganic. This recalls Fox's statement above regarding the lack of bifurication between human and non-human realms, just as it can also be read as an extrapolation of Morton's ecosophical premise that there is no 'Nature', only ecology.

In his discussion of the 'dog box' episode in *The Carhullan Army*, in which Sister experiences a brutal reconditioning through several days' incarceration in a coffin-shaped box, Lea (2016: 175–6) describes the uncovering of the 'authenticity of her deconstructed animality', a process of 'stripping away of the ground cover of socialized identity, to tap into the igneous sub-strata of selfhood'. In terms of Serres's work, the 'sub-strata of selfhood' is *sedimentary*, rather than igneous, and contains multitudes: all phases of evolution of all life, our primordial inheritance. Beneath our human consciousness there is our mammalian brain, and then our reptilian brain within that. Underscoring our phylogenetic inheritance, Serres writes of the human relationship to *matter*. The selfhood which is excavated in Hall's work is not simply a baseline for *human* identity here. For example, Serres's genotypic memory can be connected to Hall's parallel exploration of lupine and human reproduction in *The Wolf Border*, and the spare, lean bodies of the Carhullan women in *The Carhullan Army* – 'creatures who bore no sense of category' (Hall, 2007: 118). The magical realism of 'Mrs Fox' allows for a very literal rendering of such slippage between distinct categories of species, of course, but Hall's work oscillates around this idea of the human as being animal and therefore within the class of animal species, as opposed to being its binary superior. Furthermore, human inheritance is not purely animal but also inanimate: consider *Haweswater* and Isaac's love of freezing his brain in the frosty streams of Mardale (Hall, 2002: 77), this habit taken to its apotheosis in his eventual merging (in death) with the benthic layer of the Haweswater reservoir. In the same novel, we also read episodes suggestive of the merging of human and rock: Jack Ligget's fatal rock-climb in *Haweswater*, prefigured in Paul Levell's paintings, which depict 'vast amalgams of environment and humanity. People of kept stone' (Hall, 2002: 185). A similar scenario is suggested in the narration of Peter Caldicutt while trapped in a landslide of stone on the moor in *How to Paint a Dead Man*.

The merging of humans and environment is a persistent feature of Hall's writing which resists analysis in postmodern terms. The 'post' now seems exhausted. As O'Donnell (2012: 431) notes, reworking the phrasing of John Barth's 1967 essay 'The Literature of Exhaustion', writers today can be said to operate with postmodernism under their belts but not on their backs: writers like Hall may use the techniques, they may even share some concerns, but the key difference between the postmodern then and the no-longer-postmodern now is our relationship to the natural world – to *real* nature, and our acknowledgement of the imperative status of ecosystemic health. In *The Oxford Handbook of Ecocriticism* Helena Feder (2014) calls for a change in

> our conception of the human and the nonhuman, of animality itself [...] The realization that the human animal is one of many life forms engaged in the interwoven (indeed, co-creating) process of nature and culture (or naturecultures) is the first step toward a post-humanist multiculturalism, an ecocultural materialist practice – toward concepts of subjectivity and knowledge, and knowledge itself transformed by interconnected social and ecological worlds. (Feder, 2014: 235)

There is a persistent flow of ideas, themes and questions on these topics that surface in different ways throughout Hall's work, all of them reaching a confluence which reads as a persuasive statement about our status as natural beings and our essential embeddedness within the ecosystem; this is what makes Hall part of a generation which steps beyond postmodernism with work that embodies, instead, an ecocentric approach.

The exploration of the ecologically embedded human, which Hall's work has consistently encompassed, is of deep cultural significance in a geological stage that is being referred to as Anthropocene (however informally) and goes some way towards an address of the strange 'transit lounge outside of history' that is Morton's (2013: 4) description of postmodern culture. In order to achieve this, the concept of human identity needs to be recast, moving away from a dualistic view of human culture and nature in opposition, thought to be problematic for Morton in particular and deep green ecosophy in general, and awakening a 'dormant' genotypic memory of the type Serres indicates (Serres, 2018). In the following sections of the chapter, I offer two principal ways in which this is grasped in Hall's writing: first, by deconstructing individualism in favour of identity forms which are conceived of as plural and, second, by recasting the human as an animal. The first step of this approach is particularly evident in *How to Paint a Dead Man*, and it is this text to which I will now turn.

Human Being

Hall's 2009 novel is written as a fugue composed of four characters whose narratives interweave: the historical Italian artist, Giorgio Morandi (1890–1964), whose (fictional) post-Second World War diaries are translated into the novel by Tom, the younger brother of Giorgio's sometime pupil, Annette. These translated diary entries form Giorgio's first-person narrative passages. Annette is a blind teenager who forms a bond with Giorgio through a mutual love of art and her experiences are narrated in the third person. Moving the action over from 1960s Italy to 1990s Britain, we read the third-person narration of Peter Caldicutt, a middle-aged landscape artist who was inspired by Morandi's work. It is Susan Caldicutt – Peter's daughter – who opens and closes this unusual novel, this time in a moment which we can assume is contemporary with its publication.

Susan's narrative takes us through a period of intense grief following the recent death of her twin brother, Danny, just six weeks and fourteen days prior, as we are told in the close of her first narration (Hall, 2009: 8). Susan's narration is written in the present tense using the second-person perspective which expresses both the disorientation brought on by catastrophic loss (she no longer has her corresponding coordinate, her twin) and the fundamental necessity of duality as a basis for her coherent identity – a view which implies the rejection of conventional notions of Western individualism by Hall's only example of a contemporary narrator in her novels.[3] Susan is aware of the atypical nature of her sense of self: she knows she is not 'like the rest of the psychically circumscribed automatons of the world' (Hall, 2009: 6), as she has led a life in which her consciousness and her view of herself have – naturally, authentically – been bound up with Danny's. Susan and Danny are dizygotic twins: each twin is genetically unique but shares an intense telepathic bond. This literary conceit foregrounds the determining role that biology plays in the formation of human consciousness. Like Roy's earlier text, Hall's masterstroke of narrative positioning here portrays the exquisite pain of losing one's *anima*. Towards the end of the opening chapter, we read:

> You are not yearning for improvement. You don't want to be reborn from a womb of material idealism. You don't wish to emerge, perfect and bright, out of the modern western chrysalis. You are not interested in living magnificently and utterly, certain that in this life you have triumphed. All you want is to be yourself again, because the identity that was once yours has vanished. Though a familiar face is reflected in the mirror, its anima is missing. *You* are absent. (Hall, 2009: 8)

Rather than Western individualism (whether that pertains to the positivistic cultural idealism of modernity or a capitalist logic of postmodernity), Susan yearns for a lost connection to the other living being who completed her sense of identity. The correction of self-perspective which had been attempted by a course of paediatric psychological therapy only resulted in Susan and Danny's concealment of their hybrid identity. The anima – Danny's feminine identity – must be restored in order to heal Susan's fractured sense of self. The novel's close remains resolutely in favour of biological and psychological connection as a natural predisposition for Susan whose healing is not achieved on individualistic terms. This conclusion demonstrates the novel's preoccupation with the idea of interconnection over individualism, a concern also apparent in its four-part narrative structure.

Interspersed with the other three principal characters of the novel, Susan's narrative passages trace the journey of her attempt to find some kind of balance for this loss via an intense sexual affair with her married work colleague, Tom (the aforementioned Italian diary translator). This takes place while she simultaneously becomes increasingly distanced from her own partner, Nathan. Susan's narrative closes the novel with a scene in which we are given the suggestion that she reaches a point of such resolution while doing a pregnancy test. Just before she sees the blue line develop, we read:

> This world can accommodate your situation, as it accommodates all situations. And your body will keep explaining to you how it works, this original experiment, this lifelong gift. Your body will keep describing how, for the time being at least, there is no escape from this particular vessel. These are your atoms. This is your consciousness. These are your experiences – your successes and mistakes. This is your first and final chance, your one and only biography. This is the existential container, the bowl of your life's soup, wherein something can be made sense of, wherein there is a cure, wherein you are. (Hall, 2009: 286)

The insistence on the material, bodily reality of human nature is strong here. The staccato sentences indicate an anchoring within the physical, natural, *real* realm, while the emphasis on particularity prevents the narrative from lapsing into a problematic universalism. Serres's notion of genotypic memory is evident in the insistence on the body's innate knowledge, as it will remember and execute the dictates of its archaic inheritance, 'explaining' to Susan how it works. As Susan sees the blue line appear, confirming the pregnancy, her husband calls for her and she replies: "'Yes,' you say. "I'm here'" (Hall, 2009: 286). Notably, Hall maintains the second-person narrative perspective through to Susan's final line, something that Daniel Lea

(2016: 183) interprets as an 'affirmation of herself as a singularity', the process of grieving for her twin reaching a new stage as she accepts the redrawn limits of her selfhood. However, this is the point at which she recognizes that she has become *two* again, the developing foetus within her shows Susan reaching a stage where her identity is, once again, inconceivable in singular terms. The foetus seems to be the answer to her missing anima – both the sense and the cure contemplated just before seeing the test's result. In retrospect, her intense affair with Tom was the body's answer to the situation she found herself in after Danny's death and the new child becomes the cadence to this novel's fugal structure, harmonising the four contrapuntal 'melodies' of Anette, Giorgio, Peter and Susan. The novel persists in its move away from individualism in favour of illustrating our interconnection across continents and through history. In ontological terms, it operates at a level that disturbs conventional concepts of selfhood. The exploration of these unconventional forms is a recurrent theme in Hall's work. Redrawing the parameters of human identity and creating a fictional space in which identity can be conceived of differently results in a novel which posits a version of selfhood that allows for the possibility of a greater sense of interconnection with other people, but also with the world around us. *How to Paint a Dead Man* shows us that we are not a collection of individuals, pitted against the wild environs which we sculpt to our ends.[4]

As in *The Carhullan Army*, the wild environs of the uplands play an important part in *How to Paint a Dead Man* throughout the narrative passages of Susan's father, Peter, giving him time to consider his own life, his mortality and the nature of human existence while trapped in a rock-fall on the moors. In a much less threatening scene, we have a dialogue about 'being' played out for us in quite explicit terms as Peter sits in the bath. Here he recalls his first wife, Raymelia, nearly 20 years earlier: 'Yes. He remembers Raymie. Bleeding from her nostrils as if she would never stop. Narcotic pioneer, showing them all how it was done. Holding forth about post-modern art and the inauthentic project of being' (Hall, 2009: 54). Raymie's view of human identity is proven to be catastrophically bad for her, and Peter ends up with little option but to extract himself from their toxic marriage. Contrast this memory of Raymie and her fascination with the concept of the inauthentic self against Peter's view of his own, now middle-aged body, in the bath:

> [W]ild man of the moors. He looks at his leg hairs swaying in the bath's current, like the manes of the fell ponies in the wind at the top of the valley. His cock hairs are turning grey, like the strands of fireweed caught in the elm trees in the garth. Crab ladder. Hernia scar. Patch of rabbit-skin glue. (Hall, 2009: 55)

Peter is recognizing here the extent to which his body has aged to resemble his surroundings, a landscape with which he has identified for a long time and which he paints obsessively. Rabbit-skin glue is a sizing agent used in the production of gesso paint and made from the collagen extracted from rabbit skin. With this detail, the link between art, the body and material nature are referenced again and connect to Morandi's preferred method of sourcing pigment for paint directly from rocks. Listed directly after the crab ladder and hernia scar in this way, the rabbit-skin glue becomes an integrated aspect of Peter's body, a nexus in which art, nature and identity combine, as we also see with the tattoo work of Cy and Riley in *The Electric Michelangelo*. Peter's body – his art – his environment: boundaries blur and evoke a strikingly different philosophy of human identity to Raymie's. In this 1990s moment of narration, the postmodern *then* is contrasted sharply with the no-longer-postmodern *now*, and the present moment of the narrative instead meditates upon this deep connection between a body and its local ecology. Peter's narration here indicates that there is an authentic self, rooted in one's natural surroundings, to the extent that he begins to see his own body as part of that landscape, evoking camouflage; indeed, at one point he almost disappears into a landscape of fallen rocks.

For another positive example of identity perceived in collective terms, I will conclude this section with Grace's view of Brooklyn life in *The Electric Michelangelo*. Even while living on the streets as a new immigrant to the USA following the global displacements of the Second World War, Grace sees the possibility of human interconnection, which is expressed here in naturalistic terms:

> The secret was that if the city tipped just so against the light you could see a fine web between corresponding human hearts throughout it, like a spider's web revealed in the grass on the steppe in the morning dew against the sun. It connected all paths and all peoples with a frail strength. (Hall, 2004: 215)

Hall's work pushes against the myth of human individualism in several ways, and this impulse in the writing connects to a wider thesis in which ideas of who and what we are as a species gets redrawn. In Hall's fictional worlds, humanity is conceived of as an interconnected web but, furthermore, these bodies are the bodies of *animals* and it is the contemporary representation of our animal self to which I will now turn.

The Human Animal

Explorations of our animal self feature most prominently in Hall's work in writing about sex, pregnancy, birth and motherhood, a collection of themes which begins to emerge on the final pages of *How to Paint a Dead Man*. Hall's work does not celebrate an archaic Earthmother ideal, a paradigm which affirms patriarchal binary hierarchies about women being 'closer to nature' because their bodily abilities. Rather, the picture of sex, pregnancy, birth and motherhood is here an ambivalent, complex one: sex is driven by instinct, bodily need and chemical attraction; pregnancy and motherhood are rarely seen as the apotheosis of womanhood. Instead, in Hall's novels, the central female protagonists (Janet, Rachel, Sister and Susan) come to motherhood reluctantly, accidentally or not at all. Birth is sometimes dramatic and harrowing (see the first chapter of *Haweswater*), and sometimes controlled and clinical (Rachel Caine's caesarean delivery in *The Wolf Border*). For Hall's mothers, babies are neither burdens nor blessings, the rosy glow of the post-partum moment is found to be a myth and the writing works to dismantle such expectations. The human animal's means of reproduction here work to resituate the political within the realm of the natural in literature which appears to be working to free reproduction from conventional cultural patriarchal codes and consider it instead as an essential aspect of animal existence – quite literally so in the case of the short story 'Mrs Fox'. Accusations of idealism are averted insofar as this animal realm then often rubs up against the social one bringing conflict into the text (as indicated at the end of *How to Paint a Dead Man* and Susan's closing dilemma).

In approaching this aspect of Hall's work, it is first worth noting that a significant amount of work is done to unshackle conventional associations between sex and romance in favour of a focus on the mammalian state: hormones, pheromones, the working of instinct. We read this in *Haweswater* (which, of all Hall's texts is the one with the most identifiable 'love story' element) as Janet searches for Jack in the darkness with her hands held out in front of her one night, guided by these human animal instincts:

> Her blood pulls and she trusts it. Her fingers brush past his face. The figure recoils, startled, as if a large moth has alighted on his shoulder, releasing a stifled cry. He hears someone inhale, the growl of energy gathering somewhere in a near portion of darkness. He is being attacked. Then her hands touch again, more certain this time, and he knows it is a friend. (Hall, 2002: 129)

This is just one occasion on which we hear this animal noise coming from Janet – if we look back to the scene in Janet's childhood when she saves her father from being gored to death by a bull, we read that she startled the bull by leaping onto its head from a tree with a 'cry, a throaty half-growl, half hiss' (Hall, 2002: 28). Such actions lead her father to conclude, in a passage of focalized narration, that Janet 'terrorizes the old notions, batters her way through and out the other side. There are no absolutes to be found in the blood on her wrists, and under her nails. She has feral qualities not belonging to either sex' (Hall, 2002: 73).

There are parallels here between the portrayal of Janet and Sister's description of the Carhullan Unit on the verge of their military coup. Sister speaks of the work that their leader, Jackie, has carried out in her extreme training routine, saying:

> She did not make monsters of us. She simply gave us the power to remake ourselves into those inviolable creatures the God of Equality had intended us to be. We knew she was deconstructing the old, disabled versions of our sex, and that her ruthlessness was adopted because those constructs were built to endure. She broke down the walls that had kept us contained. (Hall, 2007: 187)

The writing works towards an insistence on the authenticity of our animal selves in ways which do much to sever conventional human gender norms. Instead, it advocates the primacy of the animal state while also suggesting that the connection with the wild is the very thing which gives Janet and Sister the impetus for their violent interventions *into* politics and history.

Bearing this sense of the dual address of gender and human identity in mind, we turn to *The Wolf Border*, Hall's most sustained exploration of reproduction as a function of our mammalian identity. As Rachel returns from the Doctor's surgery where she has raised the possibility of a termination, she thinks of the wolves she has observed in whom 'instinct activates' and 'parenting is intuited': unlike Rachel, 'they have no choice' (Hall, 2004: 108). Rachel is caught between an already developing sense of acceptance of the pregnancy which seems to her composed of 'some rhythm – circadian, immune, hormonal, she does not know which exactly' (Hall, 2004: 105), and a life-plan which did not feature motherhood. This point of indecision illustrates a self deeply split between the options available through modern medicine and an infinitely more complex, animal self. As Rachel thinks to herself, 'What use are the higher faculties now … Cognition and invention, the internal combustion engine, intermittent wipers, peace treaties and poetry, the Homo Sapiens' thumb and tongue? Is optionality really evolutionary ascent when it leads to paralysis?' (Hall, 2004: 108). All advancements, modern and ancient, even evolutionary adaptations such as the opposable thumb and language – of what significance are they when faced with stages in one's life in which one is confronted by the substrata of their animal state? Here, the memory of Serres's genotype is shown to be in conflict with the advantages of modernity as well as with some of the significant evolutionary adaptations. Following Serres's (2018: 24) argument that 'hominization made us into monsters of forgetfulness', Rachel's mothering seems to be part of a journey of remembering, connected to similar disavowals of monstrosity in relation to Sister and Janet, as seen here above.

The manner in which Rachel's son, Charlie, is born once again brings this contrast of 'the vast archaism of the flesh and the Earth' and the advancements of modern science (Serres, 2017: 25). A natural birth would have corresponded well with the novel's exploration of wildness and mammalian ontology (as it does so very powerfully in *Haweswater*'s first chapter) but this baby is breach and Rachel has a planned caesarean section. In this twenty-first century, high-tech, sterile enclosure – the operating theatre – Rachel's long-held ambivalence about her pregnancy gives way entirely to her maternal instincts. These instincts are not in line with the conventional image of the mother experiencing a passive emotional connection to her child. Instead, Rachel experiences the assertive maternal instincts of a wild creature. As her son is pulled from her body and taken away to be cleaned, we read:

> Don't take him, she thinks. Give him to me, he's mine ... She wants to get up and go over there, pick him up. The surgeons are at her waist, taking too long. She doesn't care. There seems to be no need for anything else now. There is no wound. The only wound is life, recklessly creating it, knowing that it will never be safe, it will never last; it will only ever be real. (Hall, 2004: 254)

It is significant that the word 'real' closes off a long chapter entitled 'We are all Red on the Inside', flattening out any sense of human superiority over other animals because it all comes down to this: sex, birth and death – all animals are 'gradations within an essential sameness of being' to borrow Kate Soper's (1995: 50) phrase. Hall does not give us a romanticized portrait of new motherhood, but rather a possessive, protective animal claiming her young, while accepting the vulnerability, brevity and arbitrariness of life. With such scenes, Hall's work is entering heavily contested territory, particularly in the face of third-wave feminism with its developed notions of a gender spectrum and resistance to essentializing paradigms. Yet even in our transgender age, pregnancy and birth are still only possible within the female body and to bypass this topic in writing would be to ignore a hugely significant aspect of the (potential) bodily experience of the female human mammal, as well as to elide a crucial aspect of the continuation of our species (it being a moot point whether this is possible or even desirable). With regards to the male of the species, there is no analogue and so, in Hall's work, we look to other aspects which demonstrate a different view of the human animal in relation to male characters.

In *The Electric Michelangelo* the caustic, alcoholic tattooist, Eliot Riley, forms a counterpart to Reeda, the mother of protagonist Cyril Parks. By day, Reeda runs a boarding house for the elderly and consumptive in Morecambe, but by night she practices as an illegal home-abortionist for 'girls in trouble', as they were euphemistically referred to during this inter-war period. Hall's (2004: 27) sympathetic portrait of Reeda's care displays her as administering over the shadowy border between life and death, performing 'rituals in blood, aspects of the human body which lived beyond official stewardship and out towards an altogether stranger keeping'. The narration makes it clear that there has been a long attachment between Reeda and Riley and the two characters fulfil the role of parents for Cyril, following the early death of his own father at sea. After his mother dies, Cyril commits himself to Riley's business and cares for him in his self-destructive later years. In a move away from conventional gender norms, Reeda intercedes between life and death, whereas Riley brings new life into the world through his work as a tattooist. In relation to both Riley and Cyril's work as tattooists, the dialogue between nature and nurture is played out on the surface of the body through the process of being tattooed which enables a fuller expression of the animal self as it takes on its 'natural markings' using 'all the aspects of chromatic nature' to '[bring] forth self' (Hall, 2004: 96, 131, 149). On one of many drunken nights, Riley tells Cyril:

> Boy, come here. Listen. I'm a fucking midwife, boy, that's what I do, spread their fucking legs open and I catch their little babies and all their shit and blood from pushing and they never even bloody know it

... hahaha ... they never know they're birthing themselves, a fucking midwife I am. I am. (Hall, 2004: 94)

Riley implies a view of identity in which surface features are indicative of the most profound depths of self: apparently superficial tattoos, which postmodern theory might have regarded as constructed aspects of the performed self (Butler, 1988), are actually manifestations of various drives within us. In the apprenticeship, Riley makes Cyril work on himself first with a 'bamboo block and a hammer' (Hall, 2004: 99), a detail which draws our attention to the ancient, global tradition of tattooing. While this shows Riley's respect for the place of art as a crucial aspect of human nature, it also references periods of ancient and prehistoric human existence in which the dividing line between nature and human culture may have been a lot more fluid than it is in the present moment of the novel. In acquiring these markings, the tattooed body displays its authentic coherence, which is tied very tightly, in the language of this text, to the mammalian body: viviparous birthing and animal markings.

In addition to Hall's writing about the human animal, her work also provides several examples of non-human animals, which are always freighted with import regarding their position in relation to both humans and the ecosystem we all share. We see the somewhat more conventional domestication of animals in Giorgio's deep bond with the feral dog Benicio in *How to Paint a Dead Man*, and Grace's unusual cohabitation with her horse, Max, in *The Electric Michelangelo*. Also present in the work, however, are less conventional examples of interaction across species boundaries. Two episodes which resonate strongly are the slow death of the abused horse in 'Butcher's Perfume' and Jack Liggett ordering the poaching of the eagle in *Haweswater*. When presented with the dead eagle, Jack Liggett immediately regrets engaging the services of a poacher to kill the eagle for him, a creature which is described through his focalized narrative as 'perversely beautiful, fallen' (Hall, 2002: 201). Like Coleridge's Ancient Mariner, Jack acknowledges the bird's exquisite beauty and suffers deep regret for his actions, but Hall grants Jack none of Coleridge's redemption and Jack dies falling from a cliff face as he makes a frantic bid to put the dead eagle back into its nest. Retribution is taken away from the plot development and put into the hands of the horse-loving Slessor family in 'Butcher's Perfume', in which the abuser of the horse, Lenny Miller, has vengeance wrought upon him by the men who whip the 'putty' from his spine with a riding crop, leaving him paraplegic (Hall, 2011: 36). The two scenes of senseless animal suffering and death are points in Hall's oeuvre where her writing takes on a truly arresting quality, suggestive of a deep empathy for the other animals with whom we share this planet. The horse and the eagle take on a sacred quality in these scenes, evoking Rachel Caine's respectful distance from the wolves under her care in *The Wolf Border* whom she regards as '[t]he god of all dogs' (Hall, 2015: 6).

In the bleak short story 'Later, His Ghost', non-human animal life has been all but wiped from the locality of the narrative's British setting. So evocative of Cormac McCarthy's *The Road* (2006), this short story speculates a world in which the Gulf Stream has shifted off course, bringing about apocalyptic climatic conditions in the UK which are hostile to all life except the rats who can escape underground. Some human life is hanging on by its fingertips in a British town-scape partly eroded by severe winds in which our young male protagonist ventures out to scavenge in abandoned houses for fragments of Shakespeare's *The Tempest*. These he intends to present to his companion, Helene McDowell, a former English teacher at his old school, who is now heavily pregnant following a rape in this hellish speculative near-future moment. The protagonist's desperately naive and simplistic narration is buoyed up by three principal ideas: the quest for more fragments of *The Tempest*; the prospect of surprising Helene with a two-course Christmas dinner of food from scavenged jars (the narration all taking place on 23 December); and the memory, from two years ago, of seeing a stag in the vicinity:

> [A] fantastic thing. It was reddish, six points on each antler, standing perfectly still, like something from the middle of a forest, as if it had always stood there, as if tree after tree had been stripped away, until the forest had gone and there was nothing left to shield it. (Hall, 2017: 114)

The repeated phrase 'as if' attests to the boy's innocence: deforestation is precisely what has happened: tree after tree had indeed been stripped away, not just in the once densely-forested UK but in many locations around the globe, contributing to the process of global warming and resultant climate crisis that, it is indicated here, have shifted the Gulf Steam's course. The memory appears in a scene in which the boy considers his freshly damaged ankle, an injury about which he does not seem too concerned but which bears doom-laden insinuations from a narrative voice which indicates that his injury will shortly lead to him becoming the 'ghost' of the story's title. A striking textual correspondence is set up for us here as we recall that while Peter Caldicutt is trapped in the rock-fall in *How to Paint a Dead Man*, also with a damaged ankle, he too recalls once seeing a stag by the river 'with bloody velvets' (Hall, 2009: 85). Here we are given two points at which our protagonists are rendered suddenly very vulnerable with an ankle injury that will halt/slow their progress, allow infection into the body and, potentially, end their lives. At these moments, the two protagonists bring to memory their sighting of a stag, the largest wild land mammal in the British Isles. The power of the stag is contrasted, in each case, with the relatively feeble, injured human, the contrast serving as a reminder of personal frailty for Peter, but taking on a much wider, and far more poignant, significance in the case of the boy's story in 'Later, His Ghost' as he seems unaware of both his immediate vulnerability and of the vulnerability of human life on a planet so drastically altered by climatic disorder. In the present moment of *How to Paint a Dead Man*, we know that stags still exist in the UK; 'Later, His Ghost' is narrated from a speculative future-present in which stags are probably now all gone, soon to be followed by humans.

In her monograph, *Climate Crisis and the 21st-Century British Novel*, Astrid Bracke (2018: 87) discusses wilderness in *The Wolf Border* as a postmillennial fiction, stating 'In twenty-first-century novels, I'd argue, the desire for and appearance of the wild is yet another way in which contemporary fictions renegotiate contemporary climate crisis'. A consideration of Hall's work indicates that the human-animal's dependence on a stable ecosystem has become *the* formative creative context for literature in the opening stage of this twenty-first century, as contemporary culture goes through a redefinition of itself and its relation to the ecosystem. Serres's genotypic memory offers a profound way of conceptualising the human in relation to a new kind of Grand Narrative with a value that is as absolute as it is universal. This Grand Narrative offers us the possibility of connecting to a sense of the authentic which is so at odds with a postmodernism whose preoccupation with systems of meaning left it blind to the deep material processes that shape the larger ecological systems on which humans – and life itself – depend. In his conclusion piece for the anthology *Supplanting the Postmodern*, Nicholas Stavris (2015: 353) writes that we are 'living in this "techno-scientific world", now even more so than ever before. However, what has been steadily unfolding is a demand for simplicity, authenticity, and sincerity, a demand that is supplanting postmodern concerns for fragmentation and distortion' Hall's work achieves this through a process of redefining human identity away from individualism, and then recasting the human as part of the animal life on this planet (including the ways in which we interrelate with other species). The literature discussed here presents many instances of humans extracted from conventional social situations and instead stripped back to reveal a bare essence of our species. This literary incursion strikes out from the fragmentation and surface play of twentieth-century art and into the heart of ontological concerns engendered by our growing cultural awareness of ecological disruption.

Notes

1 The term 'cli-fi' has gained currency in the twenty-first century following its emergence in media circles, rather than academic publication. As the term is now widely adopted by ecocritics, Gregers Andersen (2016: 865) proposes that it 'should only be used to describe fictions of various genres that employ the specific scientific paradigm of anthropogenic climate change in their plot. That is, to describe fictions that explicitly use humanity's emissions of greenhouse gasses as some kind of driver in their world-making.'

2 For developments along these lines, see the work of Patricia Waugh (1989), Christopher Norris (1993), Terry Eagleton (1996) and Wendy Wheeler (1999).
3 Rachel Caine's present becomes a speculative one over the course of *The Wolf Border*; *The Carhullan Army* is set in a future-present, and Hall's other two novels – *Haweswater* and *The Electric Michelangelo* – are historical.
4 As a balance to this proposition, however, Hall's writing also explores the negative outcome of situations in which a sense of self is so dissolved as to become untenable. In the short story 'Case Study 2', for instance, we see the child subject, Christopher, as an example of a communal identification being taken to extremes (Hall, 2017). From early childhood, Christopher has been conditioned not to think of himself as 'I' at all but only as 'we' or 'us', in a narrative that seems to encapsulate in brief some of the more troubling aspects of communal identification at work in the farmstead of *The Carhullan Army*.

Works Cited

Andersen, G. (2016) 'Cli-fi and the Uncanny', *ISLE: Interdisciplinary Studies in Literature and Environment* 23(4): 855–66.

Barth, J. (1967) 'The Literature of Exhaustion', *Atlantic Monthly* 220: 29–34.

Bracke, A. (2018) *Climate Crisis and the 21st-Century British Novel*. London: Bloomsbury.

Butler, J. (1988) 'Performative Acts and Gender Constitution: An Essay in Phenomenology and Feminist Theory', *Theatre Journal* 40(4): 519–31.

Eagleton, T. (1996) *The Illusions of Postmodernism*. Blackwell: Oxford.

Farman, J. C., Gardiner, B. G., Shanklin, J. D. (1985) 'Large Losses of Total Ozone in Antarctica Reveal Seasonal ClO_x/NO_x Interaction', *Nature* 315(16): 207–10.

Feder, H. (2014) 'Ecocriticism, Posthumanism, and the Biological Idea of Culture', in G. Garrard (ed.) *The Oxford Handbook of Ecocriticism*, pp. 225–40. Oxford: Oxford University Press.

Fox, W. (1984) 'Deep Ecology: The New Philosophy of Our Time?', *The Ecologist* 14(5–6): 194–200.

Hall, S. (2002) *Haweswater*. London: Faber and Faber.

Hall, S. (2004) *The Electric Michelangelo*. London: Faber and Faber.

Hall, S. (2007) *The Carhullan Army*. London: Faber and Faber.

Hall, S. (2009) *How to Paint a Dead Man*. London: Faber and Faber.

Hall, S. (2011) *The Beautiful Indifference*. London: Faber and Faber.

Hall, S. (2015) *The Wolf Border*. London: Faber and Faber.

Hall, S. (2017) *Madame Zero*. London: Faber and Faber.

Hochman, J. (2000) 'Green Cultural Studies' in L. Coupe (ed.) *The Green Studies Reader: From Romanticism to Ecocriticism*, 187–92. London: Routledge.

Lea, D. (2012) 'The Anxieties of Authenticity in Post-2000 British Fiction', *Modern Fiction Studies* 58(3): 459–76.

Lea, D. (2016) *Twenty-first Century Fiction*. Manchester: Manchester University Press.

Morton, T. (2013) *Hyperobjects: Philosophy and Ecology after the End of the World*. Minneapolis: University of Minnesota Press.

Norris, C. (1993) *The Truth about Postmodernism*. Oxford: Blackwell.

O'Donnell, P. (2012) 'New British Fiction', *Modern Fiction Studies* 58(3): 429–35.

Serres, M. (2018) *The Incandescent*, trans. R. Burks. London: Bloomsbury Academic.

Smith, J. and G. Garrard (2017) *The New Nature Writing*. London: Bloomsbury.

Soper, K. (1995) *What is Nature? Culture, Politics and the Non-Human*. Oxford: Blackwell.

Stavris, N. (2015) 'The Anxieties of the Present', in D. Rudrumand and N. Stavris (eds) *Supplanting the Postmodern: An Anthology of Writings on the Arts and Culture of the Early 21st Century*, pp. 349–64. London: Bloomsbury

Waugh, P. (1989) *Feminine Fictions: Revisiting the Postmodern*. London: Routledge.

Wheeler, W. (1999) *A New Modernity: Change in Science, Literature and Politics*. London: Laurence & Wishart.

2

VITAL ANIMALS IN NIETZSCHE, GARNETT AND HALL

Elke D'hoker

Animals abound in Sarah Hall's fiction. In most novels, they are central presences, whether as companions, substitutes or foils for the protagonists. Think of Grace's horse in *The Electric Michelangelo*, the golden eagle in *Haweswater*, the wolves in *The Wolf Border* or the sheep in *The Carhullan Army*. Even more prevalent in Hall's work are animal metaphors, which serve to foreground the characters' bodies and instincts, ferocity and desire. The closeness between human and non-human animals suggested by these stylistic and narrative linkages is further literalized in 'Mrs Fox', where the female protagonist transforms into a fox. As critics have noted, Hall's foregrounding of animals, both real and symbolic, in her fiction suggests a deconstruction of the traditional boundaries between humans and animals. For Daniel Lea (2016: 193), for instance, both 'Mrs Fox' and *The Wolf Border* highlight 'the porosity between human and non-human animality' and in a discussion of the story 'Bees', Christiane Hansen (2019: 182) argues that 'the fox encounter comes to question the foundations of the human–animal divide in Western thought'.

In a contemporary context of man-made climate change and looming ecological disaster, Hall's exploration of human–animal relations and her questioning of the categorical, binary distinction between animal and human seem especially topical. They resonate with the recent posthumanist critique of the notions of human singularity and supremacy, central tenets of Western humanism, for their complicity with abuse, racial and gendered oppression, and the destruction of the eco-system (Braidotti, 2017: 26–8). Instead of the anthropocentric species hierarchy, Aristotle's 'Great Chain of Being', which puts man at the top of the scale as the measure of all things (Clutton-Brock, 1995: 427), animal studies scholars have proposed an alternative way of thinking, based on our 'being-in-relation' with non-human animals (Haraway, 2003: 12), or what David Herman (2018: x) calls the 'co-constitutive relationality between humans and other animals'. From a slightly different angle, new materialist philosophers have similarly insisted on the centrality of the body and, by extension, matter, as what we share with other animals and the natural world. In short, Hall's insistent foregrounding of the embodied and embedded nature of her protagonists and their close links with non-human animals clearly ties in with these wider cultural concerns and critical re-evaluations.

Yet, while posthumanist, neo-materialist and animal studies scholars typically celebrate this trans-species relationality and shared embodiment, Hall's fiction also explores the dark side of our human–animal natures. Several of her novels and stories gauge the violence and destruction to which our instincts, drives and desires can bring us. Moreover, in her stories and novels, Hall is not just concerned with what we share with other animals but also what distinguishes us, what it is that makes us human. In this chapter, I propose to trace both these explorations in Hall's oeuvre through a reading of the different animal figurations in her short fiction. Hall's short stories, published in the collections *The Beautiful Indifference* (2011) and *Madame Zero* (2017) offer many examples of animal–human encounters and tropes within a relatively short frame. Moreover, the short story's generic ties to the traditions of the tale and the animal fable also enable Hall to move more freely between realism and fantasy in her short fiction than in her novels. This is most apparent in 'Mrs Fox', the story that won the BBC short story Award in 2013 and was published as a separate booklet in 2014, before becoming the opening story of *Madame Zero*.

In the first part of this chapter, therefore, I will read this story of human–animal transformation in the context of other tales of metamorphosis, in particular David Garnett's *Lady into Fox* which forms the model for Hall's story. In a second part, I will expand my enquiry to other animal–human pairings, both stylistically and in terms of plot, in Hall's short fiction. I consider these in the light of recent insights from animal studies and critical posthumanism, before, thirdly, exploring Hall's affinity with Nietzsche's animal philosophy. Nietzsche's concepts of animal forgetfulness, the gift-giving virtue and the overman will, in a final part, allow me to probe Hall's exploration of exploration of the distinction between human and other animals in some of the central stories from *Madame Zero*.

Becoming Animal: Metamorphosis in Garnett and Hall

Western literature has a long tradition of tales of animal transformation, going back to Ovid's *Metamorphoses*, where human beings change into animals, often as a punishment from the gods. Following the Aristotelean 'Scale of Nature', the transformation is typically presented as a degradation and accompanied by a nostalgic longing for a previous mode of existence (Gymich and Segao Costa, 2006: 69). In Mediaeval literature, Caroline Walker Bynum (2001) has argued, hybrids and metamorphoses abound as an expression of the fear of otherness, of the 'self in dialogue with another' (hybridity) or 'the self becoming other' (metamorphosis) (Herman, 2018: 51). An engagement with otherness also underlies many modernist accounts of metamorphosis, most famously Kafka's *Metamorphosis*, where Gregor's sudden physical transformation spurs an extended and agonizing process of mental change in which human thoughts and perceptions are opposed to an alien way of experiencing the world. In postmodern literature, to the contrary, animal–human metamorphosis and hybridity are part of a playful celebration of flux and heterogeneity or, as in Angela Carter's animal tales, an expression of desire, passion and power (Pollock, 2000: 38).

While Hall seems to share with Carter a belief in a human–animal continuum centred on the body and sexuality, the immediate inspiration for 'Mrs Fox' is a modernist tale of transformation: David Garnett's *Lady into Fox* (1922). Hall inserts a playful nod to Garnett's novella in 'Mrs Fox', by calling the protagonist 'Sophia Garnett' and having the husband consult the library to find an explanation for his wife's transformation and bringing home 'medical texts and a slender yellow volume from the twenties' (2017: 26, 16). Like 'Mrs Fox', *Lady into Fox* revolves around a husband's discovery that his wife has suddenly turned into a fox. As in Hall's story, Garnett's Mr Tebrick tries at first to preserve the illusion that Silvia is still his wife – he puts clothes on her and keeps her inside – but in the end he sets her free. He meets 'his vixen' again in spring when she shows him her cubs. Throughout the summer he visits them and plays with them, but also worries for them and feels called upon to protect them. Only at the end do the two stories diverge. In *Lady into Fox*, Mr Tebrick's fears are realized as Silvia is pursued by the hunters' dogs and dies in his arms. 'Mrs Fox', on the other hand, has an open ending with the husband worrying about the foxes' safety – 'The woods are temporary and the city is rapacious' (Hall, 2017: 27) – and idly imagining his wife's return.

Unlike in most tales of transformation, the emphasis in 'Mrs Fox' and *Lady into Fox* is not on the metamorphosed being, but on the response of the husband, whose perspective shapes the narrative. Both stories thus invite being read as parables of a love that is tested yet endures; as allegories of a lover coming to terms with the fundamental otherness of his loved one. In *Lady into Fox*, the transformation could be read as a metaphor for Silvia's 'true' nature – instinctive, embodied, desiring – which has been repressed by the strict codes of genteel femininity. In 'Mrs Fox', on the other hand, Sophia's transformation could be understood as a metaphor for the physical and psychological changes that come with pregnancy and first-time motherhood (one of the first signs of Sophia's metamorphosis is morning sickness) and that demand a readjustment of the partner as well. Yet reading these stories as allegorical tales of change and otherness threatens to bypass the very real presence of the animals in both stories as well as the human–animal interactions that are at the heart of the stories. Moreover, as in all tales of metamorphosis, the process of human–animal transformation itself asks us to reconsider human proximity to animals. In order to gauge the extent to which 'Mrs Fox' radically dismantles or only temporarily suspends the human–animal binary and traditional species hierarchy, I will investigate more in detail Hall's representation of the process and consequences of this transformation. A comparison with the highly similar development in *Lady Into Fox* will also bring to light the impact of contemporary ecological awareness and changed gender ideologies on this representation.

For all their similarities, the stories show some remarkable differences as far as the process of metamorphosis is concerned. In Garnett's novella (1922/2013: 5), a very sudden physical transformation – '*where his wife had been the moment before was a small fox, of a very bright red*' – is followed by a slow mental transformation on the part of the wife. At first, Silvia still eats at the table, plays cards, enjoys music and stories and even observes Sunday rest. Only gradually does her animal nature assert itself: she tears up all her clothes, looks for ways to escape, chases ducks and, finally, devours a rabbit. In 'Mrs Fox', by contrast, mental and physical change take place simultaneously: after the metamorphosis Sophia immediately starts behaving as a real fox. Moreover, it is the physical transformation that is related in great detail, as the husband witnesses his wife's body changing during an early morning walk on the heath:

> She picks up her pace and begins to walk strangely on the tips of her toes, her knees bent, her heels lifted. Then she leans forward and in a keen, awkward position begins to run. She runs hard [...] She crouches on the path as he hurries after her, her body twitching [...] Something is wrong with her face. The bones have been re-carved. Her lips are thin and her nose is a dark blade. Teeth small and yellow. The lashes of her hazel eyes have thickened and her brows are drawn together [...] Now she is running again, on all fours, lower to earth, sleeker, fleeter. She is running and becoming smaller [...] All

vestiges shed. [...] She looks over her shoulder. Topaz eyes glinting. Scorched face. Vixen. (Hall, 2017: 8–9)

If in *Lady into Fox*, the metamorphosis is explained by Silvia's maiden name – Fox – and her abhorrence of the hunt, in 'Mrs Fox' it is through the body that the transformation is first announced and prepared for. Even when Sophia is still a woman, her body is described in animalistic terms. Her husband, for instance, notes her 'protruding bones' and the lack of 'corrugation on her rump' (Hall, 2017: 4, 2). When she vomits, similarly, she makes 'a clicking sound in her gullet' and 'a cry like a bird, but wider of throat' (Hall, 2017: 4, 6). Moreover, while *Lady into Fox* castigates even the slightest hint of instinct or desire as unladylike, 'Mrs Fox' already emphasizes Sophia's sensuality and sexual passion before the transformation. In this way, the metamorphosis from human to animal becomes a movement along a continuum, rather than a radical change. For Hall, in other words, human proximity to and affinity with animals is located in the body and its drives and desires. In fact, the very act of transformation is in 'Mrs Fox' connected to desire, it is called 'act of will' (Hall, 2017: 16, 20), and this contrasts starkly with the sense of loss and regret that traditionally accompanies metamorphoses in literature and can also be found in *Lady into Fox*. Juxtaposed to Silvia's distress and her very slow and painful relinquishing of feminine propriety, Sophia's wilful transformation reflects late-twentieth-century changes in gender ideology, which put a greater emphasis on female embodiment and allow for a freer expression of female desire and sexuality.

Yet, even if Hall's husband is considerably less upset by his wife's wildness and physicality than Mr. Tebrick, he nevertheless feels 'sickened', 'angry and ashamed' when he sees her kill a pigeon: 'He watches as she recoils and then pounces high, higher than she need, in excitement and prowess, and comes down hard on the helpless flurrying thing. She bites its iridescent neck. She twists its head. She is like machinery; the snapping and clicking of teeth' (2017: 18). As in *Lady into Fox*, this violent assertion of the fox's instincts forces the husband 'to acknowledg[e] her alterity and the futility of anthropomorphising her' (Ditter, 2019: 198). So, like Mr. Tebrick, he sets the fox free. After a winter of mourning and loss, the vixen parallel this act of love by re-establishing contact with their husbands in order to show them their offspring. This points to the continuity of sameness underlying the othering of the metamorphosis: even though they are marked by otherness and unknowability, both foxes remain, in one way or another, wives.

It is particularly this new relationship between human and animal, between the husbands and 'his' vixen, that leads in both stories to the husband's most radical self-doubts. Confronted by the 'brilliance' and 'magnificence' of the foxes as well as the love and natural harmony of their lives, the husbands start to question their own human nature, social codes and civilized conduct (Hall, 2017: 9, 28). Hall's husband realizes he can no longer speak to his wife, 'his voice sounds ridiculous to his own ears, a cacophony' and when he follows her to her den, he finds that 'his footfalls are mortifying, though he tries to tread respectfully through this palace of delicate filaments' (Hall, 2017: 17, 24). Juxtaposed to suburban fathers 'lifting their children out of car seats and up from toppled bicycles', the foxes' energetic play on the heath comes to seem more natural and harmonious (Hall, 2017: 27). The husband's 'great inspirational feeling' when watching the cubs also echoes the intense happiness of Mr. Tebrick who spends an idyllic summer with the foxes (Hall, 2017: 24). The latter realizes the 'folly' of 'all human customs and institutions' and vows 'I would exchange all my life as a man for my happiness now [...] the beasts are happier and I will deserve that happiness as best as I can' (Garnett, 1922/2013: 84).

In short, while the continuum between woman and fox in both stories deconstructs the human–animal binary, the husbands' proximity to – and, in *Lady into Fox*, emulation of – the foxes' easy existence in their natural habitats also serves to challenge the superiority of human life and civilization. In *Lady into Fox*, however, Mr Tebrick's idyllic animal existence, and the concomitant reversal of the species hierarchy, proves to be short-lived. It is destroyed by the hunters who set out to kill the foxes when autumn comes. In a climactic final scene, Mr Tebrick fully experiences what it means to be an animal, to be prey: 'before he could turn back the hounds were upon them and had pulled them down'. Yet, after this brief but radical experience of human–animal oneness, human distinction and supremacy are restored again: the fox dies, while Mr Tebrick 'recovered his reason and lived to be a great age' (Garnett, 2013: 91).[1]

Although the ending of 'Mrs Fox' is considerably more ambivalent, here too the human distinction and superiority seem reasserted at the end. Just as the hunt does not finally kill Mr Tebrick, so too the husband's worries about the foxes' survival in the face of the urban expansion and ecological destruction do not call his own safety into question. Moreover, precisely by highlighting these worries, thoughts and dreams – 'to suspend thought is impossible' – Hall draws attention to the narrator's rich mental life and distinguishes his investment in the past ('He thinks of Sophia, the woman he loved') and the future ('the mind is made perfectly of possibilities') from the foxes' instinctual immediacy (2017: 27-8).[2] The final lines of the story might seem to reassert animal superiority as the husband realizes that the loss of the fox would be more 'unendurable' than the loss of his human wife has been: 'To watch her run into the edgelands, breasting the ferns and scorching the fields, to see her disappear into the void – no – how could life mean anything without his unbelonging wife' (Hall, 2017: 28). Still, the possessive pronoun in the final phrase does hint at the husband's continued sense of mastery and ownership.

This sense of possessiveness runs in fact throughout the story: from the early statement 'she is his to kiss' to his reading of the fox's return to him in terms of 'a dog [...] returning to its master' (Hall, 2017: 10); from his sense of 'victimhood' after his wife's transformation, 'Something has been taken from him', to the proud realization that the cubs 'are, they must be, his' (Hall, 2017: 2, 10, 20, 24). Even though the husband generously relinquishes full control by allowing the fox to return to the heath, the final sentence as well as the title, 'Mrs Fox', suggest that the husband is unable to fully renounce a sense of mastery over his wife, both as woman and as animal. In this too, the story carries echoes of *Lady Into Fox*, where the husband's patriarchal authority is even more pronounced: as a landowner he is lord and master over animals, servants, and his wife alike. He also consistently refers to Silvia as 'his vixen', even though his ownership of her is undermined to an even greater extent than in 'Mrs Fox' as Silvia has mated with a dog fox to produce offspring. In short, although 'Mrs Fox' is considerably more contemporary than *Lady Into Fox* in its celebration of the female body and sexuality as the basis for a human–animal continuum, it still carries echoes of traditional patriarchal attitudes and continues to insist on a human distinctiveness that may well be superior to animal existence. Whether this is a reflection – and possibly critique of – the husband's residual anthropocentric and patriarchal worldview or rather the overall ideological stance of the story as a whole can only be decided by turning to other figurations of the animal–human relationship in Hall's short stories.

Being Animal: Predator or Prey

Although no other human–animal metamorphoses take place in Hall's fiction, in many of her stories protagonists are linked to animals, through metaphorical description, metonymical linking or both. Indeed, an encounter, interaction or contiguity with a real animal is often further underscored by metaphoric descriptions that highlight the protagonist's animal characteristics. Through both narrative and stylistic means, in other words, the short stories highlight human proximity to animals. In 'Bees', for instance, the displaced and traumatized narrator draws strength from an epiphanic, early-morning encounter with a fox. The fox is 'fearless', 'unapologetic' as 'if it owns this city enclosure' (Hall, 2011: 85). It is described as 'a candid little hunter' that 'crouches for a moment, then springs up on its back legs. The jaws open and snap shut, and as it lands it shakes its red head furiously'. The adjectives fierce, fearless, furious echo those used in 'Butcher's Perfume' to describe the protagonist's friend, Manda Slessor, who is 'fierce', a 'fighter', with a 'pedigree', 'fire-dog eyes', 'that got set off easily, like a dog chained up all its life and kicked about, pone to attack for no other provocation than it catches you looking its way' (Hall, 2011: 4-6). In fact, the entire Slessor family, which so fascinates the protagonist, is given animalistic characteristics through metonymic association – they are a proud horse-breeding and dog-owning family – as well as metaphoric description: the parents are said to 'have paired by feral instinct, like wolves'. A traumatic encounter with a maltreated, dying horse then puts Kathleen's relation to Manda and her family in a new light.

Another woman–dog alliance can be found in 'She Murdered Mortal He', where the female protagonist strikes up a friendship with a large stray dog, which comes to act out her anger at the lover who jilted her. In 'The Nightlong River', to give another example, the female narrator feels as powerful as a dog or predator when hunting mink with her brothers:

> We were in the hinterlands, a wilding place, where the reign was ours entirely. We were the wolves. We were the lions [...] Sometimes I imagined I could, like the dogs, detect the waft of mink through the ferns [...] And when an animal blurted from its hole [...] my heart banged up towards my throat, and my eye focused. (Hall, 2011: 160–1)

In 'Goodnight Nobody' from *Madame Zero*, finally, Jem sees her mother in terms of the animal–human hybrid from *Thundercats*, 'Mumm-Ra', because of her 'power' and 'strength', her seeming mastery over death, and because she 'could sense things coming like a dog could' (Hall, 2017: 127, 130).

These examples further confirm Hall's dismantling of the human–animal binary, which was also evident in 'Mrs Fox'. Moreover, they highlight again that, for Hall, the proximity between animal and human is located in the body, with its instincts and desires. Moreover, in most stories this animal connection confers a sense of vitality, power and strength on the protagonists, which is further underscored by the opposition between the instinctual, fierce and natural behaviour of the animals (and animal-like protagonists) and the rules and laws of civilized behaviour, which come to seem very repressive, artificial and stale by comparison. For the Slessor family, for instance, 'all the laws of the town, the curfews and fines, the borstal and jail time, mattered not' (Hall, 2011: 16) and this stance is vindicated by their outsmarting the police at the end of the story. In 'The Beautiful Indifference', on the other hand, the protagonist places feeling over reading – 'she disliked books [...] Her preference was for company, the tactile world, atoms', and sexual passion over civilized conversation:

> She still found it remarkable: the spurs of desire, and the way desire interfered with all else. They were perfectly capable of having conversations, about politics, their occupations, anything. But they were not capable of corralling the animal necessity of ruining each other first. (Hall, 2011: 43, 47)

This questioning of the established hierarchies of reason over instinct and civilization over nature is also expressed by Hall in her preface to the short story anthology *Sex & Death*, which she edited together with Peter Hobbs: 'What civil lives we lead. So mannered, so controlled. Everything tidy and safe [...] But underneath, closer than we dare to think, is the reddish nature of humanity, the strong meat of our anatomy. The force that drives us on, generation after generation' (Hall and Hobbs, 2016: 1).

Hall's editing of a short story anthology on these very issues underlines the timely nature of her emphasis on embodiment, her exploration of human–animal interactions, and her questioning of the binary opposition between animal and human. Indeed, the relationship between humans and animals has become a central concern in animal studies, new materialism, ecocriticism and posthumanism in recent years. In her *Companion Species Manifesto*, for instance, Donna Haraway (2003: 12) argues for our 'being-in-relation-to-one-another', for a recognition of the 'co-constitutive relationship' of humans and animals, which we also saw at work in stories like 'Butcher's Perfume' and 'She Murdered Mortal He'. For Rosi Braidotti (2013: 67–8), on the other hand, 'becoming-animal' is an important step in the posthumanist overcoming of the anthropocentric, exclusionary and ultimately destructive legacy of Western humanism. Deconstructing the species hierarchy with its radical distinctions between human, animal and the rest of nature is for Braidotti part of a more general dismantling of all self-other binaries in favour of a neo-materialist embracing of multiplicity, relationality, and change. While Hall seems to agree with Braidotti that our embodied and embedded existence puts human beings on a par with other animals, instances of 'becoming animal' in Hall's fiction are considerably less all-embracing and less self-effacing than the transformation Braidotti (2013: 136–7; 2017: 31-5) calls for, whereby 'becoming imperceptible' is the true goal of an inclusive and egalitarian embracing of what Aristotle called *zoē*, or all of life. Hall's animal–human imaginaries, to the contrary, show a marked preference for mammals over birds or insects, for the strong, solitary animals over the herds, and for fierce predators over their prey.

In this way, Hall's configuration of animal–human relations also differs from the emphasis on a shared creaturely precariousness that marks the approach of prominent post-humanist animal studies scholars like Anat Pick, Cary Wolfe and David Herman. For Wolfe (2010: 80), for instance, 'the key link between animal and human beings' is 'their shared finitude as embodied, vulnerable beings'. Taking his cue from Simone Weil's argument that 'The vulnerability of precious things is beautiful because vulnerability is a mark of existence', Anat Pick (2011: 3) similarly argues for an understanding of human–animal commonality in terms of a shared vulnerability which has only become more pressing in the face of global warming and ecological destruction. Or, as David Herman (2016: 3) puts it, 'the status of being a creature subject to the requirements of the surrounding environment, the vicissitudes of time, and the vulnerabilities of the body, emphasises the fundamental continuity between humans and other animals'.

In spite of a common emphasis on materiality and embodiment, Hall's staging of human–animal relations and a human–animal continuum seems far removed from these ethics and poetics of the 'creaturely', based on a shared vulnerability. Instead, Hall's stories highlight the power and vitality of animals, and of the protagonists in touch with their animal being, even when other creatures – bees, pigeons, geese or rabbits – are hunted and killed in the process. Moreover, as we have seen, human beings are not as threatened by ecological destruction as the foxes in 'Mrs Fox', nor are they as vulnerable in the face of the climate crisis depicted in 'Later, His Ghost', where animals have all but disappeared. I would argue, therefore, that Hall's depiction of the interaction and affinity between humans and animals owes less to contemporary ecocritical or posthumanist approaches than to an older, philosophical tradition of naturalism that found one of its most imaginative expressions in what Vanessa Lemm (2009) has called, Nietzsche's 'animal philosophy'.

Animal Forgetfulness in Nietzsche and Hall

More than with contemporary animal studies, Hall's representations of animals and animal–human connections shares an affinity with the way Nietzsche places the animal, and 'the continuity of the animal, the human and the overhuman' (Lemm, 2009: 3), at the centre of his philosophy. Like Hall, Nietzsche opposes the vitality, energy and immediacy of the animal to the artificial existence and restrictive codes of civilization. For Nietzsche, human beings have strayed from their animal natures under the influence of civilization, with its 'willed and forced animal taming' (cited in Lemm, 2009: 11). Rather than being 'the crown of creation', therefore, the human being is 'the most unsuccessful animal, the sickliest, the one most dangerously strayed from its instincts' (cited Lemm, 2009: 14). Like Hall, moreover, Nietzsche seems to specifically think of the strong animals or predators here: the eagle and lion are key symbols in *Zarathustra* and in the essay 'Homer's Contest', he praises the ancient Greeks for their 'trait of cruelty, of tiger-like pleasure in destruction' (cited Lemm, 2009: 16). Moreover, if in Hall's stories, the strongest characters seem to be those who are in touch with their animal instincts and desires, also Nietzsche argues that human beings have 'to return to animality and animal forgetfulness' in order 'overcome the human', much like Zarathustra is led by the animals towards the Übermensch or 'overhuman' (Lemm, 2009: 15). An important characteristic of the animal in this respect is 'forgetfulness', the ability to be 'contained in the present' and, hence to be courageous and 'honest' (cited Lemm 2009, 114). Lemm summarizes Nietzsche's idea of animal forgetfulness as follows:

> Forgetfulness is a blind passion, a kind of frenzy and stupidity. Without forgetfulness, the human animal would not dare take risks; it would not give itself and throw itself into its life and its actions. It

is a frenzy (*Wahn*) that enhances the human animal's activity and increases its vitality. Forgetfulness narrows down, centers, and concentrates the perspective: to 'forget most things so as to do one thing'. In the human animal, forgetfulness gives rise to a higher, more virtuous, and more generous form of human animal life than an all-too-human memory. It leads the human animal to its highest purpose, which is, according to Nietzsche, to perish in the pursuit of one's dearest values and highest aims. (Lemm, 2009: 93)

In Hall's stories too, the most powerful and vital protagonists are characterized by this forgetfulness. The hunting girl in 'The Nightlong River', for instance, reflects on the recent death of her best friend as follows,

The truth of death is a peculiar thing. When they leave us the beloved are as if they never were. They vanish from this earth and vanish from the air. What remains are moors and mountains, the solid world upon which we find ourselves, and in which we reign. We are the wolves. We are the lions. (Hall, 2011: 165)

The sentiment is echoed by the protagonist of 'She Murdered Mortal He', who has almost forgotten her ex-lover after an exhilarating walk through the African jungle and along the shore: 'She could accept the end now. She could embrace it. No one was irreplaceable. No one. He could go. She would let him go […] Let him join the men of the past. Her old lovers were ghosts. None of them had survived; none were missed' (Hall, 2011: 143). Similarly, at the end of 'Butcher's Perfume', Manda has already forgotten about the mistreated horse and its owner, while the narrator 'thought about the man, lying lame in a hospital bed' (Hall, 2001: 37). Both these stories, however, also register a sense of uneasiness about the animal forgetfulness and single-mindedness of these female characters. In 'Butcher's Perfume', Kathleen scans her friend's face for 'some sign of disturbance', but 'saw nothing favourable' (2011: 3), while the title of 'She Murdered Mortal He' hints at the darker meaning of the protagonist's exorcizing of her ex-lover, who is mortally wounded by the wild dog she has taken a liking to.

In 'The Beautiful Indifference' too, the protagonist's animal forgetfulness, her frenzied embracing of the moment in a passionate affair with a much younger lover, takes on a darker undercurrent as the story progresses. Initially, her reckless celebration of the body and instincts over reason and propriety, her preference for life over literature, seems a positive thing, with her friend's disapproval – 'Being with him means you can defer all the rest […] keep avoiding the hard stuff' – amounting to little more than the jealous voice of conventional femininity (Hall, 2011: 44). Yet, the protagonist's animal forgetfulness, artificially enhanced by the pills of paracetamol she takes thrice in the story, comes to seem more and more like an intentional numbing in the face of the trauma of her mother's death, possibly through suicide. In this, she comes to resemble the bolted horse that she encounters in the climactic scene of the story. The horse is blindly 'hammering down the street', '[i]ts breast working like a machine', 'its eye white-cupped and livid' and the protagonist thinks, 'Someone would have to catch it before it damaged itself' (Hall, 2011: 61–2). In view of the story's hinting at the protagonist's own suicide at the end of the story, these lines come to seem ominously prophetic.

A final grim questioning of human animality can be found in 'Evie', the last story of *Madame Zero*. As another story of a woman's transformation told from the perspective of her husband, 'Evie' forms an interesting counterpart to the opening story, 'Mrs Fox'. At the start of the story, Alex is surprised to note an increased craving for sweets and chocolate in his wife: 'She went with a predatory look to the cupboards. She wasn't thinking, just acting on impulse. She was drinking more too. Wine with dinner every night, a few extra glasses at the weekend; becoming gently hedonistic' (Hall, 2017: 152). Alex is annoyed at first, 'She was acting a little irresponsibly', and then wonders whether 'she might be pregnant, and hormonal' (Hall, 2017: 155). Yet he ends up embracing her new hedonism and, in particular, her increased sexual desire: 'The rules were gone. It was easy to say these things; easy to undo himself. They'd suddenly found each other, through irrepression, means he did not quite understand. Her age, hormones, a revival of some lost appetite, the arrival of a new one; it didn't matter, he didn't care' (Hall, 2017: 166). Evie's impulsive, instinctual behaviour and her uninhibited sexual passion are initially reminiscent of other sexually liberated characters in Hall's stories: Sophia in 'Mrs Fox', the protagonist of 'The Beautiful Indifference', or the wife and mother who visits a sex agency in 'The Agency'. Moreover, Evie's explanation for her changed behaviour – 'Her body finally knew what it was meant for' – or her exhortation, 'We only live. We only live, Alex', seem to echo Nietzsche's rejection of the restrictive codes of 'civilized' behaviour and his celebration of animal forgetfulness as a vitalistic embrace of life (Hall, 2017: 166, 168). Yet, the turning-point in the story reveals Evie's transformation to have been the result of a brain tumour. Her initial 'wild' and 'predatory' behaviour is now likened to that of a cow: 'She was making long, low sounds, bellows, almost cowlike. There was a smell like offal' (Hall, 2017: 172). After the diagnosis has been made, Evie still has instinctive cravings, but 'she knew what it was now. She was self-conscious, and fought for rationality' (Hall, 2017: 175). As in 'Mrs Fox', the ending of the story thus seems to reassert reason and self-conscious thought as markers of human distinctiveness and superiority. In a similar way, Nietzsche's celebration of animals and animal life ultimately serves a reassertion of human superiority, more particularly through the figure of the 'Übermensch'.

Becoming Overhuman: Responsibility and Gift-Giving

For Nietzsche, as we have seen, human beings need to reconnect to animal life and animal forgetfulness. Yet, this is not an end in itself, rather a means of becoming 'overhuman' in 'a movement of excess and an extension of the human that leads it beyond its all-too-human form', to a vitalistic embracing of the future as an 'eternal recurrence of the same' (Lemm, 2009: 23). Apart from this commitment to the future – as opposed to both the animal's being in the moment and human being's resentful focus on the past (Lemm , 2009: 2) – the overhuman is for Nietzsche characterized by an ethics of 'gift-giving' and 'freedom as responsibility' (Lemm, 2009: 30). In *Zarathustra*, Nietzsche praises the 'overhuman' as one 'whose soul squanders itself, who wants no thanks and returns none: for he always gives away and does not want to preserve himself' and as one 'whose soul is overfull, so that he forgets himself' (Nietzsche, 1883/2005: 14). In this extraordinary generosity, 'the relationship between the self and the other is not symmetrical' (Lemm, 2009: 61). Rather it is an expression of 'power, for it is the complete affirmation of life which is capable of embracing existence while it resists every negative or life-denying ideal' (White, 2016: 352). Similarly, 'the gift-giving virtue is 'useless' because it cannot be measured in the ordinary terms of social utility, and it is not the means to any further values'. Moreover, White continues, the gift-giving virtue is for Nietzsche 'the 'highest' virtue, because it is an expression of the most complete affirmation of life, and there is nothing beyond life that could lead to a higher transcendence'.

In Hall's stories too, the virtue of gift-giving recurs as a superior human quality. As in Nietzsche, moreover, it is especially associated with those protagonists, often though not always female, who have been given animal characteristics through metonymic or metaphoric associations. 'Butcher's Perfume', for instance, ends with Mandy and her mother giving 'a new pony' to Kathleen, thus drawing her further into the fierce and independent Slessor clan (Hall, 2011: 37). In 'The Nightlong River', the protagonist hunts mink to make the Christmas gift of a mink coat for her dying friend, while in 'The Agency', the flamboyant Anthea offers the business card of the agency to her discontented friend: 'This is for you, darling, she said, passing the card to me. One shouldn't have to go on feeling so embarrassed about oneself. I am a great believer in private acts' (Hall, 2011: 96). In 'Mrs Fox' too, gift-giving occurs when the husband 'takes from his pocket the little purple ball Sophia used to keep in her purse' and leaves it near the entrance to the foxes' den (Hall, 2017: 27).

Perhaps the most compelling example of a Nietzschean gift-giving that draws on animal renewal can be found in 'Later, His Ghost.' In a dystopian world in which violent winds have all but obliterated human and animal life, the narrator imagines himself like an animal in order to get up and venture outside:

> because it was too difficult today, he thought, *Buffalo*. He pictured a buffalo. It was enormous and black-brown. It had a giant head and the shoulders of a weightlifter, a tapered back end, small upturned horns. The image came from a picture he'd kept in a box in the bunker [...]

> The buffalo looked permanently, structurally braced. (Hall, 2017: 101)

Like the young woman in 'The Nightlong River', the young man in 'Later, His Ghost' risks his own life on dangerous missions into the ruined town in order to find enough pages of Shakespeare's *The Tempest*, so that he can present the book as a Christmas gift to Helene, the pregnant woman he's taken into his home. Moreover, '[a]s well as the surprise gift, he'd been planning their Christmas meal. He'd had a tin of smoked pheasant pâté for two years, it was too special to eat by himself […] It was important to try to celebrate' (Hall, 2017: 105). Although the protagonist has been drawing on animal-like strength and instincts to survive in this hostile world, the story emphasizes that it is his generosity, optimism and self-consciousness that make him human:

> On the way out he saw his own reflection in the dusty, cracked hall mirror […] His coat hood was drawn tightly around his head; he was earless and bug-eyed, and one eye lens was shattered. The metallic tape around his neck shone like scales. He looked like some kind of demon. Maybe that's what he was, maybe that's what he'd become. But he felt human […] He could use a can opener. And he liked Christmas. (Hall, 2017: 119)

The gifts in these stories are not sensible, utilitarian or reversible; they are not caught up in a logic of give and take. Rather they are an expression of freedom and an excess of strength: they go from those who are powerful to those that are weaker or in need. As in Nietzsche, gift-giving is thus also associated with the responsibility that comes from freedom and power: as when the anaesthesiologist in 'Theatre 6' assists a pregnant woman in spite of government regulation or when the young girl in 'Goodnight Nobody' travels on her own to the morgue to bring her mother the sandwiches she had forgotten. As we have seen, similar notions of responsibility and superiority characterized the husband–fox or human–animal relation in 'Mrs Fox', where they also served to underline human distinctiveness over and against a shared animal embodiment.

Throughout Hall's short fiction, then, animal metaphors as well as human–animal encounters and transformations clearly foreground the body, with its instincts, needs and desires, as the basis of a human–animal continuum that connects us to animate life around us. Moreover, like Nietzsche, Hall suggests that being aware of this shared embodiment, being in touch with this animal life may result in a sense of freedom, power and vitality that rivals, or overcomes, an all too restrictive and repressive 'civilised' behaviour. Yet, if Hall's animal imagery thus challenges the traditional binary that represents animals as humanity's radical 'other', her stories also explore what distinguishes human from other animals: be it reason, self-consciousness, a concern with past and future or an ethics of gift-giving that draws on individual freedom and strength to freely give to those more vulnerable. In this way, Hall stops short of the more radical – but perhaps also more facile – embracing of a shared creaturely vulnerability or pan-*zoē*-affinity advocated in posthumanism and animal studies. Instead, following Nietzsche, Hall seems to suggest that a renewed proximity to animal life is necessary for an overcoming of the limited, 'all-too-human' human, in order to become the 'overhuman', a hybrid creature imagined by Hall in 'Later, His Ghost' as a Shakespeare-quoting demon and by Nietzsche in 'The Genius of Culture', as 'a centaur, half-animal, half-man', with 'angel's wings upon its head' (Nietzsche, 1876/1996: 115).

Notes

1 In his analysis of human-to-animal metamorphoses, Timothy Baker (2019: 83) argues that Silvia's death is necessary to restore patriarchal order and authority, given the challenges Silvia presents to species and gender hierarchies.

2 Both Timothy Baker (2019: 88) and Julia Ditter (2019: 201), however, read this ending – with its emphasis on the possibility of further transformations – as the ultimate confirmation of the story's critique of human–animal binaries and its celebration of hybridity, impermanence and change. Yet, the story very clearly presents this final image as the content of the husband's wishful dream or imagined vision, which in itself marks the difference between the human husband and his animal wife

and points to his maturation and development as much as – hypothetically – to that of his wife.

Works Cited

Baker, T. C. (2019) *Writing Animals: Language, Suffering and Animality in Twenty-First-Century Fiction*. Cham: Palgrave Macmillan.
Braidotti, R. (2013) *The Posthuman*. Cambridge: Polity Press.
Braidotti, R. (2017) 'Four Theses on Posthuman Feminism', in R. Grusin (ed.) *Anthropocene Feminism*, pp. 21–48. Minneapolis: University of Minnesota Press.
Bynum, C. (2001) *Metamorphosis and Identity*. New York: Zone Books.
Clutton-Brock, J. (1995) 'Aristotle, the Scale of Nature, and Modern Attitudes to Animals', *Social Research* 62(3): 421-40.
Ditter, J. (2019) 'Human into Animal: Post-anthropomorphic Transformations in Sarah Hall's "Mrs Fox"', in B. Korte and L. Lojo-Rodríguez (eds) *Borders and Border Crossings in the Contemporary British Short Story*, pp. 187–204. London: Palgrave Macmillan.
Garnett, D. (1922/2013) *Lady Into Fox*. Mineola, NY: Dover.
Gymnich, M. and Segao Costa, A. (2006) 'Of Humans, Pigs, Fish and Apes: The Literary Motif of Human-Animal Metamorphosis and its Multiple Functions in Contemporary Fiction', *L'Esprit Créateur* 46(2): 68–88.
Hall, S. (2011) *The Beautiful Indifference*. London: Faber.
Hall, S. (2017) *Madame Zero*. London: Faber.
Hall, S. and Hobbes, P. (eds) (2016) *Sex & Death: Stories*. London: Faber and Faber.
Hansen, C. (2019) 'Indifferent Borders: Confined and Liminal Spaces in Sarah Hall's "Bees"', in B. Korte and L. Lojo-Rodríguez (eds) *Borders and Border Crossings in the Contemporary British Short Story*, pp. 171–86. London: Palgrave Macmillan.
Haraway, D. (2003) *The Companion Species Manifesto: Dogs, People, and Significant Otherness*. Chicago, IL: Prickly Paradigm.
Herman, D. (2016) 'Introduction', in D. Herman (ed.) *Creatural Fictions: Human-Animal Relationships in Twentieth- and Twenty-First-Century Literature*, pp. 1–15. New York: Palgrave Macmillan.
Herman, D. (2018) *Narratology Beyond the Human. Storytelling and Animal Life*. Oxford: Oxford University Press.
Hall, S. and Hobbs, P. (eds) (2016) Sex & Death: Stories. London: Faber and Faber. Lea, D. (2017) *Twenty-First-Century Fiction: Contemporary British Voices*. Manchester: Manchester University Press.

Lemm, V. (2009) *Nietzsche's Animal Philosophy: Culture, Politics and the Animality of the Human Being*. New York: Fordham University Press.

Nietzsche, F. (1876/1996) *Human, All Too Human*, trans. R.J. Hollingdale. Cambridge: Cambridge University Press.

Nietzsche, F. (1883/2005) *Thus Spoke Zarathustra*, trans. Graham Parke. Oxford: Oxford University Press.

Pick, A. (2011) *Creaturely Poetics: Animality and Vulnerability in Literature and Film*. New York: Columbia University Press.

Pollock, M. S. (2000) 'Angela Carter's Animal Tales: Constructing the Non-Human', *Lit: Literature Interpretation Theory* 11(1): 35–57.

White, R. (2016) 'Nietzsche on Generosity and the Gift-Giving Virtue', *British Journal for the History of Philosophy* 24(2): 348–64.

Wolfe, C. (2010) *What is Posthumanism?* Minneapolis: University of Minnesota Press.

3

Homo Sapiens
Being Human in *How to Paint a Dead Man* and *The Wolf Border*

Natalie Riley

In their introduction to the 2016 short story collection *Sex & Death*, Sarah Hall and Peter Hobbs consider the bare self that fiction reveals. At moments both ordinary and extreme, Hall and Hobbs suggest, the civil veneer of contemporary life is wrenched away, exposing the naked creature beneath. For Hall and Hobbs (2016: 1), literature offers an insight into this fundamental bedrock of human nature:

> Look at us in our ties and our stockings, taking vitamins and buying prophylactics, arranging mortgages and emptying recycle bins, ameliorating, ordering. We've almost convinced ourselves.
> But underneath, closer than we dare to think, is the reddish nature of humanity, the strong meat of our anatomy. The force that drives us on, generation after generation, the gust behind us we don't want to feel but is always felt, moves us towards the edge. How we come in, and how we go out, sex and death: these are our governing drives, our two greatest themes. The humid embrace and the cold sweat. The weight of a coffin on the shoulder, the illicit kiss or *la petite mort*; the sting of intimately split flesh and the wonder of holding a tiny howling genetic machine in our arms. These are the moments we are left

staring into the void, realising, rejoicing, or fucking it all up. (Hall and Hobbs, 2016: 1)

Edging close to the border that separates biology from biologism, Hall and Hobbs cast sex and death as organizing principles not just of the human body but also of human behaviour. It is a stark portrait, and one which shares more than a passing resemblance to the neo-Darwinism that suffused mainstream British intellectual culture during the late twentieth century. Intent upon a full description of human life in light of its evolutionary origins, neo-Darwinist theorists such as Richard Dawkins (1976) and E. O. Wilson (1978) argued that the causes of human behaviour can be divined in the processes of natural selection. This materialist agenda relies on a single, core assumption: that the human being and homo sapiens are one and the same, and can therefore be explained by those natural principles and laws that have already sufficed to explicate all other biological phenomena (Dennett, 1991: 33).[1] As Dawkins (1976: 67) infamously summarizes in *The Selfish Gene* (1976), every human being is merely 'a gene machine', and the brain that takes decisions for it nothing more than an organic device for 'individual survival and reproduction'.

The 'reddish' image of humanity offered by Hall and Hobbs (2016: 1) likewise places generation and degeneration at the heart of human experience: the governing drives of their own genetic machines – sex and death – are here representative of a fundamental and inescapable materialism which similarly situates all human life within the larger principles of biological, and more specifically, evolutionary continuity. Hall and Hobbs are not alone in their attention to the biological capabilities of the body and of fiction. New British writing has been more widely marked by the influential rise of the life sciences, with contemporary novelists such as Jeanette Winterson, Ian McEwan, Zadie Smith, Graham Swift, and A. S. Byatt all engaging with neo-Darwinian ideas (see Waugh, 2005: 63; see also Byatt, 1995). Adopting ideas and vocabularies drawn from the life sciences, novelists of the contemporary are exploring new questions about the relationship between mind and body, plasticity and determinism, and agency and causality. Peter Boxall (2013: 123) has termed the heightened attention to the material reality of the human body as the emergence of 'biological subjectivity'. Styled after Nikolas Rose's (2007: 26) 'somatic individual', the biological subject defines the re-emergence of the 'oozing stuff of life' in contemporary British fiction after the waning of postmodernism (Boxall, 2015: 76).

Sarah Hall's fiction shares this sensibility for the oozing stuff of human being. As Daniel Lea (2017: 154) has recently noted, Hall is 'a writer of shit, piss, phlegm, semen, rot, mud, and death, who sees in the depths of the human body and wildness of nature an obscene denominator which underpins all relationships'. Hall's close and concerted attention to the concrete materiality of human bodies – their physical surfaces and depths – comprises a literary response to the twenty-first century concern with embodiment. But despite the attention critics have paid to the supposedly 'natural' matters of the body in Hall's work, there has been a profound silence surrounding the biological in her novels.[2] By addressing Hall's persistent interest in the biological substratum of human life, this chapter address themes that deserve far closer examination in her work. In her two most recent novels, *How to Paint a Dead Man* (2009) and *The Wolf Border* (2015), Hall pays close attention to the biological realities and thematic potentialities of mortality and reproduction. In these novels, the material conditions of embodiment are bound up in the biological regimes of the *homo sapiens*. Our embodiment entails birth and death, but it similarly requires being, oneself, a body that is alive; open to and partaking of the sensual world, subject to decay and disintegration, and – potentially – to the visceral mess of reproduction. Hall explores how this awareness of the brute materiality of the human organism acts as a fundamental organizing principle of human existence.

Nature Morte: Still Life, Realism, and the Body in *How to Paint a Dead Man*

In Hall's 2009 novel about mortality and materiality, the governing forces of reproduction and death are explored in the form of painting known as still life. At its simplest and most conventional, the still life may be described as the artistic representation of material things. Whether natural or man-made, the objects which the still life presents to the viewer are normally the recognizable items of the domestic interior (Bryson, 1990: 13). The first of Hall's four narrators, the enigmatic still-life painter Giorgio, keeps a collection of bottles, decanters, and coffee pots which he frequently depicts in his paintings (Hall, 2009: 72). Referencing the basic, daily acts of eating and drinking, Giorgio's artefacts are typical of the objects of still life, which recall the familiar and comforting routines of the household; trivial and often overlooked 'acts of bodily survival and self-maintenance' (Bryson, 1990: 14). As Giorgio tells his young student, Annette Tambroni, however, there is often a much graver symbolism at work in these seemingly realistic paintings. Later, in her own narrative, Annette remembers how Giorgio had spent all afternoon describing the still lives of 'the artists of Holland' (Hall, 2009: 128):

> In these paintings there would often be something sinister and cautionary in the corner, a little unpleasant danger, like a fly walking towards an apple, a snail on the lip of a jug, or some mould or blemish on the rind of a Clementine. This was called symbolism. 'It is like life,' he said. 'All things desist. All things are temporary.' (Hall, 2009: 129)

Symbols of filth and decay, both fly and mould pollute the scene and turn the local site of bodily maintenance into a larger, abstract meditation on the transitory nature of life (Bryson, 1990: 107). Part of the tradition of *vanitas* (see Renger, 1997: 10), the Dutch paintings that Giorgio describes act as a discomforting reminder of the eventual corruption to which all flesh – whether animal or fruit – is vulnerable. Balanced between the celebration of an ordinary and everyday human reality, and the absolute knowledge of its ephemerality, the still life in *How to Paint a Dead Man* stages the twin tensions of realism and symbolism, generation and degeneration, and the competing human drives towards life and death.

We can easily consider these contradictions at the heart of the still life as being emblematic of wider thematic tensions surrounding death and materiality which are played out in *How to Paint a Dead Man*'s four interlinked narratives. The literary techniques employed in the novel have been likened to other forms of painting; most notably to the self-portrait and to 'accretive realism', as described by Cennino Cennini in the novel's epigraph (Lea, 2017: 177; Vice, 2017: 75). An awareness of the still life as a continual intertextual and ekphrastic referent in Hall's novel, however, adds a further layer of understanding to her text. As in the genre of painting, reminders of human mortality hang in the corner of each of the four narrative frames that Hall constructs. Each of her characters is bereaved, and the spectre of death and the mortification of the body hangs over each offered narrative. The aged painter, Giorgio, suffering from advanced lung cancer and increasingly immobile, spends his final months teaching in 1960s San Lorenzo. It is here that Giorgio meets Annette, whose own narrative will take place several years after his death. Like her art teacher, Annette's life is gradually restricted before her horrendous murder – not by the congenital impairment that leaves her blind, but by her family's growing desire to keep her safe from harm. A more temporary constraint is placed on the middle-aged landscape painter, Peter Caldicutt. Giorgio's former penfriend, and now father-of-two, Peter finds himself trapped in a narrow ravine and is gravely injured while out walking on the Cumbrian fells in the mid-1990s. In the wake of her twin brother's fatal traffic collision, Peter's daughter, Susan Caldicutt, finds herself similarly stalled. Feeling absent from her body after Danny's death, Susan stops working as a photographer and instead begins a series of secular mortifications of the flesh. Mixing illness, injury, and death, each of these four narratives mirrors the form of the still life writ large – undertaking an examination of the tensions between life and death, and exploring the inescapable materiality of the body.

While as a still life artist Giorgio has always been in the business of attending closely to the ephemeral nature of things, his recent diagnosis of terminal lung cancer has made his awareness of his own mortality particularly keen. It is precisely the discovery of the body's 'errors,' as Giorgio observes, that serve to remind us most of our biological nature (Hall, 2009: 11). Giorgio perspective echoes the work of Jonathan Cole and Shaun Gallagher (2016: 379), who posit the idea that illness is an embodied experience that can make the body

– and its fleshy components – feel suddenly more present.[3] The everyday tasks of our bodies do not consume our attention in same way when healthy – illness, however, as an embodied experience, creates an experiential shift in our sense of agency, ensuring that the body is increasingly experienced as an object to be considered, and perhaps managed (Cole and Gallagher, 2016: 379).

Confined by ill-health to his hilltop estate, Serra Partucci, Giorgio is acutely aware of the material limitations that now govern his body, and he worries about the toll that his increasingly sedentary existence will take on his mental life. Above all, he dreads a particular 'paralysis of the mind' that he has witnessed in friends and colleagues, and which he believes is caused by physical 'immobility' (Hall, 2009: 40). For Giorgio, this sign of a direct and abiding link between mind and body serves as a daunting reminder of his own mortality. Giorgio is his body, and when his body dies, so will he. Yet, in spite of the existential dread which could accompany this realization, Giorgio evinces the quiet fatalism of the still life itself: an artform which 'accepts the material fate of living in a creaturely universe, subject to limitation and routine' (Bryson, 1990: 95). On Giorgio's part, this comprises an acceptance of the prospect of death as the unavoidable price that we pay for the contract of life; the interweaving of which begins at birth, Giorgio reflects, and against which there is no fighting the inevitable trajectory:

> Our minds are born nervous, in darkness. We are subterranean beings. We must learn by the senses and continue to be instinctual, to use the antennae. The oils of lavender bring sleep when we apply them to the pillow. Aniseed stirs us. In the museums, we must believe in the Dutch trick, the red deer, and the monk beneath the vast sky. (Hall, 2009: 280)

Only because we are embodied, Giorgio argues, can we sense the workings of the material world and can they, in turn, move us – even though to be embodied is also to be mortal, fragile, and ultimately finite. Sensuous experience is both the price we pay for our material existence, and its very consolation; a dichotomy enacted in the still life as a delicate balance between the celebration of material abundance and the knowledge of its absolute ephemerality – between the generative and degenerative realities of life and death. It is evident, then, why Giorgio has pursued the still life as art form for the vast majority of his professional existence, convinced that it offers a means of understanding the 'intimacy' that the human body shares with things: 'How well I know life. I understand water in its glass. As the afternoon circles, shadows move behind the objects on the table' (Hall, 2009: 16). Only because life is inherently and invariably material, does the very act of painting a still life offer the opportunity for a lyrical reflection on our material existence marked by the inevitability of death and decay.

For Peter Caldicutt, the second of the novel's aging artists, this direct and abiding link between mind and body proves to be a subject of equal concern, and one which forces him to consider the body's biological nature. Like Giorgio, Peter has been thinking about what it means for the body to be in decline, and of how this transformation may affect his mental life. Stretched out in his bath, Peter cannot help but note the physical symptoms of aging. Cataloguing these signs like the objects of a still life, he observes how his 'cock hairs are turning grey, like the strands of fireweed caught in the elm trees in the garth. Crab ladder. Hernia scar. Patch of rabbit-skin glue' (Hall, 2009: 55). Each of these visible marks functions as a *memento mori*, leading Peter to wonder:

> Is everyone in his generation taking gingko biloba, doing brain aerobics and writing pompous memoirs? Or are they all crumbling mentally, having heart attacks while shopping for tweed jackets, or banging their secretaries, or emptying their colostomies? Dear God, are they officially old? (Hall, 2009: 54)

Despite this ironic distance, Peter cannot avoid the fact that he is now closer to the end of his life than he is to its start. His sense of increasing physical frailty is brought into sharp relief when Peter heads out walking in the Cumbrian fells in search of a subject for one of his landscape paintings. When Peter slips and falls, he finds that his leg is caught in a narrow ravine. Wedged tight, Peter makes several attempts to free himself, but each time he is thwarted by some powerful agency of self-preservation beyond his conscious control:

> The pain increases, eating through his cells. He tries to remain there. But some cautious auxiliary lobe in his brain is firing and any minute now it is going to rescue him by over-riding the decision to self-harm. He can't. He can't do it. He lifts back up, his whole body weak and shaking. (Hall, 2009: 220)

For Peter, pain is a somatic experience which transforms his sense of agency, highlighting the degree of separation between his conscious self-determination, and an independent, unconscious imperative towards self-preservation. In order for Peter to extricate himself from the ravine in which he is trapped, he must reach an accommodation with this alternate, bodily agency rooted in an appreciation of the complex biological processes of the body. His successive attempts to simply overrule this over-riding impulse, to 'fight the threshold' of his own body, prove to be unsuccessful:

> He reaches down into the crucible, between the stones, to the point of compression. He reaches further through the agony, and touches the leather of his boot [...]. But pain in his leg is speaking directly to his brain, wanting to shut him down. He claws at the laces frantically, tugs at the fastening until the struggle is too intense. (Hall, 2009: 275–6).

Instead, it is only when Peter fully appreciates the underlying purpose of this bodily agency that he finally discovers the means of extricating himself. Just as the firing of the auxiliary lobe constitutes an unconscious act of self-preservation, so too Peter must consciously decide, more than anything, that he 'wants to live', that he 'wants to go home' (Hall, 2009: 275); a determination which echoes his earlier decision to save himself and abandon his first wife, Raymie, to her self-destructive spiral. Torn between painful recollections of his youth and an agonizing present, Peter comes to the realization that it is only a similar determination to survive at any cost which will allow him to free himself from his present predicament. As he asks himself, rhetorically, what 'other choices are there really, other than to say, I am this, and I am here?' (Hall, 2009: 275). Rather than trying to directly oppose the unconscious, cautious imperative of his brain, Peter instead finds the determination he needs by tapping into the same underlying, biological imperative for survival. It is only this determination to live which can offer a sufficient enough motivation to allow Peter to endure the pain he experiences. Only then is Peter finally able to free himself from the ravine.

Like Giorgio, and her father, Susan Caldicutt also displays an intuitive sense of the close and direct relationship between mind and body, though her own concern is framed almost exclusively in terms of her understanding of twenty-first century biology. Susan, then, functions as a particularly lurid example of Rose's somatic individual, who comes to experience and articulate her corporeal reality through the language of biomedicine and the life sciences (Hall, 2009: 26). This tendency has emerged alongside an increasing belief that corporeal reality can be modified at will to meet the desires and designs of consumers, via the deployment of various medical and scientific technologies. As Rose (2007: 11) proceeds to explain, such a conviction is founded on the belief that the body might be perfected through diet, pharmaceuticals, and cosmetic surgery, amongst other biomedical means.

The contemporary London of Hall's novel is one which is firmly situated within this posthuman milieu. As Susan observes of her contemporaries, it seems as if 'identity can be chosen' and that '[p]eople are aware of the heart, slopping about like a piece of lively meat inside the chest, as if it isn't snug, as if it hasn't been fitted right' (Hall, 2009: 7). Whether we look to our nervous systems, our genetics, or to neo-Darwinian natural selection, this ever-increasing tendency towards the human scale has refocused attention on the body. Yet, rather than this close attention making the body feel like home, the very basis of our material being, in Hall's contemporary London it instead leaves people feeling 'trapped inside the dull, deficient hides that Nature has unhelpfully allocated' (Hall, 2009: 7). Within this portrayal, the operations of capitalism and the clinic can be seen to reinforce each other: individuals 'are constantly told that a better incarnation lies just over the horizon' of biomedical intervention (Hall,

2009: 7). For Susan, the impetus which she sees underlying this hope for bodily perfection is the pervading human fear of mortality: 'if this is all you've got, this single chance, this brief blemished simian posing opposite you in the mirror, then hadn't it better be refined'? (Hall, 2009: 7).

Susan's own feeling of a dis-accommodation between mind and body likewise arises from a human fear of mortality; in her case that of her grief following the death of her twin brother, Danny, in a fatal traffic collision. As Susan observes, Danny's demise leaves her feeling that her mind and body are suddenly unmeshed, the traumatic event functioning as a 'reminder of what it is to be anatomised, what is it is to be made of particles, neurones, nerves and senses, what it means to be homo sapiens' (Hall, 2009: 282). But if her brother's accident serves as an acute reminder of Susan's existence as a biological entity, and by extension, of her own materiality, it is a lesson which she seems unable, at first, to accept. Rather than bringing her closer to her body, Danny's death creates in Susan a curious sense of evacuation, conveyed through the use of the second person. Within her narrative, Susan seems to speak from outside of herself, addressing herself in the second-person as she would another – a linguistic quirk which serves to emphasize the figural absence of her brother, her twin, with whom she first enacted this duality of 'you' as an intermediary term between her first-person experience and Danny's third: a conscious echo perhaps, on Hall's part, of Luria's twins, who had no word in their private language for 'I', and who instead referred to themselves interchangeably in the third person. As Susan tells herself in the novel's opening passage, with Danny now gone:

> The hands pouring the milk from the bottle were no longer yours. They felt numb, and when the bottle slipped from your grasp, smashed on the kitchen floor and cut your legs, the red drip-drip seemed inconsequential. That feeling of daily animus, that life-gust, which you have always taken for granted, was simply not there. Your body went about its business, but you were not the driving force. (Hall, 2009: 171)

Without the presence of her twin, Susan, at first, seems incapable of overcoming the evacuation of self and animus that has arisen as a result.

In her desperation to regain her lost sense of embodiment, Susan makes several unsuccessful attempts to tap into the 'true biological impetus' of 'pain and desire', 'hunger and fear' (Hall, 2009: 282). She pinches herself until red, reverses a former decade of vegetarianism, and starts a risky but sexually fulfilling affair with a colleague at the art gallery where she works (Hall, 2009: 282). Such purely sensual pursuits, however, have little impact on her feelings of dislocation. It is not until the final pages of the novel that Susan is able to unambiguously reunite her experience of mind and body. Locked in the bathroom, with her partner, Nathan, preparing their tea on the other side, Susan urinates onto a plastic pregnancy test and waits for the results. Ambivalent about the prospect of motherhood, Susan asks herself what is would mean to be pregnant:

> You have a partner who loves you, employment, a house. You have parents, talents, a salary, a vote, and firing synapses. Hitherto your body has not let you down – breasts, cervix, eyes, ovaries, cerebral functions, immune system, lungs and heart: nothing has yet malfunctioned, no dire failure has occurred, beyond the gentle degradation of ageing. If you choose to, you will live. And in your hands might be another life. (Hall, 2009: 283)

A mixture of autobiography and CT scan, Susan's deliberations re-establish the centrality of her body and its complex biological activity within her sense of self. Alongside the more typically-discussed accomplishments of employment, partner, and home, Susan reclaims her firing synapses, her healthy immune system, and her cerebral functions, as powerful and determining aspects of her identity. A significant reversal in Susan feelings of estrangement, this renewed attention to the neurobiological underpinning of her subjective experience is of course tied to her feelings surrounding her pregnancy. While the death of her twin brother results in Susan's traumatic rejection of the body – both its materiality and its mortality – it is the reminder of 'life' – both hers and another's – which forces Susan to accept the material events, and even constraints, that inflect her experience.

It is this visceral reminder of the body's biological capacity to give as well as lose life, that paves the way for Susan's return to a somatic experience of self. As Susan observes, through the process of pregnancy 'your body will keep explaining to you how it all works' (Hall, 2009: 285). To be reconciled with her embodied nature is to be reconciled with her mortality – to what Hall terms her 'first and final chance' at existence (Hall, 2009: 286). To realize this promise, Susan gives the body absolute primacy as the ground of human being and the site from which consciousness and identity emerge. Though in-and-of itself this is perhaps not a controversial claim, Susan goes further by seeming to suggest that her life is utterly determined by her body. In the face of its own reproductive agency, Susan seems to believe that she has no choice but to regain her sense of embodiment, and to allow her changing body to explain to her how and what to be. At the conclusion of Hall's novel, Susan is not just united with her body, she is thoroughly governed by it: a biologically determined vision of a wholly somatic individual in which freewill seems to recede, replaced by a biological functioning over which she envisions little to no control. It is only once this seeming surrender has occurred, and an explicit and corrective reunification of atom and consciousness has taken place, that Susan is able to re-establish her own intentional sense of self. Only at the end of the passage, at the end of the book, is she able to reclaim the first-person pronoun for the first time in the novel, responding to Nathan's inquiry with the simple but profound statement 'I'm here' (Hall, 2009: 286).

Evolutionary Erotics: Reproduction and Death in *The Wolf Border*

In her subsequent novel, *The Wolf Border* (2015), Hall again links death and reproduction. The plot centres around the decision of Rachel Caine, a zoologist, to return to the UK and oversee a rewilding project in the Cumbrian landscape in which she grew up. Informing this professional decision, is a series of profound personal tribulations with which Rachel struggles. As in *How to Paint a Dead Man*, life and death are fundamentally intertwined in *The Wolf Border* when Rachel's life is transformed by the death of her mother and the birth of her first child; the bringing of one person into the world and the letting go of another. Again, Hall positions these materialist themes alongside a scientific vocabulary which concerns genes, neurones, and hormones, as Rachel approaches questions of biology, and authenticity, through the language of evolutionary theory. Rachel's sense of the human condition, then, is one which is moulded by her understanding of biology. A dispassionate observer of herself and her fellow humans, Rachel seems to view the human body and its behaviour as that of a specimen for scientific study.

This unsentimental, biological materialism with which Rachel views the world is particularly notable in regard to her attitudes to sex. Rachel's approach to intercourse is almost exclusively mechanistic. The majority of her attention is paid to the interaction of surfaces, senses, and body parts. While sitting in a Cumbrian bar, casually cruising, Rachel imagines what it would be like to have sex with one of the patrons. Lost in her reverie, Rachel thinks of her previous sexual encounters, which have all followed a similar script. Producing a composite of her previous experiences, which blurs memories with an imagined present, Rachel details a hypothetical encounter in which the sexual act is rendered into little more than a Newtonian account of matter and mass in motion. First, she must sort 'through the bodies' she encounters until she finds what she is looking for (Hall, 2015: 38). Her selection will be based on some appealing quirk of anatomy: 'the way he carries himself, his movement, or the strength of bones' (Hall, 2015: 39). From here, the couple will travel away, perhaps to an apartment, a hotel, or convenient dirt road (Hall, 2015: 40). The sex itself will be conceived of as a similar series of motions, staged along the same causal continuum: 'He steps in, kisses her, one of evolution's stranger necessities. It does not take much to accelerate him, the angle of her body, her tongue' (Hall, 2015: 40). Accompanied only by the biologically-demanded rituals of courtship, Rachel's pared-down account renders sex at once carnal and reductive; 'just movement and noise, flesh slapping' (Hall, 2015: 41).

When she does concern herself with the complex social practices which typically surround sex (such as her discussion of kissing, above), this is only to view such conventions as having their authentic origins in the shared biological basis of our being. Divested of all but the simplest principles of evolution and mechanics, Rachel views sex as an act of the utmost authenticity. In the carnal meeting the true self is exposed: 'identity is revealed in the habit of climax; it is the real introduction' (Hall, 2015: 41). *Real* is – as discussed above – a slippery term. But here Hall invests it with the full weight of biological truth and authenticity. As in *How to Paint a Dead Man*, Rachel views the body with a primacy based on its very materiality, understood in light of evolutionary theory. The compulsion which she experiences towards sex, in its naturalistic origin, is seen as being 'automatic' and 'impossible to stop' (Hall, 2015: 41). Desire and love, then, are perceived as having their authentic basis in a residual, naturalistic self: in the idea that evolutionary instincts remain unchanged beneath the thin patina of our social lives. A conception which, in its stripping away of the civil veneer of daily life, is reminiscent of the paradigm Hall will later suggest in *Sex & Death*.

Though Rachel uses the impersonal register of evolutionary theory to posit the body as the ground of a natural self, Hall's novel highlights how Rachel's investment in these terms is not value-neutral or dispassionate. Instead, it is shown to arise from a deeply personal fear and distaste for intimacy. Rachel's fascination with the evolutionary basis for the mechanistic rituals of sex, is in marked contrast with her distaste for the complexity of familial, emotional relations; for forms of intimacy and interrelation which are typically understood as likewise sharing an ostensible, evolutionary basis and purpose. As the reader will discover, Rachel's relationship with her mother, Binny, has always been difficult. Rachel's upbringing, and that of her half-brother, Lawrence, is both unconventional and turbulent. An idiosyncracy which results in arguments at home, name-calling in school, and in Rachel feeling that she must be wholly self-reliant at a young age. The result of this imbalanced childhood is a profound emotional deficit:

for decades the members of her family have been 'orbiting each other only if it suited them, not required to show love or compassion' (Hall, 2015: 43). We are, then, invited to view Rachel's adoption of science as a way of organizing these relationships, and of justifying the paucity of her emotional connections to both Binny and Lawrence. Even Rachel's mother appears to realize that her daughter has harnessed scientific, and particularly evolutionary discourse, in order to avoid investing in the messy nature of the human relationships that she has with those closest to her. As Binny observes: '*You're always on about science. Why don't you talk about people more? Where's all your blood going, my girl?*' (Hall, 2015: 44, emphasis in original). For the reader, the answer seems evident: Rachel has invested in science because of its typical connotations of being objective, neutral, bloodless, dispassionate, and distant. All of the qualities that are diametrically opposed to the subjective messiness of the human intimacy which she fears.

When Rachel finally visits her mother after a three-year absence, and notes her pronounced decline, the spectre of Binny's impending mortality is largely seen through the lens of this dispassionate, scientific register. Rachel spends less time engaging with the intimate, emotional nature of their reunion than she does in a meticulous cataloguing of the signs of Binny's steep 'descent' (Hall, 2015: 16). In a parallel of her attitude towards sex, Rachel's first reaction to seeing her mother is to describe the transformed surfaces of Binny's body in marked detail; how her mother's hand on the doorframe 'looks fossilised, like something extracted from a bog' (Hall, 2015: 16); and how her body radiates with 'the reek of sweat and ammonia' (Hall, 2015: 16). Viewed in terms of the body alone, Rachel's once virile mother can no longer be identified. The '[s]elf-declared red-blooded sensualist' of Rachel's youth has now been reduced to 'an impotent leaking ruin' (Hall, 2015: 18). Lingering over the changes that age has created in her mother, Rachel's scientific dispassion is such that there is little emotional tenor to her description, even when she considers that the changes in her mother's body are 'flags of Rachel's future, perhaps, if it's all laid out in the genes' (Hall, 2015: 20).

Rachel's unsentimental perspective on human nature has often been viewed as an extension of her professional life (Cottrell, 2017:

683; Ya-Chu Yang, 2018: 7). As a zoologist, it is to be expected that Rachel will broadly subscribe to the ideals of scientific rationalism, which makes her lengthy discussions of biology less surprising than those of Susan Caldicutt. Yet, it is still important to note the degree of nuance present in Hall's portrayal of Rachel's evolving faith in the explanatory powers of science, a variation which is particularly notable in Rachel's ambivalent experience of pregnancy. Rachel discovers that she is pregnant only a few months after the death of her own mother, Binny. As in *How to Paint a Dead Man*, sex and death are thematically united in *The Wolf Border* when the reader learns that the date of conception is New Year's Eve; the very same night that Binny takes a fatal overdose of aspirin and amlodipine. Sex and death are juxtaposed in this revelation, just as they are in Rachel's impulsive decision to have a one-night stand with her co-worker and friend, Kyle, in a momentary act of *carpe diem*: 'So what, she thinks. Soon everything will end, even the stars' (Hall, 2015: 64).

Her subsequent, unplanned pregnancy, and the intractable complexities which it brings, forces Rachel to examine the extent to which biologism alone cannot provide a satisfactory explanation for her own experience of reproduction. Having moved back to the UK from Idaho, she visits her new GP for the first time to confirm that she is in fact pregnant, and to decide on her next course of action. Uncertain as to the appeal of motherhood, Rachel debates whether or not to terminate her pregnancy. As Rachel cannot help but note, this experience of reproduction differs greatly from that of the animals in her care. For the wolves 'there is no thought' (Hall, 2015: 107): reproduction is a drive, activated by 'instinct,' and the resulting 'parenting is intuited' (Hall, 2015: 108). Evolutionary theory would suggest that since Rachel, too, is an animal, similarly marked by a reproductive drive, '[s]houldn't she know what she wants: what to do and how to do it?' (Hall, 2015: 107). Her rather plaintive appeal breaks down at the point at which she considers human existence in its specificity:

> What use are higher faculties now, Rachel thinks, as she indicates and pulls out onto the road. Cognition and invention, the internal combustion engine, intermittent wipers, peace treaties and poetry, the

Homo Sapiens' thumb and tongue? Is optionality really evolutionary ascent when it leads to paralysis? (Hall, 2015: 108)

Though she undoubtedly wishes it were otherwise, Rachel is forced to acknowledge that the biological process of reproduction is not wholly coincident with her human experience of incipient motherhood.

As in *How to Paint a Dead Man*, then, the figure of *homo sapiens* function in *The Wolf Border* as a shorthand for the fundamental and inescapably biological basis of life. It recalls the fundamental assumption that the brain has been crafted, via natural selection, to serve the evolutionary imperatives of genetic survival and reproduction (see Tallis, 2011: 43). If the mind is largely synonymous with the brain, and the brain itself is, as Rachel implies, an evolved organ, then the mind should have adapted to encourage reproduction, the prime mechanism for the survival of our genetic material. This suggests that there should be a fundamental determinism to the way in which humans behave concerning questions of reproduction, evidence of the operation of a marked, biological imperative upon human mentation. Yet, as Rachel's own experience suggests, the evolutionary ascent which has marked the emergence of *homo sapiens* has led to an unprecedented degree of self-reflection. As Rachel's frustration illustrates, while reproduction in the abstract might be considered a universal, biological function – applicable to individual cells as much as to the production of offspring at the level of the organism – human motherhood is neither general nor universal. Rather, it is specific and, in Rachel's case, optional.

For Rachel, then, the evolutionary ascent of *homo sapiens* has only served to further distance the complexity of the human mind from the direct, biological imperatives which seem to shape the behaviour of the animals in her care. If biology alone was ever sufficient to dictate human action (or inaction), Rachel suggests that this is certainly no longer the case. Though Rachel seems to evade the responsibility of deciding whether or not to become a mother, this only echoes, rather than parallels, the behaviour of the wolves she studies: to refuse to choose is still, in-and-of itself, the exercising of a choice. Rachel's struggle thus emphasizes that though human life is framed and constrained both by wider physical laws, and the limits of our own biology, it is also underlined and structured by what Tallis (2011: 43) calls 'an infinity of abstractions, generalizations, customs, practices, norms, laws, institutions, facts, and artefacts unknown to even the most "social" of animals'. The paralysis which Rachel feels is ultimately a sign that her experience of biology is not wholly coincident with that biology itself; that mind cannot be easily reduced to merely the material functions of the brain, as yet another evolved, biochemical organ.

Rachel's dilemma concerning the disjunction between reproduction and motherhood in turn opens her eyes to the wider insufficiency of biology alone as an explanation for human behaviour more generally. Rachel and her half-brother Lawrence are brought closer together by the death of their mother and by Rachel's unexpected pregnancy. Acutely aware of the transformation in their relationship, Rachel mourns their previous lack of emotional connection:

> All those moments together when they were young and she felt nothing, an emotional deficit. She even used to think, once she'd learnt enough biology, that her programming meant she wasn't supposed to care for him – they had different genes. *Roll the other egg out of the nest and watch it smash below.* Her throat constricts. She wants to correct the error. Stupid to feel such things now, she thinks. She is strangely not herself: the power of hormones. (Hall, 2015: 126)

In acknowledging her past mistakes, there is a break in Rachel's otherwise unsentimental narration; an emotionally charged acknowledgement that in the past she has used biology as a means by which to simplify and reduce the complexity of human interconnection. This brief impulse towards sentimentality is diffused, however, in the last line quoted above, by an almost bathetic swerving to the familiar safety of the biological and the material. In evoking the spectre of the transformative power of hormones, Rachel raises the possibility that her emotional epiphany could well be driven by a material, neurochemical process.

As the above example illustrates, though Rachel has evidently moved on from a simplistic and ill-fitting neo-Darwinian explanation of her behaviour, the acknowledgement of such an 'error' does not mean the wholesale abandonment of materialism as the basis of human experience. For Rachel, in particular, and Hall's characters more generally, human existence is shown to be both inescapably material and biological, but to also comprise the social construction and individual experience of that very biology. In *The Wolf Border*, any claim to authenticity is thus shown to lie in the body, but it is in a body that is situated and contextual, touched and constructed with and by others in the social world. Emotions such as those which Rachel experiences towards her brother are thus shown to be both physiological states and psychological feelings and experiences.

It is this duality of biology and experience which is attended to carefully and sensitively in *The Wolf Border*. It is thus not biology itself which is renounced by Rachel, but rather the use of biologism as a medium of dissociation and simplification. In its inclusion of details concerning the traumatic nature of Rachel's unusual upbringing, Hall's novel invites us to see how Rachel's extreme independence in her interpersonal relationships, justified by her use of the tropes of biologism, in fact arises as a form of compensation: a sense that her earlier habits of being – her deficits of emotion and her inability to feel – are marked by a deeper 'fear, a flaw, stuntedness' (Hall, 2015: 292). Pregnancy functions as the catalyst for the transformation of this impoverishment – what Anna Cottrell (2017: 1) has termed Rachel's 'evolving notions of love' – which is, simultaneously, a transformation of the manner in which Rachel views the relationship of subjectivity and biology, mind and brain.

Perhaps the most marked example of the extent of this transformation occurs at the conclusion of the novel. Rather than avoiding the entanglements and complexities which will arise from informing Kyle that he now has a son, Charlie (a fact which thus far she has hidden), Rachel takes the decision to travel back to North America, and to introduce her child to his father. As she sits on the plane, Rachel imagines how this first contact might go. In a startling and protean metaphor, she voices her dread: 'The subject is not going to be gentle on the palate: human beings are strong meat' (Hall, 2015: 428). Dense and allusive, Rachel's chosen metaphor speaks to her fears about introducing Charlie to Kyle, of finding an explanation for her choice to bear the child, and of her choice to keep that decision secret. She anticipates that the meeting will be difficult: as tough as chewing on strong, perhaps even inedible, meat. The potentially cannibalistic sensibility here is fitting for a situation in which there is already too much human; where Charlie constitutes an unplanned increase. But because they are strong meat the three of them might also survive this initial meeting. Moving into a more optimistic frame of mind, Rachel continues: 'Perhaps there won't be too much shock. The world is used to reproduction after all. Nothing seems to stop it – not war, not science, not humanity's own incalculable stupidity' (Hall, 2015: 428).

There is an echo here of the biological drives with which this chapter began. Directly paralleling Hall's own sentiments about 'strong meat' in *Sex &Death*, Rachel presents reproduction as a fundamental, organizing principle of life. At first glance her statement seems to step back towards the lazy biological determinism that renders human behaviour an innate function of genetic and neurochemical forces – reproduction as merely a near-universal, biological process. But, as we have seen, Rachel's experience of pregnancy, birth, and motherhood are not sufficiently explained by biology alone. The metaphor of strong meat also hints at all the social, familial, and historical factors which inflect and are threaded through the material basis of her being. In each instance, as we have seen, Hall's novel stresses that there is a difference between a mechanical event and the experience of it. That while easy material explanations can offer a reductive account of human life, they cannot hope to adequately cope with the full complexity of the biosocial nature of human experience. In *The Wolf Border*, as in *How to Paint a Dead Man*, Hall lingers over these differences, paying close attention to what biology can and cannot disclose, while at the same time celebrating the very real predicaments of material being. As Hall's work deftly points out, there is a difference between accepting that to be human is to be biological and proposing that to be human is *merely* biological. Ultimately, Hall's characters do not fall on the side of the former – even if their relationship to these discourses remains troubled and, at times, troubling.

Notes

1 In *Consciousness Explained*, Daniel Dennett details the broad characteristics of a materialist stance at some length: 'The prevailing wisdom, variously expressed and argued for, is *materialism*: there is only one sort of stuff, namely *matter* – the physical stuff of physics, chemistry and physiology – and the mind is somehow nothing but a physical phenomenon. In short, the mind is the brain. According to the materialists, we can (in principle!) account for every mental phenomenon using the same physical principles, laws and raw materials that suffice to explain radioactivity, continental drift, photosynthesis, reproduction, nutrition and growth' (Dennett, 1991: 33).

2 Hall's bodies are often considered within the politicized framework of the 'natural', a trend that began with her earlier novels *Haweswater* (2002), and *The Carhullan Army* (2007). See, for example, Pollard (2017) and Walezak (2019).

3 Cole and Gallagher are writing within a wider phenomenological tradition that commonly maintains that illness and associated experiences can disrupt a more habitual or transparent feeling of embodiment. For similar works, see Leder (1990) and Gallagher and Zahavi (2012).

Works Cited

Boxall, P. (2013) *Twenty-First-Century Fiction: A Critical Introduction*. Cambridge: Cambridge University Press.

Boxall, P. (2015) *The Value of the Novel*. Cambridge: Cambridge University Press.

Bryson, N. (1990) *Looking at the Overlooked: Four Essays on Still Life Painting*. London: Reaktion.

Byatt, A. S. (1995) A New Body of Writing: Darwin and Recent British Fiction, in A.S. Byatt and Alan Hollinghurst (eds) *New Writing Vol.4*. pp.439–48. London: Vintage.

Cottrell, A. (2019) 'The Power of Love: From Feminist Utopia to the Politics of Imperceptibility in Sarah Hall's Fiction', *Textual Practice* 33(4): 679–93.

Cole, J. and Gallagher, S. (2016) 'Narrative and Clinical Neuroscience: Can Phenomenologically Informed Approaches and Empirical Work Cross-Fertilise', in A. Whitehead and A. Woods (eds) *The Edinburgh Companion to the Critical Medical Humanities*, pp. 377–94. Edinburgh: Edinburgh University Press.

Dawkins, R. (1976) *The Selfish Gene*. Oxford: Oxford University Press.

Dennett, D. (1993) *Consciousness Explained*. London: Penguin.
Gallagher, S. and Zahavi, D. (2012) *The Phenomenological Mind*. London: Routledge.
Hall, S. (2009) *How to Paint a Dead Man*. London: Faber.
Hall, S. (2016) *The Wolf Border*. London: Faber.
Hall, S. and Hobbs, P. (2016) 'Introduction', in S. Hall and P. Hobbs (eds) *Sex & Death: Stories*, pp. 1–3. London: Faber.
Lea, D. (2017) *Twenty-First Century Fiction: Contemporary British Voices*. Manchester: Manchester University Press.
Leder, D. (1990) *The Absent Body*. Chicago, IL: University of Chicago Press.
Pollard, E. (2017) '"When the Reservoir Comes": Drowned Villages, Community and Nostalgia in Contemporary British Fiction', *C21 Literature* 5(3): 1, https://doi.org/10.16995/c21.9
Renger, K. (1997) 'On the History of Research Concerning the Interpretation of Dutch Painting', in W. Frantis (ed.) *Looking at Seventeenth-Century Dutch Art: Realism Reconsidered*, pp. 9–14. Cambridge: Cambridge University Press
Rose, N. (2007) *The Politics of Life Itself: Biomedicine, Power and Subjectivity in the Twenty-first Century*. Princeton, NJ: Princeton University Press.
Tallis, R. (2011) *Aping Mankind: Neuromania, Darwinitis and the Misrepresentation of Humanity*. Durham: Acumen Publishing.
Vice, S. (2017) 'Sarah Hall: A New Kind of Storytelling', in J. Acheson (ed.) *The Contemporary British Novel Since 2000*, pp.70–8. Edinburgh: Edinburgh University Press.
Walezak, E. (2019) 'Landscape and Identity: Utopian/Dystopian Cumbria in Sarah Hall's *The Carhullan Army*', *Critique: Studies in Contemporary Fiction*, 60(1): 67–74, https://doi.org/10.1080/00111619.2018.1479242
Waugh, P. (2005) 'Science and Fiction in the 1990s', in N. Bentley (ed.) *British Fiction of the 1990s*, pp. 57–77. London, Routledge.
Wilson, E. O. (1978) *On Human Nature*. Cambridge; London: Harvard University Press.
Ya-Chu Yang, K. (2018) 'Restoring Life: Carnivore Reintroduction and (Eco)Feminist Science in Sarah Hall's *The Wolf Border*', *Women's Studies* 47(8): 829–44, https://doi.org/10.1080/00497878.2018.1524763

4

Rewilding Welfare
Sarah Hall and the State of Nature

Pieter Vermeulen

The Birth of Welfare

Haweswater, Sarah Hall's debut novel, begins with a birth scene. Ella Lightburn gives birth to Janet, the novel's heroine, and she does so alone. As Ella screams, curses, and fights 'with her own body, with God, with nature, unmaking herself' (Hall, 2002: 3), her husband stands by. He had, we learn, 'been present for the birthing of many animals' before, and was even 'accustomed to intervention [...] reaching inside the hot, rough canal of an animal himself with a bare greased arm' (Hall, 2002: 4). Yet this time is different, and Samuel is finally convinced of his own uselessness and leaves to rejoin 'the men of the village' in the kitchen downstairs, 'sitting, standing, smoking' (Hall, 2002: 5). The women of the village stay around, but they can do no more than instruct Ella 'to be calm and breathe' and 'to control her pain. She could not' (Hall, 2002: 4). Nor is there a doctor to assist, as 'Dr Saul Firth was absent, and, surely by now, unreachable' (Hall, 2002: 4). Ella's act of self-unmaking, a process in which 'slowly

99

she came apart' (Hall, 2002: 3), is then also a momentous demonstration of self-reliance.

In *The Wolf Border*, Hall's fifth novel, we see Rachel Caine, that novel's heroine, signing into a hospital to give birth in her turn. Thirteen years separate the two novels, and there is a remarkable change in the way the process of giving birth is described. In the 2015 novel, it is rendered less as a process of coming apart, but rather as one of carefully being 'opened [...] up' (Hall, 2015: 251). Unlike Ella, Rachel is duly surrounded, supported, and sedated, even if the father is not in the picture (he is on the other side of the Atlantic, ignorant of his fatherhood). Instead, representatives of the welfare state competently assume the role of caretakers: there is a nurse, a midwife, an anaesthetist, a consultant, surgeons, and painkillers (Hall, 2015: 250–3). The process does not leave Rachel unmade: the next chapter finds her a few months later, inside her house, being taken care of: 'The last few months,' we read, 'the world has come to her: deliveries of food and equipment, the midwife and healthcare work, the men in her life, work' (Hall, 2015: 257).

If giving birth was, in Sarah Hall's fiction, still a heroic confrontation with the wildness of nature in 2002, in *The Wolf Border*, it is an experience in which the institutions of the welfare state play their part.[1] Of course, this shift can partly be explained by pointing to the different historical settings of the novels: *Haweswater* covers the first few decades of the twentieth century, when there were no robust and universal welfare provisions in place in the UK (the Beveridge Report, which inaugurated the shift to state-provided and legally-mandated welfare in which I am interested in this chapter, was drafted in 1942), while *The Wolf Border* is set in the present (or, given the far-reaching deprivatization schemes it situates in Scotland, in an only slightly speculative near future). *The Wolf Border* organizes its geography around a somewhat schematic opposition between a society without any social safety net (the USA) and one that has adequate and generous welfare provisions in place (the novel's unravelling UK). This opposition was not yet in place in the *Electric Michelangelo*, another novel that traffics between these two sites: New York here 'contain[s] all the indistinct chaos and divergence and eccentric myth of the old world' (Hall, 2004: 172), while Coney Island is the 'richer, zany American relative' to Morecambe, the town from where the protagonist hails (Hall, 2004: 182). The centrality of this opposition – on which Rachel reflects at different moments in the novel, and which features in the plot by her move from the USA to the UK – shows how crucially concerned Hall's work is with the relation between human flourishing and state institutions. Nor is it merely anachronistic to look for the missing traces of the welfare state in *Haweswater*. As Bruce Robbins has shown, many nineteenth- and twentieth-century novels feature stand-ins for the welfare state that remind readers that human (and, most notably, protagonists') thriving depends on mediators and patrons. For Robbins (2007: 72), such novels do the cultural work of legitimizing the welfare state, that 'politically ambiguous mode of social organization' that at the same time regulates and preserves corporate capitalism.

It is significant, then, that in the birth scene that opens *Haweswater*, neither the husband, the doctor, nor the women of the village are made to assume the role of midwifing such a welfare state imaginary. In a reading of Dickens' *Great Expectations*, Robbins (2007: 42) remarks that 'the role of benefactor might be an endpoint of upward mobility as well as its proximate cause'. In *The Wolf Border*, Rachel is not only aided by the beneficial ministrations of the welfare state, as we have seen, but she is also herself employed as a benefactor for the wellbeing of a group of wolves. The novel more confidently repeats a pattern already intimated in *The Electric Michelangelo*, where the protagonist begins his trajectory as a tattoo-artist as an apprentice only to end the novel himself as the mentor of a young artist. Rachel is a highly-skilled and well-paid professional (and the novel makes clear that career advancement is an important concern for her [Hall, 2015: 32, 329]), yet she is also a carer; she embodies the insight that the market and the welfare state depend on one another – that welfare-state institutions are complementary with 'the enlarged market for professional service and expertise that the welfare state has always implied' (Robbins, 2007: 7).

The elaborate and remarkably consistent welfare state imaginary of *The Wolf Border* and the conspicuous lack of it in *Haweswater* cannot simply be reduced to elements of the novels' historical veracity. If the contrast between the 'chilly' room where Ella Lightburn gives birth, whose 'walls [are] glowing with cold' (Hall, 2002: 3), and the comfortable room where Rachel Caine and her baby are 'wrapped up warm by the fire' (Hall, 2015: 257) reflects an historical difference between two moments in British history, the two novels' divergent imaginings of welfare do more than that: they signal a key development in Hall's oeuvre. This development, I argue in this chapter, reorganizes the central coordinates of her novelistic work: the issue of female self-assertion and freedom, the ambivalent attractions of motherhood, and the call of the wild. By putting the novel in dialogue with recent developments in the environmental humanities and in the interdisciplinary study of neoliberalism (the governmental logic that has been dismantling the welfare state over the last few decades), I show how *The Wolf Border*'s hesitant appreciation of the beneficial role of state institutions develops in tandem with its revised understanding of the wilderness. This shift, I argue, is less an achieved insight than an abiding concern for the novel – a concern for which the wolves serve as flexible and fungible figures. *Haweswater* still sees the entanglement of state and capital as a bad thing: in this novel, an organic community which persists in 'an intricate union' with nature and in which 'bonds [a]re strong and necessary and abundantly understood' (Hall, 2002: 112, 6) finds itself flooded by the combined evil forces of industry, the military, and the state. In *The Wolf Border*, life – including natural life, including the wolves – operates *within* the confines of the state, a state that first cares for Rachel's dying mother and later for her infant son, and a state of which Rachel's employer – a quaint aristocratic Liberal Democrat – is very much a pillar.

The Wolf Border's shift toward a reluctant acceptance of the institutions of the welfare state has few precedents in Hall's novels. For the first time, freedom implies a negotiation with institutions and a willingness to dwell within their confines rather than a resolute resistance to them. Such a position is emphatically missing in novels like *The Electric Michelangelo* and *How to Paint a Dead Man*, for instance. The story of the former novel begins at the time of the First World War in a privately-run guest house for consumptives, in which the protagonist's mother acts 'as both bed-nurse and hostess' (Hall, 2004: 11); soon, the institution dies with her. When the story moves its protagonist to the USA, it enters a world similarly bereft of stable and secure institutions: the care for premature infants is paid for by displaying them in a baby incubator exhibition, and the psychiatric hospital where an assailant is put up cannot protect him from a revenge attack. In the four narrative strands of *How to Paint a Dead Man*, state institutions offer no help for the novel's two main thematic interests: art and what we could call the calamities of life. Susan, the artist who is recovering from the loss of her twin brother, opens the novel by recalling painful and woefully ineffective doctor visits from her youth, an ordeal for which her mother later apologizes. Her father Peter, a landscape artists, with cheerful cynicism, emphasizes he made a name for himself without public commission: 'I have worked,' he says, 'despite every establishment and have known obstacles and ridicule before any favour' (Hall, 2009: 74). (In a comparable way, *The Electric Michelangelo*'s fascination with tattooing is linked to its status as an industry that is 'wholly self-sufficient and home-skilled' [Hall, 2004: 98].) Annette, the blind Italian girl, is simply dismissed from a school that is unable to cater for her caring needs. The only person living through state support is Susan's friend Nicki, who is in an irreversible coma after the emergency services failed to show in time when she collapsed in an asthma attack on the moor (Hall, 2009: 64). The novel's representation of the state's support system, then, is at the same time a stark reminder of its inability to foster a more valuable life for Nicki. Real life, it seems, in *How to Paint a Dead Man*, as in *Haweswater*, is lived outside the state: in the wild, in nature. And if the ordeal of Peter, who gets stuck amid the rocks that he has earlier so successfully converted into landscape paintings, underlines that life amid the elements can be brute and nasty, the novel still implies such unbuffered exposure to danger is what makes life worth living in the first place.

The anti-statism of *The Carhullan Army* is at least as pronounced. Set in a near-future dystopian Britain, this novel is organized around the opposition between, on the one hand, hyperregulated areas in which women are 'fitted' with contraceptive devices that they must at all times be ready to display 'to the monitors in the backs of cruisers' (Hall, 2007: 27) and, on the other, a 'serious' and 'honest' life on the woman-only farm that persists 'off record' and beyond regulation (Hall, 2007: 103, 15, 17). For Deborah Lilley (2016: 61, 65), the Carhullan farm serves as a 'transformative retreat' and affords a 'sense of pastoral restoration' in a landscape that stands out from an environment marked by the debris of the industrial future past. When the novel's main character (known only under the name of 'Sister') is fitted with a 'regulator,' there is a medical professional at hand, but her request to be seen by a female doctor is ignored; there are also painkillers, but there is no one who cares enough to remind her to take them (Hall, 2007: 28). Although the contraptions of welfare are in place in 'the official zones' (Hall, 2007: 7), then, the novel can only imagine them as apparatuses of control and inflictors of humiliation and pain. Life, as in *How to Paint a Dead Man*, as in *Haweswater*, is elsewhere – in what the novel calls 'the other half of the landscape, the other half of Britain' (Hall, 2007: 15). This other half is imagined as untainted by the compromises of social institutions: Sister here believes herself to be 'no longer complicit in a wrecked and regulated existence' (Hall, 2007: 41), as '[t]here [a]re no regulations out here. There [is] no human mess, no chaos, poorly managed, and barely liveable' (Hall, 2007: 17).

As in the other novels, the point is not that the farm serves as a site of utopian bliss; it is rather that even the violence and mishaps here have an aura of authenticity and freedom that institutions, in these novels' imaginary, serve to stifle. Remarkably, Sister describes her transition from an intrusive, violent, and humiliating state to the more generous life on the farm as a process of becoming 'an unmade person' (Hall, 2007: 94), using the same phrase that describes Ella Lightburn's limit experience at the beginning of *Haweswater*. In these novels, nature and the wild, it seems, reliably serve as restorative sites in which the intrusions by the state can be undone. It is this dispensation, I argue, that *The Wolf Border* will begin to revise.

Wolves, Wilderness, Welfare

The Wolf Border by no means unambiguously embraces the institutions that Hall's earlier novels shun. One sign of its lingering ambiguity about boring, unglamorous limitations is that Rachel's mother quasi-deliberately ends her life in her care-home apartment, as if administered life is not enough; another is an offhand remark about a midwife, who is described as 'past retirement age but not, it seems, retiring anytime soon' (Hall, 2015: 206), as if there is a certain allure in relentlessly pursuing a vocation and declining the option of state-assisted old age. For all these and other signs of hesitation, *The Wolf Border* at least entertains the possibility that the operations of the state can be anything more than destructive and diminishing, and that there is such a thing as a *beneficial* state, a state that fosters the lives of its citizens without diminishing the dignity of these lives by robbing them of their (illusory) self-reliance. The novel explores this possibility by entangling the confusions of early motherhood with the attempt to reintroduce wolves into northern England. If the former theme features Rachel as both a provider and a beneficiary of care (for her son and by the welfare state respectively), the latter more resolutely sees her emerge as a benefactor for the welfare of the wolves.

In Rachel's first conversation with her doctor, who is provided for her through the UK's state-run National Health Service, the care presented is anything but the degrading and intrusive intervention from *The Carhullan Army*: the doctor notes that she will be contacted for 'possible screening. But I'm not going to push you. You're on our system, which is good' (Hall, 2015: 106). Later on, the midwife is always reliably on call: 'I've got NHS enhanced reception,' she notes, 'so you can get me anytime' (Hall, 2015: 206). Such unobtrusive reliability looks a lot like the way Rachel and her team go on to monitor the wolves: the wolves are tracked and fed, but in a self-effacing way that avoids direct confrontation with human carers. The novel's descriptions of institutional care are remarkable for conveying a sense of tact and tenderness – as when a nurse apologizes that the ultrasound gel 'will be a little cold' (Hall, 2015: 136) – which is not very different from the way the wolves' territory is described: walking along the fence, Rachel notes '[t]here are no barbs and it is not electric,' which surprises her, as 'she had expected something more industrial-looking – penal even' (Hall, 2015: 131–2). If these examples may suggest that the novel is organized around an analogy between Rachel and the wolves – both get offspring, both physically escape their habitat – such a reading obscures a slightly different and more relevant analogy: that between Rachel's care for the lives of the wolves and the way the welfare state quietly facilitates her life as a working mother. For Rachel, in other words, her developing relation to the wolves is a way for her to work through her own reliance on state institutions – the awareness that life necessarily takes place *within* the confines of the state, and not outside of it in some putative untouched wilderness.

This revised understanding of the wilderness finds itself in tune with developments in the fields of ecocriticism and of the environmental humanities, fields in which the wilderness is no longer what it used to be. In early environmental writing, especially in a US context, wilderness was conceived as society's other; it was seen as 'nature in a state uncontaminated by civilization' (Garrard, 2004: 59), an easily idealized realm divorced from technological and industrial pollution and corruption. As the field of ecocriticism cast a more self-critical eye on environmentalist discourse, it soon discovered this outright separation between human action and wild nature to be untenable. Environmental historian William Cronon's classic essay 'The Trouble with Wilderness' not only unsettles this distinction on conceptual grounds, it also points to the considerable social and political costs incurred by maintaining it. Cronon (1996) observes that the very opposition between wilderness and civilization is a construction that emerges *from within* civilization, and thus starts from a position of alienation from nature. The celebration of wilderness, Cronon (1996: 17) notes, 'has been an activity mainly for well-to-do city folks' cast out from an intimate participation in the rhythms of the natural world. Glorifications of the wilderness, Cronon (1996: 17) continues, 'embod[y] a dualistic vision in which the human is entirely outside the natural', avoiding the difficult issue of how to construct viable ways to live together and to design a sustainable relation to nature.

As 'our working and domestic lives are [considered] effectively irredeemable alongside this ideal' (Garrard, 2004: 71), the idea of wilderness demoralizes all efforts at social and environmental change. And designing a nurturing and sustainable relationship to nature is a crucial challenge: 'To the extent that biological diversity [...] is likely to survive in the future only by the most vigilant and self-conscious management of the ecosystems that sustain it, the ideology of wilderness,' Cronon (1996: 18) notes, 'is potentially in direct conflict with the very thing it encourages us to protect'.

Cronon's essay makes it possible to see that the opposition between wilderness and civilization is only one of three templates for understanding the human impact on the natural world: first, there is a premodern human life magically in sync with the rhythms of nature; second, there is modern civilization's glamorization of an undebased wilderness it knows itself to be irrevocably divorced from; and third, there is the option of a more vigilant and careful management of nature, driven by an awareness of reciprocal dependence rather than fantasies of purity and authenticity. This third option is the one Cronon prefers, and it is the one *The Wolf Border*, on my reading, works to accommodate. Hall's earlier novels did not decisively move from the first and second to the third template. *Haweswater*, for instance, hovers between the first and third templates as it offers an elegiac exercise in coming to terms with the loss of a primal unity and with the inevitability of an irrevocably humanized world. *The Carhullan Army*, in turn, adopts the second frame as it imagines Britain as split in two halves – one wild, one micromanaged – with one half somehow escaping all contamination by the other. It is only in *The Wolf Border* that the question of how to manage nature in a less destructive way takes centre stage.

We can assess the difference between *Haweswater* and *The Wolf Border* by comparing the ways they process the fantasy of reciprocal attunement between human and natural life. *Haweswater*, as I noted, is organized around the opposition between an organic community in which people's 'knowledge of the place is as unconscious and simple as the mechanisms of breathing' (Hall, 2002: 112) on the one hand and the aligned forces of modernity on the other. For people belonging to the 'intricate union' of landscape and community, the opposition between wilderness and culture makes no sense and appears as an affectation of city folk. Jack, the representative of the Waterworks who comes to reside in the village and begins an affair with Janet, is seen as '[o]ne of those classless types who believes that this place is about scenery and escape, and getting' something out that hasn't bin put in!' (Hall, 2002: 180) – as someone, in other words, sufficiently alienated from natural life to believe in a separation between civilization and the wilderness. Jack believes such alienation can be overcome, yet the novel does not share this belief: it sends him to his death during an absurd excursion because of his lack of intimacy with the landscape, and his death inspires Janet to become a kind of proto-suicide bomber at the end of the novel. Only death reconnects Jack to the landscape, as '[a] ghost in the elements' that is 'shouting through the soil [...] faintly' (Hall, 2002: 229). The novel's formal choices further underline its inability to imagine a productive encounter between Jack and Janet: the start of their affair is narrated in the subjunctive mode as a matter of speculation, not fact (Hall, 2002: 113–15). This hesitation permeates the whole novel through the intermittent and often surprising tense shifts, which evoke an omniscient narrator, shuttling between past and present tense, who finds herself unable to find her temporal footing in recounting a world that, even if she knows it to be lost, continues to haunt her. Indeed, if the novel is convinced that alienation cannot be undone, this does not mean that it quite knows what to believe instead. In *Haweswater*, the loss of rural connectedness is not compensated for by a different vision of the common good; the unity with nature is only something to be lamented, which is reflected in the novel's elegiac tone. When one of the characters asks in exasperation 'What of us after dam?' (Hall, 2002: 111), the novel has not imagined an answer. And if the character is consoled by the assurance 'Give it a while [...] Summet'll cum' (Hall, 2002: 111), this 'summet' has failed to materialize by the point in time the novel is narrated from – that is, the present.

This lack of a vision of the common good is most apparent when we look at the nature of the Manchester City Waterworks that is tasked with organizing the controlled flooding of the village. The

Waterworks is emphatically no private company, but rather combines the interests of government and industry. The Haweswater Reservoir is deemed necessary because Manchester needs water 'for its thirsty people, for its industries which had tripled in size since the start of the century' (Hall, 2002: 49). It is because the 'country' needs more water supplies that the organic way of life in the village is undone. It is the Waterworks and its terraforming powers, then, that stand in for the compromised alliance of industrial capitalism (which brings the 'thirsty people' to Manchester in the first place) and the state that would, after the Second World War, enable the elaboration of universal welfare institutions. *Haweswater* is unable to imagine the difference between beneficial – if inevitably compromised – state action and the rampant capitalist exploitation the welfare state is supposed to constrain: the improvised town for the workers is compared to 'one of the Western gold-rush towns of the previous mid-century, born [...] out of the desire for profit' (Hall, 2002: 168); the project is described as an enterprise that relentlessly converts individuals into indistinct biomass when we read that '[t]he hundreds of men working on the project suffered thousands of fingers broken, re-broken, toes fractured' (Hall, 2002: 166). The aggressiveness of these formulations shows *Haweswater* acting out its dismay over the displacement of a more intimate relation with nature. While it pointedly refuses the compensatory fantasy of an untainted wilderness it diagnoses the character of Jack with, it nevertheless fails to imagine a reciprocally sustaining relation between nature and civilization.

The Wolf Border, like *Haweswater*, officially refuses the division between wilderness and civilization, dismissing it *not*, this time, as the product of city life, but as a mark of immaturity. Thinking back to her youth in the Lake District, Rachel notes that '[s]he did not know it then, but in reality [the moors were] a kempt place, cultivated, even the high grassland covering the fells was manmade' (Hall, 2002: 29). Later in the novel, she wonders whether Sylvia, the earl's daughter who takes on the wolves as a pet project, is naïve enough to consider the wolves' habitat 'a boil-in-the-bag Eden, with no human interface' (Hall, 2002: 339). If Sylvia resists the wolves' invasive sterilization, it is because it serves as '[a] reminder that the enclosure is governed, that it still requires management' (Hall, 2002: 339). Rachel accepts the thorough entanglement of human and nonhuman worlds and is committed to the challenge of finding a sustainable form of nature management that actively shapes rather than passively conserves the wild. Her commitment, the novel notes, is to the belief that 'the country as a whole will one day re-wild,' that one day, 'there will be a place, again, where the streetlights end and wilderness begins' (Hall, 2002: 234). It is this place the novel explicitly calls 'the wolf border.' Wilderness, in this dispensation, is not a pristine state in which a 'self-willed' nature is left alone, but a domain that, in the words of environmental writer Emma Marris (2015), is 'managed as wilderness,' that is, 'managed as if [it] were wilderness'. The border between the wild and the domesticated is not pre-given but rather instituted by human intervention.

This shift is in keeping with contemporary conservation practices, which increasingly recognize the ineluctability of human intervention because, as Marris (2015) writes, '[t]oday we can't withdraw without blood on our hands' . Human action has an impact upon the life-world of plants and animals to such an extent that preventing species from going extinct now requires further active intervention. As Jamie Lorimer (2015: 5) has remarked, this places conservation at the heart of contemporary environmental challenges , as it is an issue that engages with concerns over human impact and responsibility that are customarily grouped under the rubric of the Anthropocene. Marris' insights in her successful book *Rambunctious Garden: Saving Nature in a Post-Wild World* (2011) resonate with those of so-called New Conservationists like Peter Kareiva and Joseph Mascaro and move beyond the 'Old Conservationist' emphasis on keeping wilderness intact and restoring decaying ecosystems – an emphasis phrased most memorably, perhaps, by American president Theodore Roosevelt, when he noted, in relation to the Grand Canyon, 'leave it as it is. You cannot improve on it. The ages have been at work on it, and man can only mar it' (cited in Marris, 2015). As Jamie Lorimer (2015: 5) notes, such traditional conservation is 'reactive' as '[i]t seeks to preserve a fixed Nature from modern, urban, and industrial Society by enclosing it in National Parks'. In an English context, it also misrecognizes how thoroughly human cultivation has shaped the land for thousands of years.

For New Conservationists, the preservation and restoration of pre-human worlds have become obsolete projects in a post-wild world thoroughly shaped by human action; saving nature now requires removing or resettling species, deploying non-native species, or supporting new ecosystems in humanized environments. A preservationist ethic insisting on purity and non-intervention merely puts a brake on adequate action. For New Conservationists, non-intervention is neither a goal nor a virtue, as the relevant choice is between good interventions and bad interventions – between effective and destructive wildlife management. Nature cannot be left to its own devices as if it persisted apart from civilization; what is needed, instead, is ways to accommodate 'wildness at the heart of contemporary life' as part of a settlement that sustains rather than alienates life (Lorimer, 2015: 11). *The Wolf Border* suggests that such a dispensation not only requires an altered relation to nature, but also different conceptions of welfare and of the market.

The Market and the State of Nature

The Wolf Border's engagement with the distinction between good and bad nature management resonates with its exploration of beneficial state intervention. If New Conservationist practices can be described as 'modes of biopolitics shaping future world through the operations of assemblages of scientific knowledge, administration, and practice' (Lorimer, 2015: 6), their proximity to the very life-shaping apparatuses that the welfare state unleashes on human populations is clear. *The Wolf Border* explores the distinctions between a form of life management that sustains human flourishing and one that depletes life – between, say, a welfare state in which the NHS quietly supports single mothers and a neoliberal state in which citizens are forced to buy health insurance provided by the market. Rachel's decision to move back to the UK is triggered by the realization, when she discovers she is pregnant, that 'there is no additional rider to her policy; she is not covered [...] She'll have to find a doctor and pay for it herself' (Hall, 2015: 72–3). Rachel does not want such exposure to the contingencies of the market, and the next scene in the novel finds her accepting the job offer in the UK and the protection by the NHS that comes with it.

It is the figure of the wolf that keeps the novel's sociopolitical and environmental lines of enquiry together. If wolves have recently served as the charismatic poster animals for rewilding programs, they also circulate in the contemporary imagination as symbols of the predatory nature of neoliberalism (understood as a mode of life management in the service of capital rather human flourishing). The most famous instance of the wolf as the 'newly returned symbol of all things wild' (Marris, 2017) is no doubt the case of the Yellowstone National Park, in which the reintroduction of wolves has allegedly led to a stabilization of the ecosystem. As Emma Marris (2017) underlines, these wolves now inhabit thoroughly human-inflected lifeworlds rather than pristine habitats: they have not simply 'restored a lost component to western ecosystems,' but have in fact 'returned to a place much changed'.

But if wolves in Hall's novel and in conservationist practice are elements in the management of the biosphere, they still figure in the popular imagination as icons of unadulterated wildness. The iconography of neoliberalism is one site where such images circulate. In discussions of neoliberalism's gradual erosion of life-worlds and its 'stealth revolution' (to deploy Wendy Brown's [2015] term), the image of neoliberal power players like the International Monetary Fund or the infamous 'Troika' devastating the Greek economy as wolves in sheep's clothing is prevalent. A title like *The Wolf of Wall Street* (2014) – a film based on the life of stockbroker Jordan Belford – exemplifies an imaginary that sees the world of global finance as an unforgiving food chain in which the apex predators destroy lesser life forms lest they be eaten themselves. In another film about the 2008 financial crisis, *Margin Call* (2012), which chronicles the fall of Lehman Brothers, the moment when Sam Rogers (played by Kevin Spacey) realizes that his bank is fatally overleveraged is scored with Phosphorescent's 'Wolves.' This song's plaintive lyrics – 'Mama, there's wolves in the house/ Mama, they won't let me out' – hints at the inherent instability of this food chain: financial predators are, in the world of contemporary finance, also always potentially the prey of other predators. Man, in this neoliberal dispensation, is imagined as a wolf to other men.

But what does this mean, exactly? The phrase *homo homini lupus* (man is a wolf to man) is a classic of political theory: originating in Thomas Hobbes' *De Cive*, but with antecedents dating back to the Roman playwright Plautus, the phrase expresses the 'brutish, anarchical, and violent condition of man in the natural state' (Rossello, 2012: 255). While the phrase is often taken as a mere metaphor (man is *like* a wolf) in what Diego Rossello (2012: 257) has called the 'humanist consensus' around Hobbes' state of nature, it involves a much more conflicted trafficking between animal and human (animal) realms: human life is never definitely separated from the animal realm, and the imposition of human civilization to secure human life from the threat of other lives (Hobbes' famous Leviathan) is beset by a persistent lycanthropy. *The Wolf Border*'s sustained exploration of the analogies between (caring for) wolves and (caring for) human lives, then, draws attention to the conflicts, anxieties, and desires that continue to haunt the division between the wildness of wolves and the civilization of humans. It shows that the state of nature does not so much name an illusory state *before* civilization but is an illusion of wildness cultivated as an illusory alternative *to* social life – as the site of experiences that are supposedly truer and more authentic than the comfort and dullness of administered life.

Under neoliberalism, such a state of nature that transforms humans into wolves is not called the wilderness; it is called the market. Like the wilderness, the market serves as a carefully curated but purportedly spontaneous site of asociality; like the wilderness, it is supposed to provide experiences that are more redemptive, authentic, and truthful than the convenience and indulgences provided by social institutions. The state of nature 'renders self-preservation the primary impulse of human being', a situation that 'leads to an intolerable state of insecurity' (Elliot, 2018: 70, 71). This precarity sanctions all kinds of aggressive and pre-emptive self-defence as, Jane Elliott (2018: 72) writes, 'threat to survival necessarily releases Man from normative strictures'. In neoliberal thought, this release from social norms and this exposure to risk, chaos, and danger is precisely what makes the market a privileged source of value and truth. This glorification of exposure to market forces is most visibly reflected in the lionization of the figure of the entrepreneur. The entrepreneur, in the work of neoliberal precursors like Ludwig von Mises and Wilhelm Röpke, is someone who is brave enough to expose himself to the only available source of economic information – that is, the price signals that make up the market. If, as neoliberalism assumes in the wake of Friedrich Hayek, it is impossible to acquire all necessary information to understand (let alone plan) the economy, the willingness to surrender to the market, as 'the most advanced epistemological system available to humans' (Beaumont and Kelly, 2018), signifies a purer and more intense mode of existence (Davies, 2018: 149–75; Stedman Jones, 2012: 49–73). Neoliberalism, in other words, codifies an opposition between entrepreneurial 'risk-taking thrill seekers' on the one hand and 'dull drones' participating in the welfare state on the other (Mirowski, 2014: 119). Entrepreneurs, in this worldview, 'bask in the unknowable risk of a chaotic future, prostrating [themselves] before the inscrutable market with its Delphic valuations' (Mirowski, 2019: 9).

The analogy between the wilderness and the market also helps us understand why neoliberalism insists on maintaining this site of illusory wildness. In the previous section, we saw how the wilderness operates as the illusory other of social life that, because it appears as unassailable, demoralizes efforts to imagine more sustainable ways of living. For neoliberalism, the exaltation of the market makes it possible to extend the model of entrepreneurship and force citizens to become, in Michel Foucault's (2008: 226) famous phrase, 'entrepreneurs of [the] self' and to accustom them to dwindling welfare provisions. In environmental thought, an awareness of the constructedness of the wilderness can open up avenues towards an imagining of a more sustainable management of life; in a comparable way, recent scholarship on neoliberalism has emphasized the untenability of the separation between the market and the social. The idea of such a separation is customarily traced back to Karl Polanyi's notion of a 'double movement' in which market forces tend to disembed themselves from social institutions, which then invites a countermovement by social forces to re-embed market dynamics. Recent scholarship has explicitly taken issue with the idea of the 'growing externality of economy and sociality' (Konings, 2015: 2), and has emphasized that social and economic developments are part of the same dynamic. What looks like the emergence of an autonomous and rigorously nontransparent market is in fact part of a coordinated effort to reorganize society in a way that also recodes family relations, gender roles, and private morality in conservative ways (Cooper, 2017: 7–24; Kotsko, 2018: 69-79).

In *The Wolf Border*, Rachel's discovery that she is not covered by her insurance is a reminder that contemporary neoliberalism has wilfully reinstituted something very much like a state of nature – a carefully cultivated state of precarity and exposure to the sovereign force of the market. But if Hobbes' fictional state of nature *predates* the institution of the state, neoliberalism's market-building *deliberately designs* the institutions of the state in such a way that it exposes individuals to the contingencies of the market. Neoliberal markets are the result of something very much like a rewilding project: if markets look sublime and overwhelming and ineffable, they do so by design – a design that supports the demands of capital at the expense of the security and sovereignty of citizens. *The Wolf Border*'s sustained analogy between natural and human life-management, then, leverages Hall's long-standing fascination with the attractions of the wild for a shift from an anti-statist position to a novel appreciation of the welfare state.

Wolves of Welfare

The insight that there is nothing natural about markets is a potentially useful one. The awareness that 'creating the conditions for a worldwide, self-regulating market' requires careful planning, legislating, and institution-building (Kotsko, 2018: 69) makes clear that such institutions are subject to change – that, in other words, the neoliberal entrepreneur of the self can transform into a different kind of human animal that maintains a more nurturing and caring relationship to the institutions that sustain it. In *The Wolf Border*, it is the analogous insight – unavailable, I argue, in Hall's earlier novels – that there is nothing pristine about the lives of wolves that makes it possible for the novel to imagine a regime of care for them. If there is no such thing as an un-instituted, spontaneous market, and if there is no market that is not encased by national and global institutions, it is a small step to the realization that *different* institutions can be designed. A proper understanding of neoliberalism's institution-building lifts the old liberal taboo on state intervention – very much like New Conservationist practices lift the taboo on wildlife management.

One of the most curious moments in *Haweswater* comes when the debris of Janet's terrorist attack – 'pieces of sodden dress, a candle, the ruptured detonation device' (Hall, 2005: 243) – is gathered by an unnamed navvy and buried between the 'earth-receding roots' of an oak tree, '[a]s if the ground had never been opened or disturbed at all' (Hall, 2005: 244). 'Janet Tree' ends the novel as part of local folklore: it is the name of a witch bringing death to car drivers, and especially to tourists (Hall, 2005: 258–9). Janet, in other words, survives the novel's historical setting as a monument to the irreconcilability of nature and modernity. Yet the novel leaves room for a different imaginary through the way the navvy walks out of the story: he first walks to Langwathby, and then all the way to Scotland, where, we read, 'law and language blur and at some point separate as different smoky elements under the same crown' (Hall, 2005: 244). Scotland, in other words, figures as an as yet unspecified ambition to imagine a semi-autonomous political realm – a realm that sets its own law (the etymological meaning of 'autonomy') through its variation on the English language. Here, Hall's early work at least considers the option of a different dispensation 'under the same crown' (a reference, it seems, to the 1603 Union of the Crowns, which left Scotland separate and distinct *within* the Union); of a different arrangement of nature and society that is more welcoming to a mode of human flourishing in dialogue with both.

At the end of *The Wolf Border*, the wolves escape their enclosure and flee to Scotland. The novel's geography consistently opposes England as a fully enclosed space – the enclosure is situated on 'the largest private estate in England' (Hall, 2015: 13); the estate is 'essentially feudal' (Hall, 2005: 281) – to Scotland, where, in the world of the novel, 'great swathes of foreign-owned land is being recovered,' resources are being recalibrated, and taxes are increased (Hall, 2005: 281, also 25). But if Scotland allows the novel to push its exploration of the welfare state one step further, it crucially remains a compromise with the forces of the market rather than a post-capitalist utopia. Indeed, the suspicion that the earl has masterminded the wolves' escape and the insistence that there is no clear physical border between England and Scotland, only 'intermediate lands,' 'debatable lands,' 'just a smattering of whin and rowan, barren slopes and cuttings' (Hall, 2005: 418), underline the essential continuities between the two realms. In Scotland, the wolves will continue to be discretely monitored, 'sedated and transferred' if necessary (Hall, 2005: 420), and will be sending out telemetry signals captured by transmitters, facilitating intervention if necessary (Hall, 2005: 431). By the end of the novel, then, Scotland does not simply serve as a vanishing point for the novel's uncertain politics, as it does in *Haweswater*: it serves as an occasion to upscale the confined English experiment to the scale of a whole country. The original project had 'pre-existing limits,' and while within the estate, '[t]he landscape will become healthier and more diverse,' 'outside the enclosure barren fells will remain' (Hall, 2005: 329). In the novel's Scotland, the wild is no longer a mystified and carefully circumscribed site of authenticity and intensity, but is scaled up to, in Jamie Lorimer's (2015: 11) words, a form of 'commons, the everyday affective site of human-nonhuman entanglement'. In the novel's Scotland, the wolf border is no longer a geographical marker, but has become a territorial condition, in which the market and the state operate in the service of human and animal flourishing. The novel makes it clear that this Scotland is no utopia, but a project inevitably compromised by its entanglement with the market: the wolves herald '[a] new era for Scottish ecology' (Hall, 2005: 421), an opportunity for 'eco-tourism [...] demonstrating high-revenue potential' (Hall, 2005: 420). It is not ideal, but it might be the best available option.

It is a testimony to the novel's sustained ambivalence about the attractions of the welfare state that it ends on a flight between the UK (the precise place of departure is not mentioned) and the USA. On the aeroplane, Rachel wonders whether she should 'dope' her son to help him avoid the boredom of transcontinental air travel. Perhaps, she thinks, 'it's cruel to subject a fourteen-month-old to such physical discomforts and tedium [...] but the same might be said of the terms of existence' (Hall, 2005: 426). She ultimately decides to expose him to the contingencies of airborne existence, but not without having the dope at hand, just in case. The word 'dope' recurs once more in the last pages of the book, when Rachel recognizes her dependence on her brother, who himself overcame his drug addiction in the course of the novel through her support and solidarity (Hall, 2005: 429). The caring gesture of *not* interfering in her son's exposure to boredom, in its turn, is echoed once more as the novel recounts how, right before Rachel's American trip, 'the [wolf] pack seemed to be veering too far east,' yet she ultimately decided against 'tranquilisation and transporting them' and 'hoped instinct would prevail' (Hall, 2005: 430). In this case, instinct could be trusted; yet unlike Hall's earlier novels, *The Wolf Border* no longer believes that instinct will unfailingly prevail in the encounter with 'the terms of existence,' and that provisions against such failure diminish life. If the terms of existence condemn us to live like 'wolves to man,' perhaps, there is consolation in the fact that the wildness of wolves, as the novel has taught us, is as much a labour of love as a condition of abandonment.

Note

1 Throughout this chapter, I distinguish between 'wildness,' which refers to an unruly and savage dimension of human and nonhuman lives, and 'wilderness,' which refers to particular locations untouched by human intervention; see Buell (2005: 148–9) and Huggan (2016: 152–7).

Works Cited

Beaumont, A. and Kelly, A. (2018) 'Freedom after Neoliberalism', *Open Library of Humanities* 4(2): DOI: http://doi.org/10.16995/olh.398

Brown, W. (2015) *Undoing the Demos: Neoliberalism's Stealth Revolution*. New York: Zone Books.

Buell, L. (2005) *The Future of Environmental Criticism*. Oxford: Blackwell.

Cooper, M. (2017) *Family Values: Between Neoliberalism and the New Social Conservatism*. New York: Zone Books.

Cronon, W. (1996) 'The Trouble with Wilderness: Or, Getting Back to the Wrong Nature', *Environmental History* 1(1): 7–28.

Davies, W. (2018) *Nervous States: How Feeling Took over the World*. London: Jonathan Cape.

Elliott, J. (2018) *The Microeconomic Mode: Political Subjectivity in Contemporary Popular Aesthetics*. New York: Columbia University Press.

Garrard, G. (2004) *Ecocriticism*. Abingdon: Routledge.

Foucault, M. (2008) *The Birth of Biopolitics: Lectures at the College de France, 1978–1979*. New York: Palgrave Macmillan.

Hall, S. (2002) *Haweswater*. London: Faber.

Hall, S. (2004) *The Electric Michelangelo*. London: Faber.

Hall, S. (2007) *The Carhullan Army*. London: Faber.

Hall, S. (2009) *How to Paint a Dead Man*. London: Faber.

Hall, S. (2015) *The Wolf Border*. London: Faber.

Huggan, G. (2016) 'Back to the Future: The "New Nature Writing," Ecological Boredom, and the Recall of the Wild', *Prose Studies* 38(2): 152–71.

Konings, M. (2015) *The Emotional Life of Capitalism: What Progressives have Missed*. Stanford, CA: Stanford University Press.

Kotsko, A. (2018) *Neoliberalism's Demons: On the Political Theology of Late Capital*. Stanford, CA: Stanford University Press.

Lilley, D. (2016) 'Unsettling Environments: New Pastorals in Kazuo Ishiguro's *Never Let Me Go* and Sarah Hall's *The Carhullan Army*', *Green Letters: Studies in Ecocriticism* 20(1): 60–71.

Lorimer, J. (2015) *Wildlife in the Anthropocene: Conservation after Nature*. Minneapolis: Minnesota University Press.

Marris, E. (2011) *Rambunctious Garden: Saving Nature in a Post-Wild World*. New York: Bloomsbury.

Marris, E. (2015) 'Handle with Care', *Orion Magazine* (May/June), URL: https://orionmagazine.org/article/handle-with-care/

Marris, E. (2017) 'A Very Old Man for a Wolf', *Outside* (30 Oct.), URL: https://www.outsideonline.com/2255971/adventure-very-old-man-wolf

Mirowski, P. (2014) *Never Let a Serious Crisis Go to Waste: How Neoliberalism Survived the Financial Meltdown*. London: Verso Books.

Mirowski, P. (2018) 'Hell is Truth Seen too Late', *Boundary 2* 46(1): 1–53.

Robbins, B. (2007) *Upward Mobility and the Common Good: Toward a Literary History of the Welfare State*. Princeton, NJ: Princeton University Press.

Rossello, D. (2012) 'Hobbes and the Wolf-Man: Melancholy and Animality in Modern Sovereignty', *New Literary History* 43(2): 255–79.

Stedman Jones, D. (2012) *Masters of the Universe: Hayek, Friedman, and the Birth of Neoliberal Politics*. Princeton, NJ: Princeton University Press.

5

POST-BRITISH POLITICS AND SARAH HALL'S NORTH

Chloé Ashbridge

By the time her fourth novel, *The Carhullan Army* (2007), was published, Sarah Hall had already gained a reputation among reviewers as a writer with a strong 'regional voice' (Hore, 2007). Her literary career to date reveals a longstanding preoccupation with 'the North': all of her novels are set – at least partly – in North-West England and are characterized by a particular interest in Cumbria. Hall's earliest writing demonstrates a preoccupation with reconciling the particularity of civic regionalism with the agenda of the British state. In her rural tragedy, *Haweswater* (2002), modern industrialization threatens Mardale's agricultural community in plans to flood the village to make way for a reservoir providing water for the industrial city of Manchester. The novel ends with the death of Isaac Lightburn, a member of the family central to the novel and its close-knit community, whose drowned body in the reservoir emblematizes the irreconcilability of local priorities with the unceasing forward momentum of twentieth-century British urban modernity. *The Carhullan Army* amplifies this disconnection between region and nation, articulating the catastrophic consequences of Britain's global endeavours. Set in the not-so-distant future, the bursting of the River Thames has led to the flooding of Westminster and the subsequent economic collapse of Britain. There are no governmental structures to be found, only propaganda and the repressive totalitarian apparatus of a state body termed 'The Authority' (Hall, 2007: 15). Escape from this controlled society is only possible for the protagonist by undertaking a treacherous journey to a feminist ecotopia in a mountainous area of North-West England, where a movement to challenge The Authority is in the making.

Yet, the political energies of 'the North' that emerge in *The Carhullan Army* find a more historical expression in *The Wolf Border* (2015). Hall (2017: n.p.) has noted that she intended *The Wolf Border* to be a state-of-the-nation novel, suggesting a wider exploration of twenty-first-century Britain than has previously been the case in her work. Here, tensions between the North and Westminster occur against the wider constitutional backdrop of a successful Scottish Independence referendum, imagining both an independent Scotland and the end of the Union. In *The Wolf Border*, it is precisely Hall's engagement with 'the North' within an increasingly unstable national frame that provides the novel with regional devolutionary promise, with Cumbria becoming a site of post-British potential. Despite being a concern to which Hall consistently returns in her novels and short stories, the cultural and political significance of 'the North' in her work has yet to be closely examined. Given that the roots of regionalism in England are primarily to be found in the regions of the North-East, an area which has played a disproportionate role in the debate about regional devolution in England (Tomaney, 2000: 158), the location of Hall's work is politically significant.

Hall's exploration of 'the North' intervenes in political arguments advanced by the New Left regarding the future of the British Union. In his landmark study *The Break-Up of Britain*, Tom Nairn (1977: 12) proposed that the British state was in crisis, describing the Union as a 'general mass' now subject to 'territorial disintegration' and unable to unify its competing internal nationalisms in the wake of the disillusion of Empire. In the first of a large body of scholarship dedicated to the future of Scotland and the British Union, Nairn predicted that increased pressure for devolution in Scotland and Wales was to leave the British state with little structural integrity. Twenty years later, the New Labour government of 1997 proposed the matter of devolution to Scotland, Wales, and London as a way of addressing this concern. Yet, the establishment of devolved parliaments in Scotland and Wales during the 1990s did not end the debate about the tenability of the British Union. Nairn's study continued to influence a whole generation of scholarship on the question of British identities in general, and on Scotland and England in particular.[1] The devolution of government to Scotland especially not only re-energized discussion surrounding 'the break-up of Britain' (Nairn, 1977: 1), but, as Claire Westall and Michael Gardiner (2013: 119) have identified, raised the question as to whether membership of the British Union could be entirely re-negotiated from the inside out – England included. England became less 'the gaping hole' (Hazell, 2000: 1) in the devolution question and increasingly took centre-stage in the debate about what it meant to be English in the wake of Britain's perceived imminent break-up.

But what makes England such a peculiar case is the easy slippage that is often noticed in the relationship between England and Britain, a slippage that is best encapsulated in the term 'Anglo-Britain'. The fact that they are essentially 'two sides of the same coin' is precisely what makes conceiving of England-without-Britain – or Britain-without-England – just short of an impossibility (Kumar, 2015: 4). One missing 'institution' in England is a national literature, a literature of England, rather than the more imperial formation of 'English Literature' (Gardiner, 2013: 8). The 'English Question', then, 'is still missing the single most significant area of negotiation – literary culture' (Westall and Gardiner, 2013: 6). Indeed, beyond Westall and Gardiner's *Literature of an Independent England* (2013), there has been little attention paid to contemporary writers whose work attempts to imagine a 'placed' national England in a post-devolution era, and which might provide an innovative literary intervention within these national debates. This chapter proposes that Sarah Hall is one such writer.

What would we find, then, if we were to read Hall's writing in terms of the literary 'English Question'? What contribution might literature set in and about the rural North make towards decoupling England from Britain and shifting meanings of Englishness in the wake of Britain's constitutional uncertainty? Hall's work demands that we think these questions through, presenting a vision of the English rural landscape imbued with regional political autonomy. Contrary to Anna Cottrell's (2017: 4) assertion that Hall's preference for the regional is 'hardly new or daring', I want to suggest that the rural 'North' is a privileged site from which Hall stages post-British politics and evokes the prospect of an independent England. This chapter thus explores how Hall demonstrates a consistent preoccupation with what Robert Hazell (2000: 21) observes as the two narratives of devolution in England: a 'UK version, about rebalancing England's place in the Union post-devolution' and 'an English version, about decentralizing the government of England'. Indeed, Hall's work appears to operate at the intersection of the two; it is concerned with the possibility – or rather, the impossibility – of effective regional government in England while the nation remains part of the Union. Taken together, *Haweswater*, *The Carhullan Army*, and *The Wolf Border* offer only an emerging vision of post-British autonomy for England that is never fully realized. Equivocating between a commitment to the disruptive politics of rural wilderness and pastoral retreat, the post-British potential of her novels ultimately remains contained within, and undermined by, the ideological structures that serve the priorities of the nation state.

Region and Nation

While Hall's first novel, *Haweswater*, foregrounds the tensions between region and nation that she returns to in her more recent work, the prospect of a post-British England is, in this novel, far from reach. In contrast to the organized dissent of *The Carhullan Army*, *Haweswater*'s North is unable to present a challenge to the dominance of Britain's industrial vision: regional unrest only ever amounting to mere 'rumblings' (Hall, 2002: 91) among the community. Upon hearing of plans to flood the village, a local farmer reflects that 'Parliament was a long way south, remote from the valleys of the

North of England, and its workings were seldom this far-reaching. But its law was final' (Hall, 2002: 53). The dam project sits uncomfortably alongside the agricultural priorities of the region's residents, aligning with the priorities of Westminster. The novel's contemplation on the enduring sovereignty of British state institutions points to the lack of democratic participation in England and is indicative of the novel's inability to imagine an alternative to the jurisdiction of the centralized state. Samuel Lightburn's unsuccessful attempt to foment discontent within the local community underlines the limits of current forms of parliamentary democracy; he waits for 'the multitude of voices that did not come' (Hall, 2002: 53), hinting at a democratic deficit in the area. Indeed, while Northern England's metropolitan areas have recovered from the First World War, in rural Cumbria, 'there is not much recovery yet. Tenancies do not fall from trees in this part of the country, especially now' (Hall, 2002: 108).

Haweswater's dam project forms the central antagonism in the novel; it necessitates the destruction of Mardale's rural community, with their small-scale agricultural ecosystem deemed insignificant compared to larger, state-supported industrial projects in big cities like Manchester. This dichotomy embodies the uneven development of Anglo-Britain as the conflict between the locals and the semi-fictional city corporation enacts the disjuncture between regional and state-national priorities. While the dam will invariably serve the local community, it also communicates the way British metropolitan exceptionalism hinges on the marginalization of rural communities. MCW representative, Jack Liggett, symbolizes a hegemonic, external 'other' figure in this division. Initially, Jack's presence is perceived as accidental, with locals noting how 'he could not be in the right place, must have somehow become dislodged from his metropolitan setting' (Hall, 2002: 44). At this stage in the novel, Jack occupies a vaguely colonial position, an outsider whose 'foreignness' is made conspicuous from his immediate arrival into Mardale:

> He was dressed for dinner, or a dance, like an unusual, exotic bird, its silk and sheen foreign in the cold landscape. The artist thought to himself that the man was not lost. He had come to the valley as a

man would enter a room to receive a guest – territorially, impossibly possessive, and with charm, politeness, with a tip of a hat, a warmly shaken hand. He, the stranger, assuming control. (Hall, 2002: 44)

Jack's territorial authority signifies a centralized democratic structure that neglects regional-rural priorities; as Daniel Lea puts it, Jack's 'rationality [is] based on national rather than local duty' (Hall, 2017: 158). Here, and elsewhere in the novel, Jack's role in the reservoir construction serves as a reminder of the insignificance of Northern rural communities to a national project focussed on industrial modernity.

Haweswater's insistence on Cumbrian dialect – a formal device absent elsewhere in Hall's work – also communicates the corporation's close relationship to what is represented as a Westminster-inspired wave of industrialization. This can be observed most clearly during exchanges between a local community member and a representative from Manchester: 'yor t'fella that's gonna mek lake bigga'/'Yes I am' (Hall, 2002: 81). In staging an opposition between Standard English and regional dialect, *Haweswater* gestures towards the cultural and political chasm between Jack and Mardale's agricultural community. This geographical binary establishes the complex hierarchal structures that designate the North region as England's 'other' in contrast to a dominant metropolitanism. Reciting the process of reservoir construction in oversimplifies terms, Jack views the locals' concerns as little more than a nostalgic reluctance to engage in modernization; he speaks to the locals in 'another tongue, or in abstracts far removed from the life of these men and women. His purpose was inconceivable' (Hall, 2002: 42). The perceived untranslatability of modernity to the locals in the passage drives a wedge between 'national interest' and its metropolitan discourse of development and the rural North, pointing towards the sociopolitical implications of perceptions of the region as a provincial backwater.

What is notable, however, is that Hall's fiction after *Haweswater* retreats from the use of dialect and a delimited regional mode while retaining an insistence on local identity markers. In *The Carhullan Army*, one of the first things Sister notices about Jackie is her accent sounding like 'the country's rural equivalent [of her own]' (Hall, 2007: 78). Similarly, in *The Wolf Border*, when Rachel returns to Cumbria after a period of living in the U.S., Thomas Pennington's secretary questions her authenticity: 'You're local? I don't hear an accent' (Hall, 2015: 11). Yet what distinguishes these accounts from *Haweswater*, even as they appear superficially to echo many of that novel's preoccupations and engage with a similar setting, is that their central concerns of climate change and animal conservation are inherently global while at the same time being experienced within a local frame. Janet Lightburn recognizes that she is 'in a place too remote to fall prey to political or industrial assembling. [...] Now she has had to alter her vision. She must look with new eyes' (Hall, 2002: 112). It appears that Hall herself has had to 'alter her vision', moving from a formerly politically inoperative North to recognizing the devolutionary potential of a regional voice attuned to wider national and global shifts. Hall's repositioning of the local within a wider contextual frame allows her to respond to the ways in which these shifts are experienced locally, simultaneously creating a narrative which pulls against the British centralized state form.

It is thus when Hall engages with national and global concerns – such as rewilding and climate change – that her work is able to imagine a political future for England most successfully. Hall's fiction after *Haweswater* may therefore be considered to represent a recent entry into what Gardiner (2012: 146) speculatively terms 'a minor literature of England'. Such a literature would 'return experience to local contexts, working between dialects and showing the connectedness of the many facets of the state [...] but it may also aim to thoroughly deprovincialize the writing of England' (Gardiner, 2012: 146). As the rest of this chapter will suggest, the return of political experience to England is most explicitly realized in *The Wolf Border*.

The Scottish Question

The potential for a post-British England is buttressed in the counterpoint between Northern England and the devolved nation of

Scotland that Hall sets up in *The Wolf Border*. This is not a mere geographic coincidence: the novel's familiarity with Scottish devolution highlights the exclusions inherent in Anglo-Britain. Indeed, Rachel's initial reservation about the re-wilding project concerns, notably, its location in England, a country that she considers to be 'particularly owned' (Hall, 2015: 29). Conversely, the opposite is happening further north, where land is being de-privatized and returned to public hands:

> [Rachel] is aware of the reform plans across the border – public acquisition of private land, recalibration of resources – a notion that must make the likes of Thomas Pennington more than a little uncomfortable. The BBC is full of debate about independence and the forthcoming referendum; she's been surprised by how close the polls are, how troublesome the matter is proving for Westminster. (Hall, 2015: 26)

In Scotland, the hierarchies of land ownership that have characterized the British class system since feudalism are being readily dismantled as the nation prepares to rebuild itself anew, presenting post-British Scotland as an increasingly egalitarian civic space compared to England. Hall's reference to the BBC in this scene is also an important comment on the ideological construction of Britishness. As its very name suggests, the BBC is a cultural symbol of Unionism. Jean Seaton notes, for example, that the BBC has helped to define Britain-as-nation and thus become part of Britain's unwritten constitution (Seaton, 2015: 13–14).[2] Notably, recent sociopolitical tensions throughout Britain in the post-Brexit period have seen the organization's role as 'uniting the nation' called into question, with debates concerning the contradictions in the BBC's unifying status as a nationally funded corporation in such a divided present.

In contrast to England, intertextual references to the Scottish Renaissance of the 1980s and 90s locate the perceived 'radicalism' of the newly independent nation (Hall, 2015: 281). Prior to a healthcare appointment, Rachel listens to a radio station on which Scotland's First Minister is '[g]oaded, accused of being racist, an economic dunce, but he maintained optimism, Scotland was, is, and will be a beacon of social enlightenment. He quotes one of the country's premier writers: work as in the early days of a better nation' (Hall, 2015: 102). The writer in question here is Alasdair Gray, whose fiction forms a significant contribution to the revival of Scottish literary nationalism; his dystopian novel, *Lanark* (1981), was supported by a wave of nationalist journals associated with the New Left, including *Cencrastus, New Edinburgh Review*, and *Radical Scotland*. This intertextual reference gestures towards literature's potential to accelerate a devolved national consciousness in leu of political devolution, indicating an awareness of the relationship between literary and political forms of devolution. Here, the 'early days of a better nation' refers to Scotland but may also speak to a potential independent England. Rachel's hope that 'the country as a whole will one day re-wild, whatever its man-made divisions created at the ballot box' (Hall, 2015: 234) positions Scotland as progressing towards a post-British nationhood and evokes the potential for England's own political 'rewilding'. We can therefore read *The Wolf Border*'s rewilding project as an allegory for a post-British politics of England located in the North.

Yet, it is crucial to note that Hall is careful to distinguish between cultural forms of devolution and the dissolution of the British state form. The novel highlights cultural devolution's inadequacy to yield a political praxis that transcends British state structures, simply substituting legislative power for a depoliticized civic nationalism. This sentiment echoes Christopher Whyte's assertion that 'in the absence of elected political authority [in pre-devolution Scotland], the task of representing the nation has been repeatedly devolved to its writers' (Whyte, 1998: 248). The process of cultural devolution Whyte identifies here is locatable in Hall's work. We can think of her fiction as tending to a similar task for England, speaking from a region that has been defined by longstanding socio-economic and political marginalization. For instance, *The Wolf Border* is certainly attuned to the regional and national democratic deficit throughout Britain, illustrating the ways in which both Scotland and the North of England have been disadvantaged by the British centralized state form. Even the case for Scotland's independence remains exclusively discussed by 'grey-haired' retirees and 'the district's rich', which suggests that independence from Britain may simply result in the redistribution of power between two already existing political elites (Hall, 2015: 95). This class dynamic inflecting the management of British rural space evokes the conquests of conservation charities and interest groups such as the John Muir Trust, an organization that now owns eight estates in Scotland under the remit of protecting and managing 'wild' land.[3]

Likewise, in Hall's vision of an independent Scotland, antiquated British hierarchies remain part of the political fabric and matters of 'the World Heritage status bid, new speed limits on the lakes, the Scottish polls [and] the wolf-project' remain uncomfortably upper-class affairs (Hall, 2015: 95). The end of the novel communicates a similar pessimism when the wolves' future is negotiated at Holyrood, a state-mandated institution in which authority has simply been recentralized. Hall thus remains critical of the capacity of literature as a substitute for legislative power and acknowledges the limitations of cultural devolution. Paradoxically, then, *The Wolf Border* reimagines the political narrative of Scotland while simultaneously exposing how independence is an illusion 'often projected onto the cultural sphere through its persistent lack in the political sphere' (Carruthers et al., 2004: 15). So, while Hall goes as far as imagining a post-British Scotland, she offers only a guarded prognosis for progressive politics in a country still dominated by class interests and the institutional remnants of the British state.

Rewilding and the Post-Pastoral

In terms of institutions of the British state, the pastoral idyll has functioned as a stand-in for a civic English nationalism. As Ian Baucom (1994: 4) has previously explained, the pastoral idyll has been deployed as a synecdoche for the nation's space and mobilized after Empire to prevent the emergence of a political English civic nationalism. As Baucom puts it, 'struggles to control the idea of Englishness over the past 150 years have largely been struggles over places endowed with the capacity to evoke a sense of the nation's essential continuity over time'. In this sense, the simultaneously literal and metaphorical spaces of the English countryside have been understood both within and outside of literary culture as a synecdoche of England's national consciousness that constructs, maintains, and circulates myths of a unified national identity in place of a codified, *political* identity. In a similar vein, Peter Mandler (1997: 155) describes Englishness as it came to be represented in late twentieth-century literature as '[n]ostalgic, deferential and rural'. In these accounts, he suggests, Englishness 'identified the squirearchical village of Southern or "Deep England" as the template on which the national character had been formed and thus the ideal towards which it must inevitably return' (Mandler, 1997: 155). Englishness, then, has functioned more as a stretchy cultural 'template' located in the South than as an institutional national identity. In Terry Gifford's (1999/2006: 53) recent formulation, the post-pastoral resists 'the idealizing distortion of the literary construction of the pastoral'. Post-pastoral literature, according to Gifford (1999/2006: 45), 'possesses acute awareness of the culturally loaded language we use about the country, accepting responsibility for our relationship with nature and its dilemmas'. This has constitutional implications in the context of the UK, given that one of the barriers to developing English civic nationalism is that a particular kind of mythological, pastoral Englishness already exists as a key component of the national imaginary. Englishness operates as a cultural – and at times ethnic – term located in the countryside.

While the uses of the land prioritized in *Haweswater* (small-scale agriculture), *The Carhullan Army* (environmental sustainability), and *The Wolf Border* (rewilding) create the conditions for deconstructing the pastoral idyll, their depiction of rural space overlays multiple pastoral and post-pastoral modes. From its opening pages, *Haweswater* appears to possess a commitment to the post-pastoral. Mardale is far from a place of rural retreat, but a place of home and work for tenant farmers and 'a little agriculture where the soil was deep enough' (Hall, 2002: 29). The complexities of the land and the reality of farming practices is starkly visceral, puncturing any association of space with an image of a 'green and pleasant land'. Janet's intricate familiarity with agricultural practices emphasizes their cruelty; her knowledge spans from understanding how 'pry open the mouth of an unorphaned lamb and 'to introduce milk through a fake teat' to the most efficient ways to kill livestock, 'the point on the side of a head to place the rifle barrel, exact inches from an eye, where the bullet will meet the least resistance' (Hall, 2002: 22). As the narrative voice reminds us 'there are no miracles in this dale' (Hall, 2002: 6).

Janet's affair with Jack reaffirms this post-pastoral blurring of the human and non-human, both in the instinctual physicality of their sexual encounters and the way in which Janet approaches Jack as a predator pursuing its prey; '[h]e did not know that she was more aware of his movements within the valley than he was of hers. That the direction of her walks was dependent on first pinpointing his location or hearing word of where he had been' (Hall, 2002: 119). The violence of the encounters themselves reiterates this visceral animalism: 'there were always injuries. Bruises as she struggled to leave him' and '[p]ieces of her hair torn out when she demanded he leave' (Hall, 2002: 120). Jack and Janet's bodily struggles articulate the coming together of two contradictory approaches to the land as Hall 'makes use of the staple fictional convention of the union of opposites' (Head, 2020: 356). While Jack is initially presented as an outsider due to his association with MCW, later, we learn of his familiarity with Cumbria's landscape, complicating the rural conventions of the threat of the 'outsider'. It is revealed that Jack previously visited the area as a child and knows the fells intimately, and is capable of climbing Helvellyn at night.

Jack's attitude towards his relationship with Janet also demonstrates a complex pastoralism. Aligning sexual pleasure and the recuperative effects of the land on his psyche, Jack reflects that 'the fulfilment of a high climb and the sensuality of [Janet's] body [...] brought a level of contentment beyond any he had reached in the past. The two at once seemed to offer a spiritual answer' (Hall, 2002: 147). Jack's alignment of the female body with 'nature' and the mythical properties he attributes to the combination of these acts exemplifies the colonial impulses that undercut the narrative's post-pastoral vision. Yet, his relationship with Janet does to some extent alter Jack's approach to the reservoir project and his pre-disposition to the Mardale community; he transitions from being '[o]ne of those classless types who believes that [the countryside] is about scenery and escape' (Hall,

2002: 180) to being allowed 'free passage. As if he, too, now belonged in part to the region'(Hall, 2002: 149). This relationship initiates a transformation of Jack's character and his framing in the novel – he transitions from being a figure of metropolitan dominance to possessing an intimate knowledge of Cumbria's landscape. Hall appears to be distinguishing pastoral and post-pastoral approaches the region's rural space, between Jack's territorial bravado and anthropocentric pastoral position and Janet's intimate but nevertheless anti-pastoral affinity with the land established through farming practices.

Similarly, *The Carhullan Army* disassociates rural space and pastoralism through the potential of Northern England's landscape, anticipating the role of the region in *The Wolf Border*. The fact that the novel was published in the US under the title *Daughters of the North* indicates that the region does not merely serve as the novel's setting. Set in an England overrun with environmental crisis and economic collapse, it is only in a retreat to a mountainous region in Cumbria that women are able to evade the control of The Authority. In a treatment of rural space that is continued in *The Wolf Border*, this 'raw landscape, verging on wilderness' (Hall, 2007: 50) is used as a stage for Hall's devolutionary politics. During her northward journey to what Hall describes as 'the other half of Britain' (Hall, 2007: 55), Sister is optimistic that 'alternative societies [... can] be created in these mountains' (Hall, 2007: 55), an ideal that is echoed in her subsequent reflection that 'people will learn to use the earth well. But for now, it had to be given up to another cause' (Hall, 2007: 166). *The Carhullan Army*'s literary politics rests upon the supposed 'wilderness' of the North: the urgency to decentralize state power is emphatically located in rural Northern England, presenting the region as the site for the emergence of a post-British politics. This is a venture that Sister only fully realizes towards the end of the novel, after Jackie's reminder that '[r]evolutions always begin in the mountain regions' (Hall, 2007: 195) and which is later confirmed in Sister's confession that she does not 'recognise the jurisdiction of this government' (Hall, 2007: 207). In ending the novel on an emphatic rejection of the British institutional system, Hall establishes the very concerns that *The Wolf Border* later revisits.

If *The Carhullan Army*'s dystopian vision initiates Hall's post-British project, it is in *The Wolf Border* that Hall's politics find their most successful post-pastoral outlet. In contrast to this imaginary, the post-British potential of Hall's work resides in her critical rejection of pastoral manifestations of Englishness. *The Wolf Border* performs its devolutionary politics through a refusal of the pastoral literary mode; it is exposed as placeless, ideological, and as blocking political experience in England. Through an insistence on localized, eco-critical understandings of rural places, Hall differentiates the English regions from a vision of rural England and exposes how the pastoral idyll is more suited to the global endeavours of the British Empire than a national experience of England.[4] The novel prioritizes locally particularized approaches to the rural landscape from the outset; when Rachel returns from America, she realizes that 'England is unreal, a forgotten version, with only a few pieces of evidence left to validate it' (Hall, 2015: 23). Her musing in this passage aligns the landscape with a pastoral version of Englishness, yet, when Hall evokes the landscape on a micro scale it is registered much more vividly. Upon her return to Cumbria, Rachel quickly becomes reacquainted with the 'spruce and sagebrush, the rancid vegetable smell of the paper mill downriver from the Reservation. Cumbria's signature aroma is immediately recognisable: upland pheromones' (Hall, 2015: 9). Her sensorial familiarity decouples the landscape from the mythical rural and reframes it in localized terms through the notation of specific reference points. Hall's prioritization of a local connection to Cumbria's topography – a characteristic of Rachel's role on the wolf-project – signals England's own post-pastoral return as it becomes geographically rooted and 'placed'.

The Wolf Border's accountability to the materiality of the wolves also bears out the link between the novel's rewilding project and post-British politics. The physical presence of wolves on the Annerdale estate initiates a post-pastoral reconfiguration of English rural space as the land becomes used for an ecological cause, rather than being reduced to a national iconography or object of aesthetic contemplation. Graham Huggan's explanation of the ecological value of rewilding is particularly instructive for reading the wolf-project in post-pastoral terms:

> Rewilding is not the romantic idea of restoring [natural ecosystems] to their putatively original state, which is recognised by practitioners as illusory; rather, it reflects the pragmatic need to boost their in-built capacity for regeneration, such as by performing reintroduction experiments that might encourage natural ecological processes to start. (Huggan, 2016: 169)

The Wolf Border was published during an emphatically post-pastoral moment in Britain in which there has been a significant focus on ecological conservation and rewilding; there are, for instance, parallels to be drawn between Hall's fictional Annerdale estate where the wolf enclosure is located and Paul Lister's Alladale Wilderness Reserve in the Caledonian Forest.[5] In the novel, the highly political project of rewilding contains the potential to bypass regional and, as the wolves make clear, national lines of demarcation. Indeed, the kind of post-pastoral, grounded ecology the wolf-project represents is opposed by groups who reinforce the country's 'green and pleasant land' as a synecdoche for a national consciousness. When Rachel attempts to answer the public's questions, the rallies sing a song 'written to the tune of Jerusalem' (Hall, 2015: 154). This performative ode to a mythical version of Englishness alludes to Blakean elegies of the pastoral idyll and, in drawing on a hymn frequently co-opted as England's unofficial national anthem, elevates rural space beyond a material and placed reality. In this sense, the novel's concern with rewilding appears to map onto its post-British project.

The literary function of the wolves also encodes Hall's ambivalence towards the possibility of achieving a post-British England; they become overdetermined spatial metaphors whose symbolic purpose becomes increasingly slippery. The literary wolf has long been used as a device for exploring human, political, social, and environmental preoccupations. The figure of the wolf, as Karen Jones (2011: 202) points out, is often 'a symbol of ecological vitality located in the wilderness': because of its biological proximity to the domestic dog, the wolf is a suitable device for navigating the porous boundary between civilization and 'the wild'.⁶ Likewise, in *The Wolf Border*, the wolves are indifferent to man-made boundaries; of North and South, and of wilderness and civilization. Hall's (2015: 35) intent focus on the physicality of the wolves dismantles the illusory mechanisms of the pastoral idyll, demonstrating a post-pastoral commitment to presenting 'the fact of an animal, not the myth'. Described by Rachel as creatures of 'geographic success' (Hall, 2015: 7) it is the wolves' physical presence in *The Wolf Border* that embodies the momentum for constitutional change. Indeed, the material 'fact' of the wolves punctures the pastoral throughout the text. What Rachel finds most fascinating about the wolves is their physical attributes, their 'extraordinary jaw' (Hall, 2015: 7) and 'small, clever, yellow eyes' (Hall, 2015: 253), an animal 'perfectly made' (Hall, 2015: 3). Yet the wolves are never reduced to myth: their entire journey is rendered visible, from their arrival from the US, the delivery of the pups, and the paw prints in the ground following their escape. Upon the birth of the new wolf pups, Rachel reflects that '[t]hey become almost like mascots for exactly what no one is sure, a beleaguered England, an England no longer associated with Scotland's great natural resources' (Hall, 2015: 326). Explicitly lent to a national England, the concurrent narratives of the birth of the wolves and the birth of an independent Scotland collide.

While here the wolves appear to signify the prospect of 're-wilding' England as a politically autonomous nation, they are later deployed as cultural symbols and pet projects for political figures. This slippage is most clearly observed during a passage in which the novel draws attention to how the centralized state form has accelerated regional inequality within England. As the Scottish polls tip towards a majority 'Yes-vote', Sylvia remarks that she 'would like to see a shift to more regional power, too [...] A lot of Cumbria's needs are not London's or Cornwall's. My concern is what happens in England if they go' (Hall, 2015: 179). Sylvia's comment aligns the uneven distribution of political and financial resources throughout England to its precarious position within an increasingly unstable Union. The difficulty of conceiving an independent England in the novel is partially due to a democratic deficit: as Rachel quickly becomes aware, 'regardless of democracy, the greater schemes are led by the upper echelons' (Hall,

2015: 25). Rachel's musing characterizes the 'English Question' as national only insofar as it is regional, suggesting that the discussion that surrounds the break-up of Britain must also address political, financial, and social inequality in regions within England. Nonetheless, despite Sylvia's acknowledgement of these implications, it is not long before regional any potential unrest is pacified. Rachel notes how '[t]here's been no more trouble around the fence periphery', a beneficial outcome for England's Prime Minister, who, after the Scottish 'Yes'-vote is 'desperate for good press, progressive politics – especially in the regions where there is growing agitation for devolved powers – and the project qualifies' (Hall, 2015: 260). Here, the symbolic value of the wolf-project is harnessed by political figures for their own self-legitimizing agenda – in this case, for preventing increased momentum for regional devolution in England. So, while previously the wolves symbolized the potential for a post-British England, here they are seen to potentially become part of a *state* project. The slipperiness of the wolves throughout the novel captures Hall's ambivalence towards the possibility of achieving a post-British England, especially one that is attuned to regional inequality. The wolves' various symbolic functions ultimately remain unresolved, suggesting a reading of the wolves in *The Wolf Border* as manifestations of the novel's inability to overcome the ideological stranglehold of Britain and the pastoral idyll.

Freedom and Enclosure

Pennington's vast influence over the rewilding also signifies Britain's enduring dominance over England and its regions. The uneasy tension between freedom and enclosure as part of the rewilding project articulates the politics of private and public space and their intersection with region and nation. The entire project depends upon Pennington's impulses, whose imperialist logic underscores the way ownership of and control over rural space is intrinsically political: his vast ownership of immense land alludes to the hierarchies of an anachronistic British class system. Pennignton's privatization of common land for the wolf enclosure emblematizes the lasting power of Britain's land-owning political elite and conveys Hall's pessimism towards the possibility of achieving a post-British England. As Raymond Williams (1973: 103) writes, enclosure of the commons facilitates the 'steady concentration of power in the hands of the landowners' which in turn represents 'a conscious national system and interest in the constitution of landowners as a political class'. George Monbiot (2013: 167) has also critiqued attempts to manage the rural environment in Britain through 'successive acts of enclosure 'that have led to a shrinkage of the commons'. The process of privatization Williams and Monbiot identify is embodied in the wolf enclosure and the rewilding project driven by the incalculable wealth of a member of the 'ebullient, boyish elite' (Hall, 2015: 3) who 'owns almost one fifth of [Rachel's] home country' (Hall, 2015: 15). She remains unimpressed by Pennington's expansive estate and attitude towards his 'latest environmental venture' (Hall, 2015: 15), an experiment enabled as a result of his manipulation of the Game Enclosure Bill.

In centring the wolves' rewilding on privately-owned and cultivated territory, the novel deconstructs ideas of the rural 'wild', recognizing the very idea of 'wilderness' as an impossible necessity. This paradox is illustrated when Rachel returns to Annerdale as an adult. She reflects that 'she did not know it [as a child], but in reality it was a kempt place, cultivated, even the high grassland over the fells was manmade. Though it formed her notions of beauty, true wilderness lay elsewhere' (Hall, 2015: 29). Rachel realizes that her childhood landscape has always been subject to constant human influence and regulation; it is by no means 'wild'. Her dissonance highlights the way experiences of the English landscape are contingent on modernity's innate separation from the countryside, a trope she is forced to deconstruct when she returns to Cumbria years later. Bill Devall and George Sessions (1985: 110) have previously pinpointed wilderness as fundamental to a new ecological consciousness, defining it as 'a landscape or ecosystem that has been minimally disrupted by the intervention of humans, especially the destructive technology of modern societies'. Both 'wild' enough to accommodate the wolves, yet simultaneously governed by human interests, *The Wolf Border*'s ambivalent landscape locates the contradictions embedded within notions of 'rewilding' and 'wilderness' and thus presents Hall's partial prognosis for imagining a post-British re-territorialization of rural space.

Governing interests over the land in *The Wolf Border* pertain to Pennington, the legal owner and the Earl of the Annerdale estate. Rachel and Pennington's significant ideological divisions characterize the entire wolf-project. While Rachel's ecological and professional commitment to the wolves is clear, she is never able to fully appraise the project due to 'the hegemony, the unsettling feeling of imbalance' she recognizes between her, Pennington and his loyal Gamekeeper, Michael (Hall, 2015: 29). In particular, the freighted relationship between Rachel and Michael – and the position he occupies in the social hierarchies of land management – reflects both the gendered and class-based inequalities that have facilitated the maintenance of a landowning British elite:

> [Michael] is not happy about being replaced in the chain of command. [F]or now [Rachel] holds the lateral position, perhaps even a higher position. Certainly [he is] not happy about the reconstitution of Annerdale, with its new apex predator. She represents dire competition, beyond his experience. (Hall, 2015: 117)

In contrast to Rachel's progressive approaches to the land, Michael is presented as an anachronistic symbol of feudalism. He is proud of his position on the estate and its 'old orders', opposing both the redistribution of power that the wolf project represents socially in addition to the material threat of the wolves (Hall, 2015: 117). After all, Michael's role has been secured by the fact that his father worked alongside Pennington's – his claim to the landscape is 'all in the blood' (Hall, 2015: 94). Indeed, Rachel's entry into Pennington's employ signifies the breakdown of this social order centred on ancestral lineage and class division. Rachel herself reflects that Annerdale is 'a realm so antiquated it seems impossible that it has survived reformist centuries' (Hall, 2015: 281). Here, the reconstitution of Annerdale refers to the end of a current social arrangement in the politics of land management and the emergence of a new system in which Michael's position is compromised; the reality that his legitimacy on the estate survives only as long as Pennington underwrites it is made starkly clear. In this sense, Michael's social standing on the estate is bound up in Hall's wider exploration of the logic of land management and rural decline (as seen in *Haweswater*, for example). It is notable that farmers barely appear in Hall's fiction and, in *The Wolf Border*, Pennington's concern with the rural landscape does not extend to farming purposes, but to monetizing the aesthetic value of the land in a bid for World Heritage status.

As such, *The Wolf Border* demonstrates how modern conservation strategies have gone hand-in-hand with the maintenance of land-owning class interests. The fact that Rachel has been conscripted into a role left vacant by Michael's marginalization registers this tension. Her role cannot be considered straightforwardly progressive. Although Rachel's presence on Annerdale hints at the destabilization of old class hierarchies based on ancestral lineage, in many ways she is simply replacing Michael in an already existing chain of command which ultimately continues to serve Pennington. Rachel herself 'begins to feel a little uncomfortable, part of the machinery of segregation, which always enables the elite' (Hall, 2015: 281). So, as much as Michael's resistance to the rewilding project can be read as a nostalgic desire for the continuation of British class relations, the wolves' status as symbols of England's progressive future is further problematized.

The wolves' inability to exist outside of governing structures further complicates their disruptive potential. In contrast to Rachel's local and professional credentials as a zoologist, Pennington possesses a colonial paternalism towards the land and the rewilding project; for him, the wolves are little more than an ecological experiment, a 'hope-and-glory' (Hall, 2015: 56) project key to recreating 'the British soul' (Hall, 2015: 80). Rachel's uneasiness about her living arrangements and the above-average pay gesture towards Pennington's social and professional dominance over her as the native expert. Rachel continually tries – but ultimately fails – to reconstitute their power relations and 'get to know the system' so that she may ascertain where she herself fits into it' (Hall, 2015: 84). Pennington's orchestrated release of the wolves from their enclosure reiterates Rachel's lack of agency.

Pennington's continued ownership of Annerdale signifies his absolute authority and foreshadows his ability to evade accountability over the eventual fate of the wolves. It is noteworthy that the wolves are taken first to a managed estate owned by a member of the political elite skilled at manipulating the powers at Westminster, just as their subsequent release speaks of his seemingly infinite power. Pennington's ability to dismantle the wolf-project 'as he wishes' allegorizes Westminster's state-managed devolution and allows the British state to retain its political grasp (Hall, 2015: 414). Indeed, the fate of the wolves is ultimately uncertain and becomes tied up in the Scottish Prime Minister's project of rebuilding the nation. As Rachel herself notes, 'not much has really changed [...] now our free Caledonian cousins may actually have to put theory into practice' (Hall, 2015: 413). While there are endless re-negotiations of power in the novel, the wolves remain constantly governed, even as they cross the border and enter newly independent Scottish territory.

Despite the outcome of the referendum, *The Wolf Border* imagines Anglo-Britain's ongoing cultural grip on the national imagination of England and, to some degree, Scotland. The reality that the rewilding will always remain governed is communicated when Rachel is forced to administer the wolves' invasive sterilization, a treatment she believes is 'the price of partial freedom' (Hall, 2015: 339). Through the pacification of the wolves under human influence, and given the rewilding's eventual outcome – as the Prime Minister's token gesture towards upholding Scotland's new environmental policy – it is possible to read *The Wolf Border* as a critique of devolution as it occurs within the institutional structures of the British state; in the novel, freedom from governing structures is manifested as more of a process of containment and pacification, rather than a redistribution of sovereignty. This contained, 'partial' freedom is indicated in the wolves' planned relocation to Ben Nevis, one of Scotland's most iconic cultural symbols (Hall, 2015: 430). Here, the novel retreats from its post-British project, ending instead on an image of a commodified national iconography. Scotland's most cultivated 'wild spot' functions here as a mirror image of Annerdale: Ben Nevis, host to 125,000 walkers a year, is hardly 'wild'. It is useful at this point to return to Jackie's assertion in *The Carhullan Army* that everything radical happens 'in the mountain regions' (Hall, 2007:195). While in Hall's previous novel the mountains provide a space for radical political change, *The Wolf Border*'s mountain regions are instead subject to fierce regulation. Pennington's interference in the project of Scottish independence and excitement that the wolves will become 'a new icon for a new nation' (Hall, 2015: 423) implies that the figure of the wolf will once again be reduced to its symbolic value, an 'icon' realigned with historic and geographic myth.

In this sense, the continuing sovereignty of Britain and its institutional remnants prevent the novel from achieving the post-British potential it initially imagined. When a lorry driver hits one of the stray wolves, the fatality of the novel's political project is suggested for a final time. The driver has bought into the Scottish Prime Minister's political appropriation of the wolves and wanted them to make it to Nevis, 'he was for them, a Yes voter' (Hall, 2015: 430). The syntactic ambiguity in this line enables the 'Yes' to take on a dual significance, referring to both his outlook on the wolves' reintegration and his voting choices in the referendum. What is more, the fact that the wolf subsequently dies indicates that the idea of rewilding has always been a fantasy, conveying pessimism towards post-British potential either side of the border.

Alternative Unions

There is, then, a limited degree of post-British potential to be found in Hall's representation of the North in *The Wolf Border*. However, I want to draw my argument to a close by examining one of the ironies that Hall sets up in this novel. While I have suggested that Rachel's professional narrative in many ways facilitates a post-pastoral understanding of England and English rural space, Rachel's personal narrative exists in conflict with this project insofar as the novel tends towards the pastoral mode when she forges emotional attachments. The landscape bears heavily on Rachel's emotional ties to both Alexander and his daughter, Chloe, and in the development of her familial reunion with Lawrence. While at the novel's outset Rachel does not form emotional or geographic ties, she undergoes a personal transformation in which the 'uncivilized spirit' (Lea, 2017: 154) characteristic of Hall's protagonists becomes tamed. This process of 'taming' occurs in Rachel's shift in attitude towards romantic relationships. Initially emotionally detached, her relationships with men generally end after they have had sex and consequently, 'she has never really made it past the first argument with a man' (Hall, 2015: 218). Her matter-of-fact approach towards sexual partners is aligned with her treatment of the land: it is visceral, dirty, and inherently unromantic. Indeed, she describes kissing as 'one of evolution's stranger necessities' (Hall, 2015: 40) in the same way her role as a conservationist enables her to see through Pennington's sentimentality towards the land. However, her developing relationship with Alexander and her unplanned pregnancy initiate a transformation of her character towards forms of place-bound emotional attachment. Rachel's attraction to Alexander is not instinctual. She does not immediately find him attractive and in contrast to her previous brief sexual exchanges, she gradually transitions from sex as power – from knowing someone will 'want to fuck' a woman 'like her' (Hall, 2015: 39) – to sex as an emotionally-invested act that roots her to place. When Rachel finds herself pregnant after an uncharacteristically vanilla one-night stand with her friend, Kyle, she tells her GP that she does not have relationships, 'just sex' (Hall, 2015: 81). Yet, the event of becoming pregnant instigates a softening in Rachel's approach to relationships as she moves away from what Cottrell (2017: 5) describes as 'fierce aloofness' towards a desire for place that is associated with the local.

Rachel's reunion with Lawrence – primarily achieved during walks through the countryside and watching the wolves in their enclosure – similarly evokes these pastoral tendencies. During their awkward first meeting, the potential sighting of the wolves breaks the tension in Lawrence and Rachel's reunion: Lawrence is 'taken by the exoticism' (Hall, 2015: 125) of Rachel's job and, when they reach the top of Blencathra, Rachel 'suddenly feels moved' (Hall, 2015: 126) to be with him. The unexpected emotional connection with her brother is tied to the catharsis that attends their freely roaming the rural landscape. Later, when they walk through the land surrounding the enclosure, Lawrence 'occasionally glanc[es] over, with a possessive tenderness, as if she might stumble' (Hall, 2015: 162). Indeed, it is the stability of the landscape that allows Rachel the vulnerability to establish the emotional connection to Lawrence she never had as a child. This impasse in *The Wolf Border*'s post-pastoral representation of the rural is also emphasized in Annerdale's restorative role during Lawrence's recovery from addiction. Upon the breakdown of his marriage, Lawrence is exiled from the domestic sphere and the landscape becomes a place of retreat and recovery. When Lawrence is discharged from a brief stay in hospital, he is prescribed 'recuperation and isolation in the countryside' in which Rachel's cottage 'will be a sanatorium' (Hall, 2015: 317). The novel emphatically represents the landscape as bearing restorative qualities; it enables Lawrence to undergo a process of convalescence so that he may 're-enter the world' (Hall, 2015: 354) after he has become re-domesticated. The characters' 'rewilding' in the novel therefore results in a process of taming as Hall grapples with the contradictions embedded within rewilding and wilderness. It is important to note that these passages necessitate a temporary abandonment of the novel's political project in favour of Hall's characters' personal narrative; they emphasize 'fertility, resilience, beauty, and unthreatened stability in nature', qualities that Gifford (2012: 49) attributes to the pastoral mode.

It is through Hall's refusal to neatly reconcile competing notions of pastoral and post-pastoral that the novel offers a productive engagement with the complexities of imagining a post-British England. Ultimately, *The Wolf Border* is unable to resolve its own counteracting impulses towards pastoral retreat and a post-pastoral treatment of rural space. Hall's fiction appears to operate within the 'mature environmental aesthetics' Gifford (1999: 148) sets out as a result of the post-pastoral. These aesthetics 'go beyond the closed circuit of pastoral and anti-pastoral to achieve a vision of an integrated natural world that includes the human' (Gifford, 1999: 148). We might consider Hall a part of this movement that seeks to define a pastoral that has voided the traps of idealism in seeking to find a discourse that can both celebrate and take some responsibility for nature without false consciousness. In this sense, Hall's work might be read as a *disruption* of the pastoral mode, reflecting the deeply entrenched social and political barriers to a post-British England as much as a political urgency for change.

Given the outcome of a referendum that took place the year following *The Wolf Border*'s publication, the dissolution of Britain that Hall imagines seems increasingly possible. Hall's critique of the centralized state form and vision of an Independent Scotland feels even more prescient in the context of the UK's vote to terminate its membership of the European Union in 2016. This outcome brought existing geographic, political, and socio-economic divisions throughout the archipelago into unprecedented public prominence and called into question once again the tenability of a union between the four nations that comprise the UK. Variations in support for leaving the European Union, and governmental uncertainty, have already led to further strain on Britain's constitutional integrity. In the media, the vote to Leave was perceived as less to do with European relations than with England's internal divisions, replayed as a revolt against Westminster's political elite by a disenfranchised working-class English population existing beyond the parameters of the M25. Rachel's reflection at the close of *The Wolf Border* that there is potential to change 'the fabric of British politics, state definitions [...] if people want it badly enough, if they are tired and hopeful' takes on a new significance in a post-Brexit-vote context (Hall, 2015: 423) If, then, as a consequence of Britain's deepening constitutional fissures, there lies the potential for the emergence of a national England, then placing literary politics beyond Westminster is all the more urgent. Hall's fiction suggests that the North is a privileged site for the interrogation of the centralized state form and where a post-British literature of England is most likely to be found.

Notes

1 Krishan Kumar (2015: 251) suggests that critical interest in Englishness gained traction during the 1990s, and supplies his own list of works on the subject (see also Ackroyd, 2002; Aughey, 2005; Baucom, 1999;

Featherstone, 2009; Kenny, 2014; Kumar, 2017; McLeod and Rogers, 2004; Nairn, 2000; Paxman, 1998).

2 The BBC's connection with the monarchy has further solidified its constitutional role as an obligation to presenting, and indeed preserving, a unified national image. This vision remains centred on London, despite efforts to devolve it in the establishment of a second office, BBC North, in Salford's MediaCityUK in 2011. Most recently, however, the BBC has come under attack by both tabloid newspapers and Boris Johnson for its decision to censor the lyrics of 'Rule, Britannia!' and 'Land of Hope and Glory' at the *Last Night of the Proms* in August 2020. In response to this change, the Prime Minister publicly demanded that the BBC stop the 'cringing embarrassment' about the nation's history (see Waterson, 2020).

3 See John Muir Trust (2008).

4 For an extensive analysis of the ways various and contrasting spaces in England have been used to stand for Englishness after Empire, see Baucom (1999).

5 See https://alladale.com

6 The figure of the wolf is bound up in rural images of wild Northern landscapes, particularly North America, alluded to in Rachel's initial work with wolves in Idaho.

Works Cited

Ackroyd, Peter (2002) *Albion: The Origins of the English Imagination*. London: Chatto and Windus.

Aughey, Arthur (2005) *The Politics of Englishness*. Manchester: Manchester University Press.

Baucom, I. (1999) *Out of Place: Englishness, Empire, and the Locations of Identity*. Princeton, NJ: Princeton University Press.

Carruthers, G., Goldie, D. and Renfrew, A. (eds) (2004) *Beyond Scotland: New Contexts for Twentieth-Century Scottish Literature*. Amsterdam and New York: Rodopi.

Cottrell, A. (2017) 'The Power of Love: From Feminist Utopia to the Politics of Imperceptibility in Sarah Hall's Fiction', *Textual Practice* 33(4): 679–93.

Devall, B. and Sessions, G. (1985) *Deep Ecology*. Kaysville, UT: Gibbs Smith.

Featherstone, Simon (2009) *Englishness: Twentieth-century Popular Culture and the Forming of English Identity*. Edinburgh: Edinburgh University Press.
Gardiner, M. (2012) *The Return of England in English Literature*. London: Palgrave Macmillan.
Gardiner, M. (2013) *The Constitution of English Literature: The State, The Nation, and the Canon*. London: Bloomsbury.
Gifford, T. (1999/2006) *Pastoral*. London: Taylor & Francis.
Gifford, T. (2012) 'Pastoral, Anti-Pastoral and Post-Pastoral as Reading Strategies', in S. Slovic (ed.) *Critical Insights: Nature and Environment*, pp. 42–61. Ipswich: Salem Press.
Head, D. (2021) 'The Farming Community Revisited: Complex Nostalgia in Sarah Hall and Melissa Harrison', *Green Letters – Studies in Ecocriticism*, unpublished manuscript.
Hall, S. (2002) *Haweswater*. London: Faber and Faber.
Hall, S. (2007) *The Carhullan Army*. London: Faber and Faber.
Hall, S. (2015) *The Wolf Border*. London: Faber and Faber.
Hall, S. (2017) 'Sarah Hall', *Foyles*, URL (accessed 3 September 2018): https://www.foyles.co.uk/sarah-hall
Hazell, R. (ed.) (2000) *The English Question*. Manchester: Manchester University Press.
Head, D. (2020) 'The Farming Community Revisited: Complex Nostalgia in Sarah Hall and Melissa Harrison', *Green Letters: Studies in Ecocriticism*, 24(4): 354–66, https://doi.org/10.1080/14688417.2020.1842788
Hore, R. (2007) 'The Carhullan Army, by Sarah Hall', *Independent*, 7 October 2007, URL (accessed 24 August 2018): https://www.independent.co.uk/arts-entertainment/books/reviews/the-carhullan-army-by-sarah-hall-395975.html
Huggan, G. (2016) 'Back to the Future: The "New Nature Writing", Ecological Boredom, and the Recall of the Wild', *Prose Studies* 38(2): 152–71.
John Muir Trust (2008) 'For Wild Land & Wild Places', *John Muir Trust*, URL (accessed 26 May 2020): https://www.johnmuirtrust.org/our-work
Jones, K. (2011) 'Writing the Wolf: Canine Tales and North American Environmental-Literary tradition', *Environment and History* 17(2): 201–28.
Kenny, Michael (2014) *The Politics of English Nationhood*. Oxford: Oxford University Press.

Kumar, K. (2015) *The Idea of Englishness: English Culture, National Identity and Social Thought.* London: Routledge.

Kumar, Krishnan (2017) *The Idea of Englishness: English Culture, National Identity and Social Thought.* London: Routledge.

Lea, D. (2017) *Twenty-First Century Fiction: Contemporary British Voices.* Manchester: Manchester University Press.

McLeod, John and Rogers, David (eds) (2004) *The Revision of Englishness.* Manchester: Manchester University Press.

Mandler, P. (1997) 'Against "Englishness": English Culture and the Limits to Rural Nostalgia, 1850–1940', *Transactions of the Royal Historical Society* 7: 155–75.

Monbiot, G. (2013) *Feral: Searching for Enchantment on the Frontiers of Rewilding.* London: Penguin.

Nairn, T. (1977) *The Break-Up of Britain: Crisis and Neo-Nationalism.* London: Atlantic Highlands.

Nairn, T. (2000) *After Britain: New Labour and the Return of Scotland.* London: Granta.

Paxman, Jeremy (1998) *The English: A Portrait of a People.* London: Penguin.

Seaton, J. (2015) *'Pinkoes and Traitors': The BBC and the nation, 1974–1987.* London: Profile Books.

Tomaney, J. (2000) 'The Idea of English Regionalism', in R. Hazell (ed.) *The English Question*, pp. 158–73. Manchester: Manchester University Press.

Waterson, Jim (2020) 'Proms Row: Johnson Calls for End to "cringing Embarrassment" over UK History', *Guardian* (25 August), URL (accessed 21 September 2020): https://www.theguardian.com/music/2020/aug/25/boris-johnson-scolds-bbc-over-suggestion-proms-would-drop-rule-britannia

Westall, C. and Gardiner, M. (2013) *Literature of an Independent England: Revisions of England, Englishness, and English Literature.* Basingstoke: Palgrave Macmillan.

Whyte, C. (1998) 'Masculinities in Contemporary Scottish Fiction', *Forum for Modern Language Studies* 34(2): 274–85.

Williams, Raymond (1973) *The Country and the City.* Vintage: London.

6

Borderlands
Spatializing Feminist Struggle in Sarah Hall's Fiction

Emilie Walezak

Sarah Hall's native region of Cumbria is a major source of inspiration for the writer and features prominently in the six novels she has published so far. It is, more specifically, the main location of three of her novels. Her first novel *Haweswater* (2002) is based on the true story of how the valley of Mardale was flooded in 1936 to build a reservoir meant to supply water for Manchester. The building of the reservoir serves as a background to the love story between native farmer Janet and Manchester waterworks overseer Jack. Hall's third novel *The Carhullan Army* (2007) is a speculative fiction set in a dystopian Cumbria and reproduces the testimony of Sister, who escapes the post-apocalyptic city of Rith and the Authority's regulations, to join a lesbian separatist agrarian commune in the uplands. *The Wolf Border* (2015) also has a speculative dimension in that it sets the story of the reintroduction of wild wolves in the Lakeland region of England against the dissolution of the Union as the Scottish independence referendum of 2014 is imagined by Hall to have resulted in a 'Yes' vote.

The signature of Hall as a landscape artist is the way she makes her native region into a character through spatialization. The term 'spatialization' originates in Rob Shields's introduction to the work of Marxist Henri Lefebvre on the social production of space. This chapter will demonstrate how a feminist interpretation of the three-part dialectic of Lefebvre on the social construction of space can account for Hall's brand of regional writing. The spatialization of Cumbria as 'conceived space', 'lived space', and 'perceived space', is enacted in an ecofeminist way which emphasizes the parallel exploitation of women and the land. Focusing on the contested borderlands, her novels first echo Lefebvre's important notion of 'conceived space': Hall consistently refers to judicial aspects of land administration and urban planning in parallel with women's rights, native rights, and labour laws. Secondly, her characters, inhabiting the Cumbrian landscape, exemplify 'lived space': Hall persistently depicts the variety of everyday practices in the region from the agricultural activities of shepherding to the touristic pastime of fell walking or the sport venture of night climbing. The contrast between toil and leisure allows Hall to problematize both the exploitation and the empowerment of female labourers through post-pastoral writing. Finally, her landscape writing echoes 'perceived space': Hall systematically calls on the region's past history and heritage, from the Celts through to the Romans, the border reivers, the Romantic legacy and the national park,[1] to contrast the attempts at dominating the landscape with the artistic appropriation of Cumbria. Her poetics, based on the personification of Cumbria and the 'naturification' of its inhabitants (Bradshaw, 2012: 38), points to the interrelation between humans and their environment and resignifies Cumbria as a matrix for the development of a feminist environmental ethics.

Indeed, Hall's systematic exploration of the many facets of Cumbria, its 'place-myths', which Rob Shields (2013: 31) defines as 'a topology [...] over-written with often-contradictory "place-images"', accords with a feminist environmental agenda whereby questions of land management relate to issues of women's rights, everyday spatial practices problematize women's roles and social norms, and the spatial imaginary of regional tropes questions prevailing cultural representations. Hall's geopolitical inquiry into the topography of the borderlands allows her to map the boundaries of the gender gap, of class divisions, and of the metropolitan and rural divide. All the contradictory place-images are made to resonate to portray Cumbria as a bustling terrain of vital feuds and to glocalize decisive ongoing debates about women, the environment and world politics. Her fiction invites being read along the lines of materialist ecofeminism, and in this chapter I will use its focus on women's embodiment as a mirror of ecological embeddedness to augment Lefebvre's Marxist approach to the material production of social space. Opting for the spatialization of local Cumbria allows Hall to accommodate the embodied experiences of lived space as well as the embedded involvement with the materiality of perceived space and its variable time scales ranging from the geological to the historical. Hall can thus be said to promote what Donna Haraway (1991: 194–5) calls a 'feminist accountability'. According to Haraway, 'feminist accountability requires a knowledge tuned to resonance [...] where the tones of extreme localization, of the intimately personal and individualized body, vibrate in the same field with global high tension emissions'. Hall's signature landscape writing testifies to the increasing awareness of feminist and environmental concerns that, in critical theory, seek to go beyond a dualist approach to the notions of culture and nature, man and woman, human and non-human. Hall's highly spatialized fiction explores boundary spaces which correlate Lefebvre's social space with a material feminist perspective on embodiment and embeddedness.

Conceived Space: Urban Planning and Women's Rights

Lefebvre's (1991: 38) notion of 'conceived space', which he also calls 'representations of space', is 'the space of scientists, planners, urbanists, technocratic subdividers, social engineers'. Hall's novels include a detailed outline of space production as carried out by political and economic stakeholders which she contrasts with the ostracizing experience of the populations discounted by those schemes: women, animals, natives, and the poor.

Mapping out the social dimension of spatial planning, Hall systematically incorporates issues related to the design and development of land management and the relation between built environment and community life into her novels. These novels show her keen awareness of judicial and administrative issues related to spatial planning, as she envisages material space as produced by social as well as textual forces and emblematizes how the law becomes text as well as space. Indeed, her preoccupation with the material topography of her native region is complemented by an attention to its toponymy as being revelatory of regional planning. *Haweswater* thus contextualizes its story of the drastic change brought to the rural area of Mardale to supply water for Manchester by referring prospectively to the origin of the regional entity of Cumbria. The epilogue of the novel mentions 'what is now the united county of Cumbria, what was once one of the last corners of Westmorland' (Hall, 2002: 261). It alludes to the Local Government Act of 1972, which reorganized local administration by implementing a two-tier management system of metropolitan and non-metropolitan counties and districts. It contextualizes the location historically as part of a national endeavour to organize regional development as well as cartographically by calling attention to the changing place names. But the global context in which such toponymic changes occurred is also alluded to when the text describes Janet's education in the 1910s and the changing atlas amended by the school teacher according to the extension of the British imperial dominions: 'Sometimes the world's place names are changed and Hazel Bowman will mark the changes into the atlas [...] Poetic, colourful names become practical, or flavoured with a different poetry, another country's mother-tongue' (Hall, 2002: 18–19). The story itself is based on an Act of Parliament from 1919 that gave the Manchester Corporation permission to build the reservoir to supply water for the urban conurbations of north-west England, which the novel refers to as the Haweswater Act (Hall, 2002: 50) and which gives it its title. The attention paid to the impact of national and local government decisions on the ways in which landscapes are named highlights the significant influence of politics on the environment. Space is being produced practically and commodified to serve the interests of the state in the organization of labour division according to territorial needs.

This is also dramatized in *The Carhullan Army*'s dystopian narrative, which takes place after a climatic disaster. The alteration of the place name of Penrith, abridged as Rith, bears witness to the Civil Reorganization process which has curtailed local powers in favour of the dictatorial Authority and has 'written off' (Hall, 2007a: 20) some citizens from the census who then become Unofficials, like Sister herself. In *The Wolf Border* the winter scene depicting England at a standstill recalls the apocalyptic situation in *The Carhullan Army* but it mixes additional references to the transportation networks, like the Pendolino train that serves Cumbria via the West Coast Main Line. Hall thus subtly raises the question of the privatization of the national railway network by alluding to Virgin's franchise. She also alludes to natural resources, like petrol, which echoes with the multiple allusions to Scotland's access to North Sea oil. Finally she references the ageing population, the welfare system and the risk of pandemics. In short, she depicts the now familiar apocalyptic potential of global concerns dependent on interconnected systems: 'the flights across the entire nation are grounded, and the Pendolinos south run at half speed, then are cancelled [...] the sky is as clear and dangerous as burning oxygen [...] Petrol freezes in tanks. The death rate of pensioners soars; there's talk of a flu pandemic' (Hall, 2015: 295). The novels thus reference the large spectrum of the planning process to canvas its intricate web of judicial, infrastructural and welfare networks.

In fact, *The Wolf Border* is rife with references to spatial planning, testifying to the author's growing interest in the judicial and administrative aspects of spatial organization. Its story of the reintroduction of wolves leads to additional mentions of species management like the 1981 Zoo Licensing Act (Hall, 2015: 8), the licensing laws about imported hybrid dogs (Hall, 2015: 97), or the French institutionalized destruction of wolves ordered by Charlemagne in 813 through an administration called *Louveterie* (Hall, 2015: 115). Moreover, by speculatively producing a 'yes' result in Scotland's independence referendum, the novel creates an opportunity to examine the gap between England and Scotland in terms of land use by contrasting the

Earl's private property, emblematic of the remnants of feudalism in the British system of tenancy, and the ongoing process of land reform in Scotland. The allusion to 'the reform plans across the border – public acquisition of private land, recalibration of resources' (Hall, 2015: 25) reads as a hint to the Land Reform Act of 2003 which established universal public access to land as well as community and crofting rights to buy land. The initial Act was further augmented after the publication of Hall's novel with the Community Empowerment Act of 2015 and the Land Reform Act of 2016, enforcing the right for all communities to purchase privately owned land for sustainable development. *The Carhullan Army* also alludes to the system of real property in England, especially to the law of escheat inherited from the Norman Conquest, according to which '[w]e've never owned anything, Sister. The lands of Britain belonged to the Crown, ever since the Norman Conquest' (Hall, 2007a: 104). In addition to tracing a variety of spatial modes of production (authoritarian, capitalist, sustainable), Hall's exposé of the mediating systems informing land management serves to enhance the exclusion and exploitation of women, workers, and natives.

Indeed, issues of land management and the rifts they create further connect in important ways to the feminist concerns in Hall's work. In the three novels, the treatment of women's reproduction rights correlates issues of land administration with civil rights of bodily integrity. *Haweswater* narrates the tragic love story of Cumbrian shepherdess Janet and Manchester proletarian born Jack, with the couple emblematic of the metropolitan/non-metropolitan divide. After Jack dies and the valley is flooded, the relocation of the Lightburn family with pregnant Janet to Bampton village draws a parallel between forced removal and the social status of Janet as an unmarried pregnant woman by alluding to past institutions which administered labour and poverty: 'Her mother will not have her sent to the workhouse for unmarried women in Penrith' (Hall, 2002: 208). The novel's 1936 setting implies that the Poor Law was still operative, meaning that relief for the poor was conditioned by their relocation to the workhouse. In addition, Janet, who loses her mind after Jack's death and self-mutilates, is also representative of mental health law in Britain as well as medical discourse on female mental disorders, a fate which Ella Lightburn also refuses for her daughter: 'There will be no asylum, no madhouse sanatorium for Janet Lightburn.' (Hall, 2002: 208). *Haweswater* thus narrates the romantic love story between Jack and Janet against the historical judicial background of major system alterations which point to the changes in perspective on pauper populations – the term pauper itself disappeared from the law around 1930 – while outlining the consistent exploitative streak in the treatment of women and labourers whether by law, science, or society.

Interestingly, Rachel, in *The Wolf Border*, is an unmarried pregnant woman like Janet. However, the contemporary context and the professional background of Rachel as a zoologist shift the focus from the institutional administration of pregnancy and maternity to reproduction technologies, with references to birth control, abortion, IVF and artificial insemination. Hall thus continues her exploration of the social, judicial and scientific networks that seek to control the management of women's bodies by incorporating their most recent technological dimensions. Rachel's high profile in terms of professional expertise, as well as her education by a leftist feminist single mother, mean that, despite the ambient misogyny on the estate emblematized by the gamekeeper Michael Stott, she represents a generation for whom, unarguably, '[w]omen always have a choice' (Hall, 2015: 42). The pro-choice background of *The Wolf Border* contrasts with the dystopian future of *The Carhullan Army*. The novel bases the Civil Reorganization process on birth control with the mandatory fitting of a contraceptive coil for women while the counter-resistance narrative of Sister is called 'retro-feminist' (Hall, 2007a: 50) as the lesbian agrarian commune mirrors communal endeavours from the 1970s whose separatism was meant to reconfigure the division of labour and demonstrate female competency: 'it is a twenty-first century critical dystopia in which possible responses towards the environment, fundamentalist ideologies and gender inequality are imagined and debated' (Robinson, 2013: 200). *The Carhullan Army* explicitly parallels feminism and ecology as the subjugation of women through the control of their reproductive capacity is the consequence of an economic crash and state collapse brought about by climatic disaster.

The retro-feminist tale originated in Hall's own experience of climate change with the Cumbrian floods of 2005 whereby 'the implications of an altered climate became no longer merely imaginable, but visible' (Hall, 2007b: n.p.). A recent example of the capitalist exploitation of climate change for marketing purposes was the Virgin coup after the winter floods in 2016 when the company renamed a Pendolino train 'Cumbrian Spirit' to honour the people's 'determination to continue business as usual', in the words of the general manager (Walker, 2016: n.p.).

By drawing parallels between regional and family planning, Sarah Hall shows a feminist environmental understanding of the ways in which border control, administrative divisions, species management, and the exploitation of natural resources, can be read alongside institutionalized endeavours to control women and minority groups. She thus outlines the Western capitalist masculinist disregard for the social and ecological damages engendered by a spatialized economic domination over the means of production and reproduction, or, in the words of Mary Mellor (2000: 112), how 'western society has created itself against nature using the sex/gender division of labour'. She further correlates women's experiences with that of other minority groups whose material conditions account for their social exclusion. Thus the beginning of *The Wolf Border* is set on an Indian reservation in Idaho and evokes the judicial disputes over land sovereignty while, at the same time, referring to the pro-life trend in the state as Rachel explains her return to England for an abortion: 'The state where I was living brought a new mandate – you have to have an ultrasound before having an abortion. The clinics are mostly pro-life' (Hall, 2015: 103).[2] The mother–daughter relationship, which also predominates at the beginning of the novel, further makes visible another marginalized group, the elderly, and the space of the care home to which they are confined. As Lefebvre (1991: 32) pointed out, social space correlates 'the *social relations of reproduction*, i.e. the bio-physiological relations between the sexes and between age groups, along with the specific organization of the family' with 'the *relations of production*, i.e. the division of labour and its organization in the form of hierarchical social functions'.

Hall's fiction can be interpreted from a materialist ecofeminist perspective which seeks to develop 'an ethics of social and environmental justice [...] informed by a critical awareness of the dynamics of socio-economic power' (Mellor, 2000: 120). By connecting the many ways in which women are exploited on account of their material, embodied reality – reproduction – with the spatialized means of enforcement of male domination over the social and the natural environment for a purpose of production, Hall's fiction calls for an acknowledgement of the 'sex/gender inequality in the construction of human-nature relations' (Mellor, 2000: 119). By articulating her plots around the decisive social and judicial changes for women that have occurred in the past century – women entering the labour market, financial independence, birth control, abortion, single motherhood, LGBT rights – Hall demonstrates how they are both a threat to the conservative civil space and a force for change in redefining territorial boundaries from the uplands resistance of the women fighters at Carhullan to wolf-Rachel who challenges privileged positions. In Lefebvre's Marxist terms, she contrasts the exchange value of landed property with the use value of the land. Her work expounds on the initial focus of historical materialism on class exploitation to include a feminist apprehension of sexual exploitation and gender marginalization as well as an ecological perspective on land management and the abuse of the landless and the ostracized. She equates female empowerment with the post-pastoral routine of female labourers. Post-pastoral literature, as theorized by Terry Gifford (2006: 12), offers an alternative space 'which avoids the closed circle of both 'pastoral' idealized celebration and the 'anti-pastoral' simple correction of it'. Focusing on everyday toil with the land allows Hall to develop a pragmatic approach to the lived space of the Cumbrian landscape.

Lived Space: Female Empowerment and the Everyday

'Lived space' is 'the space of "inhabitants" and "users"' (Lefebvre, 1991: 39). Lefebvre particularly emphasizes the concrete role of the body in the lived experience of space. In her novels, Hall depicts the everyday spatial practices of the Cumbrian inhabitants which testify to the reciprocal imprint of humans on the landscape and of the landscape on humans. Furthermore, she uses northern traditions and dialect to resignify regional identity after a feminist fashion. Here, I am using Judith Butler's concept of the resignification of the symbolic order as an instance of creative deviance from dominant normative signifiers. Hall re-describes the many-layered meanings of Cumbria while re-inscribing female labour in the landscape. Giving back agency to both landscape and women, she thus enacts the performativity of citationality: citing the boundaries of sex and landscape leads to transform both landscape and gender identity.

Cumbria, in Hall's writing, is a cultural landscape that anticipates the 2017 inscription of the English Lake District on UNESCO's World Heritage list. The term 'cultural landscape' originates in the 1992 World Heritage convention which defined it as 'the combined works of nature and man'.[3] Among the characteristics retained by UNESCO for the inscription of the Lakeland site as a cultural landscape, the upland farming system features prominently as it does in Hall's novels. *Haweswater* is based on a minute description of the everyday life of the rural community of Mardale focused on the agricultural activities which set the pace for the yearly routine, demonstrating that spatialization 'embraces not only spatial patterns but temporal rhythms' (Shields, 2013: 32). The novel thus mentions the autumnal shepherd's meet at the Dun Bull's Inn, when stray sheep were returned to their owner – a traditional event that is also mentioned by the nomination document dedicated to Haweswater, along with its location – and its festivities like wrestling and horse racing. The novel also refers to the haymaking period which, again, gathers the community together. Most importantly, Janet's portrait is articulated, from childhood, to agrarian life and its impact on her body. Janet is seen to participate in the killing of a lame cow and the treating of sheep against infestation (Hall, 2002: 23, 116). She knows how to read signs of sickness in the animals, how to feed orphaned lambs, how to clip and kill livestock . Her forehead bears a star-shaped scar as a 'a reminder that her life has included the sporadic brutality of her family's trade', but 'she does not consider herself unlucky or particularly broken in comparison with the rest of the valley's female population, nor is she possessed of damages out of proportion with other women of the area' (Hall, 2002: 24–5). The scene of the sheep's treatment turns to eroticism from Jack's perspective through 'the combination of agricultural odour and her attire' (Hall, 2002: 116). It is a deviant form of eroticism aroused by the embeddedness of Janet's body in the Cumbrian environment.

The Carhullan Army depicts similarly strong, agricultural women whose bodies have been modelled by the uplands so that 'they did not look like girls, middle aged and older women. They seemed to be sexless, whittled back to muscle by toil and base nourishment, creatures who bore no sense of category, no dress code other than the one they chose [...] strong, resilient' (Hall, 2007a: 118–19). The women of Carhullan refashion farming outfits to combine style and practicality: 'They were [...] dressed [...] practically, with thrift and a certain bespoke artistry. Some had overalls that seemed extreme and invented, tribal almost' (Hall, 2007a: 93). Although *The Wolf Border* adopts a different perspective on farming, as it focuses on the threat the wolves represent for the sheep, the novel does mention the practicalities of the agricultural lifestyle for women when evoking the cases of Q fever due to lambing handled by the midwife. The three novels under consideration also make use of northern dialect, notably in relation to agriculture, with such terms as cattle bothies, bields, and 'yan' (derived from sheep-counting numerals) appearing alongside others which refer to landscape features such as tarn, beck, fell, whin, and ghyll. Hall weaves together the impact of land use on the body, the seasonal routines and everyday practices so that Cumbria as a cultural landscape functions as 'a memorial to the unknown labourer' according to the definition of advisor on world heritage conservation P. J. Fowler (2001: 77), and more particularly, in Hall's case, the female labourer.

By focusing on the fell pastures of Cumbria, Hall offers a 'post-pastoral' vision of the region which matches Terry Gifford's (2012) outline. The female labourers add a feminist environmental dimension to this post-pastoral tableau. Gifford identified six features of post-pastoral writing. The elements described in the previous paragraph concur with 'awareness of the culturally loaded language we use about the country' as well as 'recognition that the exploitation of nature is often accompanied by the exploitation of the less powerful people who work with it, visit it or less obviously depend on its resources' (Gifford, 2012: 44). Gifford (2012: 44) also mentions 'awe leading to humility in the face of the destructive-creative forces of nature', which Hall's novels dramatize in relation to female labour in the sense of childbirth. *Haweswater* draws parallels between the omnipresence of water as 'a continuance of text in a land of broken fluid' (Hall, 2002: ix) with the breaking waters of delivery as the novel opens on Ella giving birth to Janet, which further connects to the flooding of the valley: 'this opening sets the tone for the novel's portrayal of water as a substance that transcends its own materiality, transforming itself back and forth across the human/non-human divide' (Lea, 2017: 157). The 'unnatural' pain of 'human birth' (Hall, 2002: 5) echoes what Lefebvre (1991: 30) calls the 'illusion of naturalness', in other words, the way 'historical and political forces' use the discourse of nature to rationalize their domination of it and conversely the way 'nature cloaks itself in nostalgias which supplant rationality' . Instead of a nostalgic approach to nature, Hall opts for post-pastoral pragmatism which, at the same time as it denounces the parallel exploitation of land and of women, also emphasizes the inexorableness of the creation/destruction process in nature when comparing, for instance, Ella's labour with snow fall: Ella can control her pain 'no more than she could control the snow falling fast and wet outside' (Hall, 2002: 4). In *The Wolf Border*, Rachel's pregnancy and experience of maternity parallels the release of the wolves and their own breeding as the key to the project's success. The killing of a young wolf by a human farmer dramatizes man's domination while the final escape of the wolves to Scotland across the border points to indomitability. The novels systematically oppose human endeavours to control the weather, the land, and the species, to the chaos wrecked by forces of diverse scales, from the viral to the atmospheric. *The Carhullan Army* presents this most dramatically: 'the Cumbrian landscape in her writing becomes the female body political – desecrated but defiant. By bringing together the themes of environmental degradation and gender politics in this dystopian speculation, Hall manages to achieve something which is both prospective and retrospective' (Lea, 2017: 171).

The experience of lived space through embodiment, especially by women characters, leads to female empowerment as, to quote Gifford's (2012: 6) last feature, they 'accept responsibility for our relationship with nature and its dilemmas'. The women's bodies echo the landscape just as the landscape echoes the human body. Janet is one with the Cumbrian environment:

> She has been pressed between two vast mountain ranges [...] each year she is re-forged. She accepts the weather and the ability of the rain to overwhelm all else. [...] Her body chemistry alters as the terrain decomposes, turns, begins again. [...] She has given herself over to this saturated strip of Westmorland. (Hall, 2002: 112)

Through labour, in both senses of the word, Hall's writing matches the pace of human biological time, emblematized by the life cycle of pregnancy and the yearly routine of agriculture, with ecological time, manifested by geological processes and weather patterns. Instead of the long-standing essentializing association of women with nature, which fostered damning patriarchal discourses on women's passivity and 'natural' subjection to biological time, Hall offers a materialist ecofeminist perspective opening on 'a wider debate about the material relations into which humans enter when confronting their embodiment and embeddedness' (Mellor, 2000: 113). The characters' embeddedness in the landscape calls for a recognition of the material basis of sociality while temporal scales draw parallels between the socioeconomic division of labour and its ecological consequences. The pragmatism of Hall's female heroines leads them to acknowledge and explore their own limits.

Despite the medical jargon zoologist Rachel uses to distance herself from her pregnancy, her childhood memories, her native region, she is depicted on the path of reconciliation. Jackie, the leader figure at Carhullan, whose 'eyes were the blue of the region's quarried stone' (Hall, 2007a: 50), defines herself as 'a dark fucking tourist, Sister, I like going to these places. It's interesting to me. I'm interested in what holds people back. And what doesn't' (Hall, 2007a: 117–18). Jackie's dark tourism of people's self-imposed borders reads as a metafictional comment on Hall's own survivalist scenarios 'where people are tested, where the urge to keep going comes to the fore' (Garvey, 2013: n.p.) and stands in opposition to traditional tourism which is yet another characteristic feature of Cumbria as a cultural landscape that recurs in the novels.

Lefebvre (1991: 354) outlines a 'three-point interaction' or movements between the consumption of space, the space of consumption and leisure which he also reformulates as a movement 'from the quotidian to the non-quotidian through festival' or 'from labour to non-labour through a putting into brackets [...] of toil'. In contrast to the women's labour, in all senses of the word, and the everyday toil with the land, tourism in the Lakeland is indeed depicted as the vector of a neo-imperialist hegemony over a region, as when city dweller Jack decides to get himself a rare golden eagle which he conceives of as the equivalent 'proletarian prize' (Hall, 2002: 200) to the imperialist trophies of colonization. All the novels refer, at one point or another, to summer residences. In *The Carhullan Army* they are connected to the North-South divide: 'People from the South had once bought retirement homes here' (Hall, 2007a: 22). In *The Wolf Border*, Scottish independence prompts speculations about 'an exodus of second-home owners' (Hall, 2015: 224). In addition, the novels allude to the major cultural references that turned the Lake District into a touristic must-see: *The Carhullan Army* mentions Alfred Wainwright's *Pictorial Guide to the Lakeland Fells* (Hall, 2007a: 11) while *Haweswater* hints at Wordsworth's *A Guide to the District of the Lakes* (Hall, 2002: 143).

Haweswater gives the most striking example of the leisure consumption of space as a masculine assault on the land which parallels the abuse of women. In his spare time, Jack indulges in the sports activity of night climbing in the fells. His climbs are characterized as attacks on the mountain side: he works 'as if aiming at volatile levels of an imaginary human body with a knife, a fist. He spins between crevices, punching shadows in the solar plexus, as if he wants to outmanoeuvre and overwhelm the nerve system of the mountain as he would an enemy. It is a strange skill, this blind murder of landscape' (Hall, 2002: 128). Such descriptions are similar to the scenes of domestic abuse and rape he witnesses from his hotel room in Penrith: a man 'kicking blood from his wife's stomach' (Hall, 2002: 91), or a young woman raped by three men (Hall, 2002: 92), and his own recourse to prostitution with the hotel owner's daughters, forcing fellatio: 'a hand over the mouth of one, forcing indentations into her cheeks, bringing her to his groin' (Hall, 2002: 92). He compares night climbing to his brutal lovemaking with Janet: 'The fulfilment of a high climb and the sensuality of release as he flooded into her body' (Hall, 2002: 147). It is telling therefore that his death arises from the realization that he is not equal to the woman he loves, nor to the landscape that has come to transform him. Jack has initially hired a poacher to get him a rare golden eagle. He dies while on a redemptive path of bringing back the dead eagle to her eyrie. The trophy eagle is female and an endangered species which disappeared from the region in 2015. The ecofeminist approach to the colonized space of the land and of the female body through consumption allows Hall to develop an alternative post-pastoral pragmatic model of female empowerment which substitutes use value for exchange value as expressed through the mutual physical relations between 'naturification of the people' and personification of the landscape (Bradshaw, 2012: 38).

Perceived Space: Regional Tropes and Resignification

To use Barthes' terminology, the Cumbria landscape is a writerly text, subjected to the many interpretations that have been made of it. It is to be read, deciphered; it is a metaphor which recurs in Hall's novels through mention of meteorologists, agriculturalists, bird-watchers, and zoologists, but it is also written over, rewritten. The water's 'voice' in *Haweswater* is 'a continuance of text' (Hall, 2002: ix), the fell peaks in *The Wolf Border* are 'a geological alphabet' (Hall, 2015: 282), and gorse in *The Carhullan Army* serves as a coded message to the citizens of Rith. The text of the North is related to a historical legacy still visible in the landscape, still present in cultural memory through texts which Hall appropriates to turn Cumbria into a particular kind of representational space. Lefebvre (1991: 39) contrasts the 'representations of space' of urban planners and military advisors who seek to dominate space, with the 'representational spaces' of inhabitants, users and artists who endeavour to appropriate space. He further connects this dichotomy to the opposition between the representations of the body and the use of the body (Lefebvre, 1991: 40). By rewriting regional tropes and resignifying the female body, Hall dramatizes the dominated/appropriated split in order to add her own signature onto the Lake District. She appropriates the Cumbrian landscape through writing in order to resignify female identity.

The plot of *The Carhullan Army* is based on the tipping point when the communal endeavour to appropriate space through agriculture turns to a terrorist attempt to dominate the terrain. It uses the region's military history as its main reference, through repeated mention of the Roman forts and reivers' fortifications. The female farmers turn into soldiers, their bodies fashioned by training in the harsh uplands. This practical remodelling of their bodies is meant to engineer a deprogramming of the cultural representations of the female body: 'to remake ourselves into those inviolable creatures the God of Equality had intended us to be. We knew she was deconstructing the old disabled versions of our sex' (Hall, 2007a: 187). Jackie is depicted as 'the clan's principal mother' (Hall, 2007a: 159) and her lineage goes back to the debatable lands: 'She's one of the border Nixons. They were the ones who went out with bulldogs to meet the reivers' (Hall, 2007a: 49). The women share a military camaraderie singing prison ballads which sound like Border songs (Hall, 2007a: 132): Hall uses the folkloric tradition and the romantic literary legacy of Walter Scott's *Minstrelsy of the Scottish Borders* to depict what looks like a female social rehabilitation centre, thus resignifying the figure of the female criminal (Walezak, 2019: 73–4). The blue tattoos sported by the women and the working of the commune recall the Celtic legacy of the Pict invaders, their matrilineal system of succession and their nomadic pastoralism. By weaving together a great variety of references to the region's military legacy, Hall appropriates the borderlands to depict a feminist venture while contrasting 'an example of environmental possibility, of true domestic renewal' and an armed attempt at domination engendered by a change in the administration of the area with the implementation of 'a new land charter' (Hall, 2007a: 166, 158).

Haweswater also refers to the long history of the region. The arrival of the army that will flood the valley and create the reservoir is compared to the Roman conquest: 'a phantom sighting of Roman legionaries, marching south from Hadrian's Wall' (Hall, 2002: 219). The migrant workers who come to work on the building of the reservoir, the navvies, are compared to the reivers: 'the valley's population [...] joked that there had not been such an influx of foreigners since the Border Raids' (Hall, 2002: 163). In addition to the city developers' plan to 'annex' the valley with a 'civilized invasion' (Hall, 2002: 53), the novel calls on the national history of Britain by anachronistically comparing the blown-up village of Mardale to 'a vision of the Blitz', with the buildings looking 'like forgotten war veterans. Or skeletal prisoners left in a concentration camp' (Hall, 2002: 226). Hall reconfigures the cultural legacy of Wordsworth's daffodils in the context of the First World War, which subtly alludes to the role of British women at home and the new labour division engendered by the war. Janet's father, Samuel, is a war veteran suffering from survivor's guilt when he meets Janet's mother, Ella, who works as a nurse in Penrith. Gathering daffodils with Ella unlocks the story of Samuel's trauma, thereby turning Wordsworth's pastoral ballad into a post-pastoral tale of female pragmatism. Ella is a compassionate woman of 'unalterable character' (Hall, 2002: 59) who responds to the call for nurses, becomes a Voluntary Aid Detachment after a two-month training, takes on 'fourteen-hour shifts' (Hall, 2002: 60) and reads psalm 23 to the dying and the wounded. The shepherd theme and 'green pastures' of the biblical text recall Wordsworth's own pastoral writing but are reconfigured in the light of Ella's unflinching temperament and resolute faith as she refuses the men's pleas for a mercy killing. She steadfastly ministers to the broken bodies and minds of her patients. The 'brutal landscape of the mind' (Hall, 2002: 62) inflicted upon shell-shocked soldiers is contrasted with the restorative Cumbrian landscape. Hall appropriates her region's cultural legacy in a manner analogous to that of a character, landscape artist Paul Levell who reads as a metafictional figure of the writer herself. Just like Paul Levell's paintings, her writing depicts 'with startling realism, almost photographic accuracy' (Hall, 2002: 38) how 'humans are jigsawed into a cliff or river, or hewn out of the landscape, a man's torso kept in a cairn of rock, a child in the womb of a mountain wall, vast amalgams of environment and humanity' (Hall, 2002: 185).

In *The Wolf Border*, too, the landscape is personified and the body is 'naturified', to borrow from Penny Bradshaw (2012: 38). The use of medical and biological terminology characterizes the landscape with the 'upland pheromones' as 'Cumbria's signature aroma' (Hall, 2015: 9), the 'spermy fragrance in the air' (Hall, 2015: 85), the 'miasma' of the waterfalls' spray (Hall, 2015: 174), 'the red bladder of the sun' (Hall, 2015: 188), the 'webbed lungs of clouds' (Hall, 2015: 218), 'hemorrhaging berries' (Hall, 2015: 273), 'measled snow' (Hall, 2015: 299). Portraying the environment as a diseased, wounded, or fertile body through the use of metaphor calls for an anthropomorphic connection with it. This connection, however, does not represent an attempt at domesticating the landscape through the familiarization of the non-human, but rather reads as a recognition of the non-human as living organisms. The metamorphosing of elemental organisms into human organs draws attention to the inescapable material interconnectivity of humans and the environment, with the recurring disease metaphors hinting at the human negative impact on the planet. The reciprocal relation means that the human body conversely morphs into the atmospheric. It features weather similes: human voices are 'like weather outside' (Hall, 2015: 188), the midwife analyses Rachel's results like 'meteorological data' (Hall, 2015: 137), as well as geological similes: Binny is compared to a 'shell', 'fossilised, like something extracted from a bog or petrified forest' (Hall, 2015: 16), Rachel's C-section has made 'a gulley' in her body (Hall, 2015: 244). It is interesting to note that while the environment is more easily transmuted into human metaphors, the human remains separate in the comparisons, which might point to humanity's difficulty to apprehend its material condition. Human beings are furthermore regularly compared to animals: sheepdogs, salmon, hawks, and bullocks (Hall, 2015: 266, 272, 274, 277). Rachel herself is a 'lupine mother figure' (Hall, 2015: 327). As Daniel Lea (2017: 193) suggests, *The*

Wolf Border 'relies on naturalist characterisation to suggest the consanguineous continuum between human and wolf'. The comparisons, however, are not designed, as is the case in many literary traditions, to demean the human, but rather to insist on the ecological relation between living entities. Hall's novel demonstrates the author's increasing consideration of human/non-human relations, a development attested to by her short story collection, *The Beautiful Indifference*, published in 2011, and the BBC National Short Story Award winning 'Mrs Fox', from 2014, which largely focus on the human/animal connection. While, from the human perspective, the wolves might represent the domination of apex predators over the environment, the novel weaves together references to history, myth and hot topics to appropriate the regional context as a crucible for world geopolitical debates.

Thus, the inevitable historical reference to the Capitoline wolf combined with the speculative success of the independence referendum read as an attempt on Hall's part to imagine a hypothetical act of refoundation of Britain. The novel repeatedly mentions stereotyped images and old-fashioned items from a bygone era of which Honor Clark, the Earl's secretary, is a representative: 'Extremely English-looking; from an England seventy years gone' (Hall, 2015: 10). Honor is like those 'English biscuits, hard as relics, like something from another century' (Hall, 2015: 45). Michael Stott, the Earl's land manager, also belongs to a former era of 'the polite rituals of British deer hunting' (Hall, 2015: 192) and 'the gentleman's smoking room' (Hall, 2015: 193), for whom Rachel 'represent[s] dire competition, beyond his experience'. Rachel, her sex and her European curriculum, are a challenge to the conservative British system: 'The systems are cracking up' (Hall, 2015: 194). In the post-Brexit context, one cannot but read the public fantasies about the wolves' threat as an allegory of the migrant crisis as they are a '*scourge* [...] *threatening* [...] *your home, your family*' (Hall, 2015: 61) which raise protests: '*We do not want this type of thing in our country*' (Hall, 2015: 117), 'If they get out, what's to stop them running riot and plundering!' (Hall, 2015: 155). In fact, the wolves are consistently depicted as ghosts; they are Seldom Seen, like the cottage where Rachel lives. Instead of the projected fantasy of invasion and domination, Hall offers a tale of appropriation as 'unbelonging, reversed' (Hall, 2015: 248). Her regional writing is neither nostalgic nor nationalist because she manages to resignify traditional tropes and to portray the territory of the United Kingdom and the European Union as ripe with possibilities while acknowledging the very real menace of dissolution. In the same way, Hall portrays empowered women while warning of the threats to their hard-won rights. The cause of women and the cause of the land systematically run parallel to each other.

In ecofeminist terms, the personification of the landscape and the 'naturification' of the people demonstrate the correlation between human embodiment as registered through biological time and environmental embeddedness as registered through ecological time. Hall's landscape writing means to contrast the 'material-semiotic' (Haraway, 1991: 208) enmeshment of bodies, texts, environments, and systems, with the western masculinist ideal of the autonomous individual. Rachel's itinerary in her novel is exemplary from that perspective. At first intent on pursuing professional achievement through mobility and by abstracting herself from kin commitments, whether to her sexual partners or her family, Rachel represents 'an idealized image of individuality' which forms the basis of 'western social and economic structures' (Mellor, 2000: 113). She is akin to the 'western economic man [...] young, fit, ambitious, mobile, and unencumbered by obligations' (Mellor, 2000: 113). The embodied experience of biological time through pregnancy operates a radical change in her so that she takes responsibility for her child, her brother, her partner's daughter, and finally her role as an unsuspecting mediator in the Earl's larger project. Her initial adoption of an individualist stance calls for a parallel with the political separatist movements spreading today across Europe, and echoes with the failed fight of the Carhullan women. Domination thrives on separation whereas Hall's appropriation of the representational spaces of Cumbria and the related embodied experiences within them reads like a call for a feminist environmental ethics acknowledging embodiment and embeddedness.

Cumbria can thus be said to be the main character in Hall's novels. The space of her native region allows the author to debate the social, scientific, and textual materializations of the feminist struggle for women's rights, of the environmental crisis of climate change, and of the larger human struggle with the environment, whether ecological or social. Hall demonstrates an awareness of the current challenges faced by humanity on a global scale, which she addresses through the local appropriation of regional space. She thus redefines regional writing using it not as a nostalgic commemoration of past ideals but as a vital speculum so as to magnify impossibly large scales through local proximity. Similarly she revisits feminism through spatialization by connecting the material-semiotic compass of embodiment – biology, law, economy, history, sociology – to the game-changing perspectives generated by the new environmental awareness of human embeddedness. Her fiction engages in the 'risky practice' of 'siting (sighting) boundaries' (Haraway, 1991: 201) with the friction area of the borderlands as the perfect place to investigate the issue as embodied by its inhabitants: 'Rachel, like Janet Lightburn, Jackie Nixon [...] before her, straddles the border between the human and non-human, drawing and channelling a fierce energy derived from the uncertainty of the both/and dichotomy' (Lea, 2017: 193). Hall's characteristic and unusual take on spatial issues of land management and her involvement in ecofeminist materialism make her a writer of note in the landscape of contemporary British fiction.

Notes

1 *The Wolf Border* was published two years before the inscription of the Lake District on UNESCO's world heritage list of cultural landscapes. The major features retained by UNESCO for the inscription of the site were its farming system and the literary legacy of the Lake poets.
2 In 2018, Idaho passed a new set of laws to further restrict women's right to terminate a pregnancy.
3 See https://whc.unesco.org/en/culturallandscape/#1 (accessed 23 April 2019).

Works Cited

Bradshaw, P. (2012) 'Cumbrians and their "ancient kingdom": Landscape, Literature and Regional Identity', in I. Convery, G. Corsane and P. Davis (eds) *Making Sense of Place: Multidisciplinary Perspectives*, pp. 33–42. Woodbridge: The Boydell Press.

Fowler P.J. (2001) 'Cultural Landscapes: Great Concept, Pity about the Phrase', *The Cultural Landscape: Planning for Sustainable Partnerships between People and Place*, pp. 64–82. London: ICOMOS-UK.

Garvey A. (2013) 'The sensual world of Sarah Hall', *Civilian*, 14 October, URL (accessed 11 August 2016): https://civilianglobal.com/arts/sarah-hall-author-lake-district-bbc-national-short-story-award/

Gifford, T. (2006) *Reconnecting with John Muir. Essays in Post-Pastoral Practice*. Athens: University of Georgia Press.

Gifford, T. (2012) 'Pastoral, Anti-Pastoral and Post-Pastoral as Reading Strategies', in S. Slovic (ed.) *Critical Insights: Nature and Environment*, pp. 42–61. Ipswich: Salam Press.

Hall, S. (2002) *Haweswater*. London: Faber and Faber.

Hall, S. (2007a) *The Carhullan Army*. London: Faber and Faber.

Hall, S. (2007b) 'Survivor's Tale', *Guardian*, 1 December, URL (accessed 21 November 2017): https://www.theguardian.com/books/2007/dec/01/featuresreviews.guardianreview16

Hall, S. (2015) *The Wolf Border*. London: Faber.

Haraway, D.J. (1991) *Simians, Cyborgs, and Women: The Reinvention of Nature*. New York: Routledge.

Lea, D. (2017) *Twenty-First Century Fiction: Contemporary British Voices*. Manchester: Manchester University Press.

Lefebvre, H. (1991). *The Production of Space*,trans. Donald Nicholson Smith. Oxford: Blackwell.

Mellor, M. (2000) 'Feminism and Environmental Ethics: A Materialist Perspective', *Ethics and the Environment* 5(1): 107–23.

Robinson, I. (2013) '"You just know when the world is about to break apart": Utopia, Dystopia and New Global Uncertainties in Sarah Hall's *The Carhullan Army*', in S. Adiseshiah and R. Hildyard (eds) *What Happens Now*, pp. 197–211. Basingstoke: Palgrave Macmillan.

Shields, R. (2013) *Spatial Questions: Cultural Topologies and Social Spatialisations*. London: SAGE.

Walezak, E. (2019) 'Landscape and Identity: Utopian/Dystopian Cumbria in Sarah Hall's *The Carhullan Army*', *Critique: Studies in Contemporary Fiction* 60(1): 69–74.

Walker, S. (2016) 'Virgin Trains unveil "The Cumbrian Spirit"', *In-Cumbria*, 3 March, URL (accessed 9 October 2018): https://www.in-cumbria.

com/Virgin-Trains-unveil-The-Cumbrian-Spirit-55a4b43e-cca2-4b13-9287-27ed5217dfd2-ds

7

La Fiaba Oscura

Narrating Italy in *How to Paint a Dead Man*

Francesca Pierini

How to Paint a Dead Man (2009), the fourth of Sarah Hall's novels, is a carefully constructed narrative, recounted in profoundly personal and potent language. Like a still-life painting, it tells a multidimensional and eventful story beneath an appearance of immobility and silence. This chapter examines the novel's adherence to the discursive tradition of representing the South in Anglophone writing, which traditionally hinges on a divide between North and South that equates the north of Europe with rationality and the south with a pre-modern kind of sensitivity, shaped by instincts and primal wisdom. The chapter, therefore, will shed light on the discursive notions and descriptive patterns that Hall uses to lend credibility to the novel's Italian sections by connecting them with established concepts that are perceived as quintessentially southern, such as religious sensitivity and closeness to the senses. The southern world depicted by Hall functions according to the rules of a pre-modern existential order in which one's role within family and community as well as one's ancestral attachment to the land account for more than individual autonomy and self-determination. Yet, I will also argue that, in spite of its adherence to this literary tradition, there are significant ways in which *How to Paint a Dead Man* departs from it. For, rather than offering the reader the trite schema of a mildly oriental (Italian) other challenging the symbolic order of the (British) self, it creates a narrative pattern of human ageing and development in which these traditional categories are blurred and opened up for interpretation.

Two Models of Development: Historical and Psychological

Anglophone fiction has a long tradition of representing Italy as Britain's other, with Italy offering a unique constellation of counter-values to British culture and its ethos. This discursive tradition runs parallel to the European discourse on the Orient, as it involves a fantasizing about the countries and cultures of the European South based on a taxonomy of places that are more or less modern, rational, archaic, timeless, and magical.[1] The tradition operates through the construction of a temporal difference, what Johannes Fabian (1983: 1) has called 'a denial of coevalness', which reiterates Italy's supposed exoticism, and, with it, a particularly complex and multi-layered notion of primitivism.[2]

In *Europe (In Theory)*, Robert M. Dainotto (2007: 4) discusses the discursive traditions behind the cultural and political divide between the North and the South in Europe. He sees them as examples of a European 'rhetorical unconscious' relating to the deeply established 'structures and paradigms that have [...] informed ideas of the continent and of its cultural identity'. Dainotto shows how the European South has often been seen as the unenlightened place of Catholicism and despotism, as a place of primitivism and closeness to the senses. Although these have mostly carried negative connotations, they receive a positive twist with Jean-Jacques Rousseau's Romantic philosophy, which construes the south of Europe as the 'incarnation of a nostalgia for an older way of living that modern Europe, with its arts and sciences, had long forgotten to remember' (Dainotto, 2007: 100). In spite of these positive connotations, however, Rousseau's perspective maintained the 'denial of coevalness' according to which France and the northern European nations are more advanced than the South of Europe. This opposition is affiliated to a taxonomic vision of the world, going back to the Enlightenment, which equates proximity to nature with a lack of rationality. In Anglophone writing in particular, Italy's alleged proximity to nature and sensual pleasures thus come to be opposed to the Anglo-Saxon inclination towards rational thinking. Both the Enlightenment and the Romantic version of this North–South dichotomy, then, hinge on an opposition between the rational and the irrational. Yet, while the first relies on the possibility of an objective access to the other (based on a superior form of rationality), the second is not concerned with establishing a primacy but expresses the desire to go back in time and reconnect with the sensual realm of experience. As I explain in further detail below, both interpretations can be traced in Hall's novel: a romantic primitivism and a sensual, anti-rational approach to life characterizes Annette's narrative, while Giorgio's story offers an invitation to transcend rationality in order to rediscover instinct.

Dainotto further shows how Hegel elaborated on these existing interpretations in his theory of history as an intelligent development, the path toward a full development of self-consciousness and freedom that humanity achieves through successive phases of self-realization, moving ahead towards the accomplishment of its destiny and spiritual potential. Hegel traces this development through different European civilizations – from ancient Greece over Rome to the modern German state – as a progressive detachment from despotic forms of power and a gradual realization of the capacity for freedom, autonomy, and self-rule. This progress culminates in the consciousness of the modern individual, who does not need external authority to live according to what is just. According to this model, some contemporary people can be considered as still living in the past, while others are perceived as living in the present. This notion opens the door for a hierarchical arrangement of civilizations and social formations based on the assumption of the existence of a higher form of self-consciousness that goes hand in hand with the modern condition.

How to Paint a Dead Man retains a flavour of this Hegelian model, as it reiterates, in part, a vision of Italy as a timeless realm dominated by oppressive religious and familial ties. It proposes a pre-modern rural setting for the stories of the Italian characters and it assigns to them a specific mark of primal innocence (Annette) and transcendental wisdom (Giorgio). At the same time, in its four-part scheme of human development, the novel assigns to Annette and Giorgio, respectively, the alpha and the omega of human life, thus excluding them from the modern/contemporary world of dynamic productivity and existence embodied by Susan and Peter. Yet, by embracing this developmental model, the novel also recasts the discursive patterns of representing Italy and Italians in a more interesting and elusive light. As I will show, *How to Paint a Dead Man* owes something to the Hegelian model adumbrated above, but not in a crudely instrumental sense. Unlike in other modern and contemporary novels,[3] no character visits Italy from a supposedly more advanced place, wishing to relinquish his/her advanced state of consciousness in order to recover something authentic. Nor is there a univocal appropriation of 'Italian-ness' on the part of a northern protagonist who is free to move back and forth across states of consciousness as he/she pleases. Nevertheless, Hall's novel does delineate a movement of progressive awareness, using a schema which traces characters as they develop through different life-stages. The novel thereby complicates a historical model of development which dichotomizes the European North and South, Italy and Britain, using a psychological model that undermines any straightforward opposition of this kind. In this movement, each character incarnates a different moment of human existence: young Annette, older Susan, mature Peter, and old Giorgio. Annette is a young blind Italian girl, over-protected by her family and gifted with a powerful imagination; Susan is a young woman grieving the sudden loss of her twin brother, Danny; Peter is a successful middle-aged man in the process of a bittersweet assessment of his past; and Giorgio is a well-known Italian artist who feels the end of his life is approaching. Whereas all characters are connected to one another in some way, stronger bonds exist between Annette and Giorgio (student-mentor) and Susan and Peter (daughter-father). All characters are depicted in a condition of stasis that grounds them physically to one place while it also helps releasing their thoughts and feelings: Annette has very little freedom of movement, impeded as she is by her blindness on the one hand, and the overwhelming presence of her mother on the other; Susan is, quite simply, paralysed with grief; Peter gets his foot stuck between heavy rocks while climbing; and Giorgio's illness restricts him to his home. In this respect too, the novel seems to be emulating the apparent immobility of a still-life painting, in which life and movement are a matter of composition, of what 'passes' between an object and the next.

In what follows, I will discuss each character in the light of his/her stage of existential awareness, while also tracing the movement of progressing consciousness which links them together. In order to make this development even clearer, however, I will rely on Jean Piaget's model of cognitive development. As Hayden White argues in *Tropics of Discourse* (1978), Piaget's model of cognitive development is also characterized by a certain Hegelian teleology as it traces the realization of consciousness articulated over four phases. Following White's reading of Piaget, the child apprehends the world through the body and no distinction is perceived between self and other: 'there is only the timeless, spaceless experience of the Same' (White, 1978: 8). The second phase sees a 'de-centration' of the ego, whereby the child becomes aware of its 'contiguity', as opposed to oneness, with the rest of the world. This realization, White glosses, is necessary to the function of speech. In the course of the third phase, the child 'becomes capable of a certain logic; he becomes capable of coordinating operations in the sense of reversibility, in the sense of the total system' (White, 1978: 8). This means that the child becomes aware of temporal processes, as well as capable of working things out in his/her head rather than experiencing them physically in a trial-and-error fashion. In the fourth phase, there is 'the dissociation of thought from its possible objects, a capacity to reflect on reflection itself' (White, 1978: 9). In other words, in this final stage, the child's thought becomes not only conscious, but self-conscious:

We may say then that, with the onset of adult consciousness, the child becomes not only capable of logic [...] but also of irony – the capacity not only to say things about the world in a particular way but also to say things about it in alternative ways – and of reflecting on this capacity of thought. (White, 1978: 9)

This Hegelian schema provides a useful tool with which to read Hall's developmental narrative pattern in *How To Paint a Dead Man*, as it shows a dynamic movement from a 'metaphorical' phase (Annette) ruled by similitude and a fundamental communion between the self and the rest of the world, over an awareness of one's own individuality (Susan), to the realization of being 'historical' (Peter) and, finally, a conquered ironic detachment (Giorgio). As I hope to show, this developmental model complicates the novel's application of the traditional binary distinctions between North and South, Britain and Italy, rationality and the senses.

Young Annette

Annette, a blind Italian florist, lives and discovers the world through the senses. The sentence that introduces this character depicts her as using her body as the key measure for everyday operations related to her work: '[i]n the cool back room of her mother's house Annette measures rose stalks with her forearm' (Hall, 2011: 26). Annette describes the world she cannot see through sounds, smells and impressions, and she translates it into a language brimming with similitudes. Annette's thoughts are often prompted by sensory experiences; her observations match memories with smells, revealing a tightly knit universe in which familiar presences and floral references combine to reflect a vivid but still acerbic understanding of the world perceived as mysterious and, at times, menacing.

A large number of Annette's similitudes stem from stereotypically Italian spaces, tropes and cultural forms: the opera – 'the perfume is insistent, a soprano pitch' (Hall, 2009: 86) – Catholic lore and superstition: the painting in the church of San Lorenzo (Hall, 2009: 29); Christ lifted by the faithful in the dark varnish, a terrible unholy face, the wounds of Sebastian (Hall, 2009: 30). Annette dreams of saints: 'Saint Catherine of Sienna visited her, and Saint Cosmos with his stethoscope. They conferred in Latin. They tangoed, like her parents in the photograph' (Hall, 2009: 164). Monthly periods are explained to Annette by her mother as the event that makes 'all girls become the monthly brides of Christ' (Hall, 2009: 168). Several descriptions and metaphors also concern food: 'on the tables are figs baked with polenta and roasted lemons, uncorked wine and pecorino' (Hall, 2009: 268); 'her voice as bitter as radicchio' (Hall, 2009: 89).

The Italian setting for Annette's narrative is depicted as rural and timeless. Once the signs of contemporaneity have been removed, all that is left is the environment appropriate to a folktale: the old town, the lake, the market, the citadel, the summer theatre, the bakery. Annette's life takes place between the school, the church, home, the country cemetery (where her father rests), and the town market. Most of Annette's relations are within the family: her mother, her uncle Marcello, and his brothers Maurizio and little Tommaso.[4] Annette's mother, in particular, is a figure that perfectly synthesizes, from a northern European standpoint, the authoritative and oppressive traits of Catholicism: 'at the front door of Castrabecco their mother stands in her long shawl and a dark dress. She holds a crucifix between her fingers' (Hall, 2009: 26). Annette's mother has lived a life strongly defined by social, religious and patriarchal conventions – she refuses, even after a long time from the death of her husband, to dismiss the attire appropriate to a widow – which she attempts to impose on her daughter. Annette's difference from her male siblings is constantly stated: 'Maurizio is a boy and the rules are different' (Hall, 2009: 27). When Annette becomes completely blind, her mother and Uncle Marcello decide that 'a frame should be placed around her life,' so to 'arrest her vitality before it has a chance to wilt' (Hall, 2009: 169).

When Annette's growth is arrested, her world of references and the similitudes prompted by her imagination become confined to the contexts of flowers/scents, food, religion, and the provincial milieu she knows so well:

> All people smell differently, like the cardamoms, and nutmegs, and Spanish chillies in the spice jars at the market. Tommaso smells of burnt milk and hyacinths. Maurizio like candle wax, chicken skin, and sometimes cologne from the pharmacy where he has flirted with the girl behind the counter. Her mother's voice always has an undercurrent of dark blue, like the night sky of the Nativity. (Hall, 2009: 188)

Annette's vivid and sensual imagination offers her a way to endure a reality of suffocating family ties and repressive social conventions. The dangers lurking in the darkness, creeping around Annette and spying on her from a distance are concrete but undefined. After being raped by 'the Bestia', an unspecified evil character, Annette's world of flowers, that reliable realm of familiar experiences, is suddenly shattered.[5]

Annette's sensual world is replaced with the dictatorial monotony of the new TV set, which takes away from her both the attention and protection of her family and her own faculty for making sense of the world through the senses: 'no perfume drifts from it [the TV], and it emanates no moods' (Hall, 2009: 224). As Annette's family officially enters the modern world, Annette too leaves her infancy behind. When that object of modernity invades her small world based on similitude and oneness, Annette has nowhere to go. She dies and, as she parts from her family and friends, she pictures for us, in a narrative scene reminiscent of Federico Fellini's final sequence of *I Vitelloni* (1953), the world that used to be so familiar to her:

> As [Annette] looks out over the town, she can see everything at once, in all directions. The courtyard of Castrabecco, and the summer theatre, the narrow citadel, and the tower of San Lorenzo. Citizens and children. On the tables are figs baked with polenta and roasted lemons, uncorked wine and pecorino. In the alleyways, old women are sitting in the shade, their legs crossed at their ankles, holding canes in their hands or kneading dough. Laundry flaps on the lines between buildings. At San Lorenzo Father Mencaroni is unfastening his belt and removing the wafers left on the plate, eating them one by one. Annette sees her mother weeping over the photograph of her papa, while the television hums and crackles, rearranging particles to make

another world. At the gardens, Uncle Marcello is conducting a ceremony; he is naming his beautiful new lily Rosaria. (Hall, 2009: 268)

Through Annette's aerial, transcendental vision, Hall composes the *tableau vivant* of a familiar world whose particles the TV is about to rearrange. The scene constitutes a telling literary instance of William Spanos' definition of *tableau vivant* as 'the schema that, from an internalized transcendental perspective, coerces the differential phenomena of being into taking their "proper place" in a sealed off, totalized field' (Spanos, 2009: 101). Annette's chapters are, for this reason, set apart from the rest of the novel and constitute a fiction within a fiction in which realistic conventions can be credibly suspended in order to make space for a self-contained dark tale of childhood fantasies and fears.

Annette's story is contextualized within a timeless space of unbroken tradition that shatters as soon as an object of modernity enters it. Her pre-modern state is connected to her way of building knowledge, a mode of thinking and learning based on the accumulation and classification of impressions and scents that Annette pairs up to build a reliable map of the world. While this mode of making sense of things provides Annette with the possibility of accessing reality, it also delimits the horizon of what can possibly be known to her. The new TV may widen the possibilities of the real, but not for Annette, whose blindness confines her to a mode of existence that can continue only as long as she perceives herself in harmonious continuity and oneness with the world of her childhood and the familiar relations that have always shaped it. Annette's timeless world of natural similitudes exclusively thus belongs to her and her chapters. By contrast, the British characters are placed within a contemporary, 'global' context, a recognizable and contingent dimension of existence dominated by present-day estrangements and alienations.

Older Susan

Annette, living in a dark space, projects a world in which she distinguishes people and objects by their voices and scents, apprehending and making sense of everything through similitudes. Susan's narrative, by contrast, tells of the excruciating experience of losing her twin brother who was so close to her that she experienced him not as other, but as same. As a child, Susan was told to see her relation to her brother in terms of contiguity rather than oneness in order to better function within the family and adequately respond to social demands.[6] She had to be taught, for example, to let Danny speak for himself. As an adult, when she loses him, she has to re-apprehend the boundaries that separate her from him and make her into a different and distinct individual.

The chapters of the novel dedicated to Susan are narrated in the second person. This narrative device functions as a marker of Susan's on-going struggle for contiguity and the gradual realization of her individual identity. As children, Susan and Danny used to live in a state clinically termed 'ulterior proximity': 'Sometimes you felt you were more at his location then you were at yours. Ulterior proximity, it's called. When you waved it wasn't to your brother, it was to yourself' (Hall, 2009: 4). When Danny dies, Susan relapses into this state during a period of existential confusion: 'You aren't feeling like yourself. You haven't been feeling like yourself for a while now, not since the accident' (Hall, 2009: 3); 'You used to feel something similar as a child, but it was less empty, less lonely then. Your brother was the same. The pair of you had a peculiar sense of each other, not as separate people but as doppelgängers, symmetries, which is quite common in twins of course' (Hall, 2009: 3).

When they were children, the bond between Susan and Danny was so strong that their nurse 'wondered about this inseparability, this double-speak. She wondered if, rather than being delightful, it was abnormal to possess a psychological satellite. She wondered how healthy the relationship was between Danny and you' (Hall, 2009: 5). A doctor taught little Susan about her singularity and distinctiveness from Danny: 'You looked at yourself in the mirror Dr. Dixon gave you to hold. You repeated the words until they stuck. *Me, me, me, I, I, I.* You wound back into yourself, like the reversing spool on your mum's sewing machine. You became a separate unit. You were cured' (Hall, 2009: 6). Danny's death plunges Susan in a second crisis of identity:

when she loses her brother, she loses the main term against which her individuality has been constructed over time: 'now he is gone, and you are here, trying to find yourself in the mess, trying to locate the intimate filaments of which you are comprised. So that from this chaos order is achieved. So that you might be restored' (Hall, 2009: 38). Susan finds comfort in a passionate affair with Tom, an Italian man married to her business partner Angela. Tom, the reader learns, is Tommaso, Annette's little brother, who is working at Susan's art gallery, translating Giorgio's diaries. The reappearance of Tommaso carries us briefly from London's contemporary milieu to the Italian timeless world of Annette's sensual scents, and to the particular one – hyacinth – Annette associates with Tom: 'It is a good fit, this indiscretion. It has the right scent. There is the match of something disturbed. It is a romance of ill-health. Like hyacinth, like sugar and must, his serum, and you taste him elsewhere' (Hall, 2009: 103).

By recasting the familiar trope of a passionate affair between a Northern European woman and a Southern man within the narrative context of a painful fight against grief, Hall avoids the usual clichés of mindless enjoyment. Still, the representation of Italy as a parallel universe dominated by natural sensations persists: it is a world capable of offering a brief respite from the pain Susan is struggling with. The passionate and sensual bond between Susan and Tommaso is destined to be short-lived and put aside in order for Susan's life to be restored. In a sense, therefore, the relationship between Susan and Tommaso still follows the conventional pattern of an encounter with otherness that contributes to the betterment or restoration of the self.

Susan's path out of grief is slow, and unfinished at the end of her chapters. We leave her when she is still fighting to regain balance, just as she discovers her pregnancy. Following Piaget, the realization of the child's sense of contiguity to the world is a necessary condition for speech. Similarly, Susan's voice is only registered at the very end of her narrative, when she replies to her partner's call with 'I am here' (Hall, 2009: 286). These words, spoken as she looks at the result of her pregnancy test are a sign of her recovery. Although she has not yet been completely 'restored,' the news of her pregnancy has shaken her out of her grieving state and Susan acknowledges, through the first person, her existence and presence to herself, to Nathan, and the rest of the world. At this point, we sense Susan will heal through acquiring a new sense of identity that is as fragile and grief-informed as it is strong in its mature conception:

> Of course they [Susan's parents] would sympathise. They love you. But they can't fix you, can't make you yourself again. No more than sex can shock your atoms, make them come alive. No more than Dr. Dixon's therapy could make of you a first person. You're comprised of a million tiny locks. There's no master key to be found, encased in the plush velvet heart, no matter how desperately you ask someone to reach in and grope around. No matter how hard you try to find it. (Hall, 2009: 205)

In short, Susan's narrative traces a progressive detachment from oneness to contiguity; a slow elaboration of pain which will carry her away from youth.

Mature Peter

In the course of the third phase of Piaget's model, the child becomes capable of coordinating operations in the sense of reversibility, and with an understanding of the process of reversibility comes a deeper understanding of time. In Michel Foucault's interpretation of this discursive trope, this phase inaugurates a reflection on what it means to be a historical being. Peter's narrative can be read in this light, as it presents a man in the process of coming to terms with the ghosts of his past and with his sense of guilt for the death of his ex-wife. Of the four main characters, Peter is the one who inhabits most fully a mature and rational way of thinking and is committed to present events. His approach to life can be situated in between Susan's self-realization through emotive turmoil and Giorgio's conquered cool irony. Peter's present-day situation (we first meet him prior to the death of his son) is comprised of a successful career, financial security, a comfortable network of family relations at the centre of which is Lydia, his wife and the mother of his children. Hall leads us through Peter's thoughts, from his sentimental lament over his children's lost infancy, to the memory of old friends; from the brief, affectionate, and profoundly sad recollection of his mother, to his first encounter with Lydia: 'how lovely she was, with her halo of brown hair on the ground. How inspiring was her calmness' (Hall, 2009: 117).

The chapters dedicated to Peter patiently follow the lead of his thoughts which are set free by a series of situations characterized by physical stasis: some pleasant (a morning lazily spent in bed; a long bath), some less so (waiting in the car for a herd of cows to vacate the road), and the main one dangerous and testing: quite ironically for a well-known landscape artist, Peter gets stuck between heavy rocks in the course of a work-related climb. At first, Peter's thoughts are steadily melancholic, but not yet painful: he remembers his father, and through his memory of him we learn of his humble origins as the son of a miner (Hall, 2009: 19). He quietly ponders over his close and relaxed relationship with his son Danny, and his equally close but tenser relationship with Susan, who demonstrates 'impatience' towards him and possesses a 'daughterly tendency to spat with her old man' (Hall, 2009: 20).

Once literally immobilized over a long period of time, and in danger to lose his life, Peter gradually becomes afraid and defenceless. It is at this point that the ghosts from his past appear before him: his ex-tutor and best friend in Liverpool, Ivan, and his ex-wife, Raymie. We learn of the destructive relationship in which they were involved and of Peter's desertion of Raymie following his need for self-preservation in the face of her damaging habits and destructive personality:

> One day, during that second New York winter, he just knew he had to go. The weather was so cold, cold enough to freeze the piss pot in the bathroom, and she was sleeping underneath every blanket they owned, maybe not sleeping but unconscious, and he, missing the way it had been, missing the calm smell of paint, went out into the blizzard. He walked all the way to the Met through the snow, without his coat, and then sat on a gallery bench for an hour in front of a now priceless painting. *Nature Morte*, 1964, the very last in the series. He'd known then that he couldn't watch her do it anymore. (Hall, 2009: 274)

The reader knows that Peter will survive somehow, be rescued or rescue himself from the trying circumstance of being trapped, since he appears in Susan's narrative, attempting to come to terms with the death of his son. Both Susan and Peter therefore manage to get themselves out of their immobilizing condition, and this makes evident a quality of dynamism and self-determination which is absent in their Italian counterparts, who are subject to a natural (and as such inexorable) decline: blindness for Annette and a lung disease for Giorgio. While Annette's deteriorating sight and Giorgio's disease cannot be stopped, Susan's grief and Peter's entrapment between rocks are trying but transitory conditions. This underlines the representation of Italy as a realm governed by inexorable laws of nature, in partial discontinuity with the modern (British) world, in which individuals have a higher capacity for self-determination and greater autonomy.

Old Giorgio

The character of Giorgio, based on the Italian artist Giorgio Morandi, who painted the *Nature Morte* Peter sees at the Met, may be understood to represent the last phase of Piaget's schema, which marks the appearance of hypothetical and deductive reasoning and 'a capacity to reflect on reflection itself' (White, 1978: 9) Giorgio's thoughts are narrated through the pages of his diary, an introspective device *par excellence* and a way to look at one's own past with emotional detachment and irony. Giorgio lives a secluded life in the countryside near Bologna. Occasionally, journalists, admirers, and art students undertake the trip to his home. Although he still dedicates himself to his art, Giorgio is in poor health. His chapters retain a quiet and profound meditative quality and we sense, from the beginning, that there are cumbersome presences in his past too, but, unlike Peter, Giorgio has made peace with them:

> There was no decision made to never leave this place, though it has been said that I renounced everything, that I suffered a great dismay and withdrew. Or that I was possessed by art, removing my heart to paint its space, its absence. This is said because of my wife and child.

I am a brute and the work denotes much calculation and control. Old news. When I hear such things I do not ask for sympathy. Whatever sins I have committed exist beyond me now. I will let Nature alone judge me; she will abominate me if it is her finding. (Hall, 2009: 13)

Giorgio's wisdom makes of him the moral compass of the novel: if all the other characters feel the limitations of their present condition (even Annette, albeit with resignation), Giorgio embraces his with a restrained attitude. In other words, a different degree of engagement with the here and now separates the British characters from the Italian ones. Chronologically, Susan and Peter occupy the central stages of adult life. Productive and self-absorbed, they are both very much involved in their current situations. Therefore, they both need a tangible obstacle put in their way (loss; a paralyzing accident) to delve deeper into themselves. The Italian characters, on the contrary, seem to be either naturally prone to inspired and emotional philosophical considerations (Giorgio), or immersed in a setting so poetic that thoroughly de-contextualizes them from the real and the mundane (Annette).[7]

Sporadically, Giorgio receives Peter's letters, informed and inquisitive, full of admiration. He wishes to reply, but, Peter having neglected to provide his own address, does so within the pages of his diary. Through Peter's letters, Giorgio gets to know him a little and is reminded of his own youth. His thoughts take us back and forth, from the most important events in his past (the first years of marriage with his beloved Dina, and the birth of their daughter), to his present-day physical decline: 'It is time to be honest. My lungs are beginning to fail. They work only to half their capacity and they commit me to the house much of the time' (Hall, 2009: 176). He wonders, '[w]hat secrets will they find beside these tarred lungs? A heart full of historic sadness perhaps. The soft blue face of Dina, like a cyanotype; the many layers of guilt and the badly repaired peace' (Hall, 2009: 178). Giorgio's last reflection on life is a hymn to instinct:

> The artistic efforts of men are indicative of our human openness, our inquisitiveness, I think. When we attempt to evaluate, or to obviate, we seldom guess correctly. Our minds are born nervous, in darkness.

> We are subterranean beings. We must learn by the senses and continue to be instinctual, to use the antennae. (Hall, 2009: 280)

There is, in these words, an invitation to go back to Annette's instinctual ways of seeing, learning, and experiencing the world through the senses. Giorgio's last reflection thus closes the development of human consciousness by returning to its beginning. Childhood and old age, both represented by Italian characters, thus become linked through the realization that rational and intellectual abilities are, respectively, not yet and no longer needed in order to apprehend the world effectively and to function within it. In a sense, one could say that the novel narrates the progression of human consciousness towards an acquired simplicity of perspective epitomized by the bottles painted by Giorgio: it takes a lifetime of learning to acquire the skills necessary to depict life's simple objects with such proficiency and clarity of mind, to be able to see order within the chaos of existence. By linking the last to the first season, Hall combines a linear with a cyclical perspective on time, 'the time of history and the time of myth' (Connor, 1996: 34). In Foucault's take on the model of progressing consciousness, the fourth phase is linked to the realization of an ultimate incommensurability between the world and language, and the consequent decline of faith in comprehensive narratives based on an assumed correspondence between the observation of phenomena and their transparent articulation through language.[8] This perspective also informs Giorgio's ironic detachment, his artistic focus on mundane objects and their apparent simplicity, and his quiet invitation to favour intuition over intellectual faculties.

Conclusions

With regard to representation of Italy, *How to Paint a Dead Man* thus assigns to the Italian characters both the most primal (intuitive Annette) and most advanced stages (ironic Giorgio) of the development of human consciousness. My analysis was inspired by the novel's steady and homogeneous, partly linear and partly cyclical development. The novel's allusion to the discursive trope of progressing consciousness invites us to reflect on the ways we construe and taxonomically distribute rational (intellectual) and emotional (sensual) human faculties, or, if one prefers, the historical and the mythical. Although Hall's novel is in line with the discursive tradition of representing Italy in Anglophone fiction to assign the more 'magical' and less rational phases of life to Italian characters, the novel does break with these traditions in refusing to subscribe to the utilitarian logic whereby the rational subject (traditionally Anglo-American) appropriates pre-modern wisdom for the achievement of a higher and more accomplished existential synthesis. Instead, subjectivity is distributed equally among the four characters and the Italian characters are not merely there to teach the British timeless lessons on the importance of nature and the senses. If there is a touch of that, perhaps coming from Giorgio, it is directed to everyone, not specifically spoken for the benefit of the British characters:

> We should not forget that when we limp away afflicted through the spirit, it is not to the factory gates or to the corporate steps we pilgrimage. Instead we go to the sea for its salt. We find shade under the sycamores on the great avenues. Or we go to the rivers where water tells us modestly of its own sickness. I cannot say that I have found peace now. But I have never loved with greater strength than in this place, with its earth the colour of *verdaccio* and its generous fruit. (Hall, 2009: 13)

If *How to Paint a Dead Man* thus reiterates some familiar tropes employed in representing Italy, by combining these tropes with a cyclical-linear narrative of human development, the novel also avoids the more stereotypical plot patterns associated with these tropes in Anglophone fiction. Instead, Hall makes a creative use of an inherited taxonomy of cultural values about the divide between North and South in Europe in the context of a larger reflection on human life and consciousness.

Notes

1 Annemarie McAllister (2007) demonstrates how a certain imagined and composite notion of 'Italian-ness' has contributed to the formation of modern British identities, arguing that such a notion functioned as a reservoir for all that was deemed discordant to the making of the British individual, collective, and national identities. Similarly, Elisabetta Girelli (2009: 10) argues that 'typecast, specific notions of Italianness have deep roots in British society, and are related to equally fixed ideas of Britishness'. See also my articles on the representation of Italian culture in popular Anglophone texts (Pierini, 2016a,b).

2 The phrase 'denial of coevalness' was coined by Johannes Fabian in his seminal critique of anthropology *Time and the Other: How Anthropology makes its Object* (1983). Fabian argues that in order for there to be an anthropological object of study, a temporal distance has to be first premised then constantly maintained in anthropological discourse, even though this discourse is presented as a work of rapprochement with the other. Observer and observed do not pertain to the same time: the observer belongs to the time of writing, whereas the observed belongs to the past. As Fabian (1983: 1) puts it, 'Anthropology's claim to power [...] belongs to its essence and is not a matter of accidental misuse. Nowhere is this more clearly visible, at least once we look for it, than in the uses of Time anthropology makes when it strives to constitute its own object – the savage, the primitive, the other.'

3 In her novel *A Visit from the Goon Squad*, for instance, Jennifer Egan (2011: 246) stages the extempory escape of one of her most conflicted protagonists, Sasha, to Naples. Egan articulates the consequent attempt made by her uncle Ted to bring her back in terms of a 'descent to Hades'. Explicitly evoking the myth of Orpheus and Eurydice, Egan summons an age-long tradition of Apollonian civilized spirits momentarily plunging into a core of dark otherness in order to recover someone else, or a part of themselves, temporarily lost to the Dionysian realm. Modern and contemporary Anglophone literature abounds in variations of this narrative: from *A Room with a View* (Forster, 1908) to *Eat Pray Love* (Gilbert, 2006), Italy serves as the ideal Dionysian setting for tales of Apollonian self-discovery.

4 Annette's mother perceives Uncle Marcello's superstitious tales –'Uncle Marcello says some people believe if you look at a poppy without making the sign of the cross it will make you go blind' (Hall, 2009: 125) – as in

opposition to her orthodox religious beliefs, but she is also superstitious herself, 'about salt and numbers and animals.' (Hall, 2009: 32) Annette's world of flowers often mixes with religious imagery: 'white lilies are for annunciation and grace, such as the angel offered to the Madonna' (Hall, 2009: 86); they 'must be trimmed under running water to prevent their white heads drooping, like nuns in prayer' (Hall, 2009: 26).

5 Annette recounts this experience, once again, through similitudes with Catholic religious lore: 'it is like the pain of the mystics, the pain of St. Theresa. She is being opened like the heart of the beloved. She is being burned alive' (Hall, 2009: 267).

6 White (1978: 8) explains the passage from oneness to contiguity as follows: 'This decentration (or displacement) is a necessary condition far what Piaget calls "the symbolical function," the most important aspect of which is speech. Only because of the possibility of apprehending relationships of contiguity is this process of symbolization, and *a fortifori*, of thought itself, rendered possible.'

7 In his review of Hall's novel for *The New York Times*, Saïd Sayrafiezadeh observes that the author's viewpoint on Italy is nostalgic and sentimental, and that, 'the mood in Italy is so constantly lyrical that everything, including dialogue and narration, take on a stilted, unnatural quality' (September 25, 2009). This article aims at investigating further, in the light of Dainotto's insights, the possible reasons behind this double discursive register within Hall's narrative: normative, (post)modern, mundane England and timeless, pre-modern, lyrical (poetic, inspired, sentimental) Italy.

8 White shows how a certain Hegelian tale of growing awareness can be discerned not only in Jean Piaget's theory of the cognitive development of the child, but also, *mutatis mutandis*, in Michel Foucault's narration, in *The Order of Things* (1966), of the 'passages' between the four main *epistemes* that characterize the modern centuries from the seventeenth century to the modern era: 'Each of the epochs of Western cultural history [...] appears to be locked within a specific mode of discourse, which at once provides its "access" to reality and delimits the horizon of what can possibly appear as real. For example, Foucault argues, in the sixteenth century the dominant mode of discourse was informed by a desire to find the Same in the Different, to determine the extent to which any given object resembled another; the sciences of the sixteenth century were obsessed, in short, with the notion of Similitude [...]. The seventeenth century set

before consciousness this apprehension of Differentness as the problem to be solved. And it proposed to solve it by disposing the world of things in the modality, not of continuity, but of contiguity'. The nineteenth century, White continues, is characterized by 'the growing consciousness of the significance of Time for the understanding of life, labor, and language, and attests, to the historicization of the human sciences [...]. The question that the human sciences had to face in the nineteenth century was, What does it mean to *have* a history? This question, Foucault maintains, signals a 'great mutation' in the consciousness of Western man, a mutation which has to do ultimately with "our modernity" [...]. The bankruptcy of the nineteenth-century investigation of the 'temporal series' was signalled by Nietzsche, who perceived correctly that the true problem which modern thought had kept hidden from itself was that of the opacity of language, the incapacity of language to serve the purpose of representation which had been foisted upon it, all unthinkingly, in the late sixteenth century'. The opacity of language is at the basis of the 'Western man's growing realization of the impossibility of ever constructing a true science of man' (White, 1978: 241–5).

Works Cited

Connor, Steven (1995) *The English Novel in History 1950–1995*. London: Routledge.

Dainotto, R. M. (2007) *Europe (in Theory)*. Durham, NC: Duke University Press.

Egan, J. (2011) *A Visit from the Goon Squad*. New York: Anchor Books.

Fabian, J. (1983) *Time and the Other: How Anthropology Makes Its Object*. New York: Columbia University Press.

Forster, E. M. (1908/2012) *A Room with a View*. London: Penguin Books.

Foucault, M. (1966/1970) *The Order of Things: An Archaeology of the Human Sciences*. New York: Random House.

Gilbert, E. (2006) *Eat, Pray, Love: One Woman's Search for Everything across Italy, India and Indonesia*. New York: Viking.

Girelli, E. (2009) *Beauty and the Beast: Italianness in British Cinema*. Bristol and Chicago: Intellect.

Hall, S. (2009) *How to Paint a Dead Man*. London: Faber.

McAllister, A. (2007) *John Bull's Italian Snakes and Ladders: English Attitudes to Italy in the Mid-nineteenth Century*. Newcastle: Cambridge Scholars Publishing.

Pierini, F. (2016a) 'The Genetic Essence of Houses and People: History as Idealization and Appropriation of an Imagined Timelessness', *Acta Universitatis Sapientiae, Philologica* 8(1): 99–116.

Pierini, F. (2016b) 'Trading Rationality for Tomatoes: The Consolidation of Anglo-American National Identities in Popular Literary Representations of Italian Culture', *Anglica: A Journal of English Studies* 25(1): 181–97.

Sayrafiezadeh, S. (2009) 'A Matter of Perspective', *New York Times* (25 September), URL (accessed 16 August 2019): https://www.nytimes.com/2009/09/27/books/review/Sayrafiezadeh-t.html

Spanos, W. (2009) *The Legacy of Edward W. Said*. Urbana: University of Illinois Press.

White, H. (1978) *Tropics of Discourse: Essays in Cultural Criticism*. Baltimore, MD: John Hopkins University Press.

8

SARAH HALL'S MATERIAL IMAGINATION

Alexander Beaumont

As we have seen over the course of this collection, Sarah Hall is a writer for whom matter matters. Her bodies are adamantly material, 'vessel[s]' composed of 'atoms' (Hall, 2009: 285). Intimate experiences are at once vivid and epiphenomenal, captured in a sometimes medicalized prose that reflects their profundity but also their corporeal, even mechanical, nature. And where medical diction is absent, Hall's description of the human animal and its social behaviour nearly always has more to do with substance and viscera than with ideals and abstraction. Yet whether described mechanically or chaotically, whether sanguinary, suppurative or seminal, the messy profusion of Hall's bodies is always the measure of their liveliness. While technology may advance, while medicine might render bodies more docile and manageable, our 'reddish nature' (Hall and Hobbs, 2016: 2) persists as a reminder of the body's capacity to outlast us. Consciousness expires, contexts change and history happens. But while our relationship with the stuff of which we are formed might shift dramatically according to the structures that bear down on us, in Hall's work that stuff always seems to remain: not constant but, rather, untimely; not transcendent but stubborn. What makes this stuff so attractive to Hall appears to be the extent to which it alternately exceeds and undermines whatever processes presume to contain or even explain it. It is in the very *thereness* of matter, its apparent resistance to philosophical abstraction and indifference to social protocols, that its interest lies.

In this respect, Hall's preoccupation with matter often confronts her readers with the very finitude that the modern, sovereign individual is everywhere encouraged to deny. This does not mean, however, that matter is fixed or inert: a notable characteristic of Hall's bodies is that, within their limits, they remain promissory – even vital. My aim in this concluding chapter is to argue that this vital finitude is indicative of Hall's material imagination more broadly, and that it is as much a characteristic of her landscapes as of the bodies that populate them. The first half of the chapter evaluates how Hall, who so evidently owes something to – and subverts – a Romantic tradition of writing about the rugged topography of northern England, represents our relationship with the stuff of the landscape. Rather than being positioned as a straightforward example of 'neo-Romantic' writing, I suggest, Hall's post-pastoral representation of 'Lakeland' is better made sense of using the critical framework adopted by figures associated with the 'material turn', a broad theoretical movement codified within the discipline of Geography as 'non-representational theory' (Thrift, 2008). Read in this way, it is possible to see how assertively Hall's work complicates popular, overdetermined constructions of the English Lake District in the significance that it accords to the material composition of a landscape that always exceeds the means by which its materiality has been made to signify within a larger system of cultural representation. The second half of the chapter returns to Hall's engagement with corporeality and addresses how her work locates a kind of vitalism in both the inertia of the corpse and the liveliness of the animal. Just like the matter of the landscape, I argue, the matter of the body resists incorporation into a conceptual schema that valorizes a fantasy of ever-increasingly sovereign subjectivity. Indeed, Hall's work evidences a thrilling preoccupation with the *end* of the sovereign subject, offering in its place a materially embodied and embedded vitalism which produces new and unsettling relationships between bodies and the landscapes in which they are situated.

Altogether, this chapter suggests, the limits put in place by Hall's representation of our physical constitution and the material geography of the landscapes in which we live open up new forms of understanding which cannot be exhausted by conceptual, discursive or more broadly cultural ways of describing the relationship between space, body and consciousness. Hall's representation of landscape challenges the notion that the latter is produced exclusively (or even primarily) by the broad discursive terrain that is labelled 'culture'. Instead of understanding meaning as something that is impressed upon the landscape by what, in a major contribution to the material turn, Sarah Whatmore (2006: 23) calls the '"in-here" of human being', Hall's fiction often decentres, etiolates or disperses subjectivity in ways that emphasize the uncanny liveliness that the matter that constitutes the landscape possesses in its own right. Likewise, Hall's representation of corporeality complicates any notion that the significance of the body lies in the – often contested – position that it occupies within cultural discourse. Instead, in her representation of the recalcitrancy of both human and non-human bodies, Hall reveals to us what the materialist feminist Elizabeth A. Wilson (1999:16) calls 'complex ontologies' that cultural theory has tended to overlook.

As Richard Grusin (2015: xi–xii) points out, the material turn is unavoidably 'opposed [...] to the more linguistic or representational turns of the 1970s through 1990s – such as the textual, cultural, ideological, or aesthetic turns' and 'challenges some of the key assumptions of social constructivism, particularly insofar as [the latter] insists that the agency, meaning, and value of nature all derive from cultural, social, or ideological inscription or construction'. This necessarily raises some intriguing questions regarding the aesthetic implications of Hall's material imagination, a question that is addressed towards the end of this chapter when I suggest that it would be a mistake to conclude that, simply because of the way in which matter facilitates a critique of representation in Hall's work, Hall therefore valorizes a straightforwardly non-representational aesthetics. An animating irony of Hall's work is that it is an attempt *within* representation to grasp how representation can end up obscuring the vitality of matter. Thus, I conclude, the effect of Hall's material imagination is to allow her fiction to exist in a curiously partial, unfinished and provocative relationship with the stuff of representation itself: that is, with language. Her work evinces a similar attitude towards the aesthetic as towards the bodies and the landscapes that appear in it: an attitude holding that matter precedes language and is, if anything, corralled, captured and even deadened when it is forced to take on a straightforwardly symbolic value. For Hall, the vitality of matter is not *produced* by language and cannot – indeed must not – be reduced to it. Words do matter; it's just that matter matters more.

Post-Pastoral Landscapes

Though scholarly appraisals of Hall's work did not begin to emerge with any consistency until the publication of *The Wolf Border* in 2015, a critical consensus rapidly emerged which positioned its author as a 'landscape artist' (Walezak, 2018: 2) whose 'literary appeal is constituted in neo-Romantic terms' and 'whose sensibilities are formed by a geographically-backed claim to belonging' (Cottrell, 2019: 682). The geography in question is, specifically, Cumbria; more expansively, it incorporates the northerly counties of England, which contain most of the country's sparsely populated uplands as well as a good proportion of its formerly industrial cities. At a mythic level, it extends to 'the North', a longstanding hyperborean spatial imaginary within European literature with lonely, wild and rapacious connotations (Davidson, 2005: 21–5). While Anna Cottrell (2019: 682) expresses some justifiable scepticism that the 'rebelliously local' aspects of Hall's work are as original as its reception might suggest, it is nonetheless the case that the way in which it represents locality conspicuously seeks to qualify its Romantic inheritance by 're-imagining versions of pastoral retreat and restoration that resist simple idealisations of nature' (Lilley, 2016: 68). At one point in *How to Paint a Dead Man*, for instance, the reader encounters the following:

> The north of your youth was practically pre-industrial. You are amazed when you hear people's ideas about idylls and pleasure grounds, the myths of the sublime. Back then it was a landscape of filth loosened

from fields, ringworm, walls of snow, and long, sickening bus rides to school. It was bad weather, burning carcasses, kids with disabilities, black-eye Fridays and badger baiting; collecting wood off the fell and trying to keep it dry under tarpaulin so the logs didn't fizzle with sap, hiss and blacken in the grate, because that was how you stayed warm. (Hall, 2009: 63–4)

Cottrell (2016: 683) notes that *The Wolf Border* 'subverts any tendencies towards the romanticization of the Cumbrian landscape', but this comment can easily be applied to Hall's earlier work as well. Instead of the pastoralism that has channelled the Romantic view of Lakeland into the recuperative imagery of the contemporary leisure industry, Hall's characterization of Cumbria in the passage above is one in which nature and culture are neither neatly dichotomized nor synthesized into a false harmony, but rather deeply and uneasily imbricated with one another. The celebrated vistas of the Lake District come to resemble a landscape that is half-finished, even half-imagined: Cumbria, in this novel as elsewhere in Hall's work, is 'pre-industrial' not in a halcyon sense, but rather in the sense that it is wilfully unable to adopt the ideal form that has been imagined for it by modernity.

This points us to an important element of Hall's work insofar as it can be read as an example of what Terry Gifford (2013: 26) has influentially termed the 'post-pastoral', a mode that is 'best used to describe works that successfully suggest a collapse of the human/nature divide while being aware of the problematics involved'. To be post-pastoral is necessarily to quarrel with any 'stable, complacent form of harmony in the human relationship with nature' (Gifford, 2013: 28). It is a mode that rejects both an heroic vision of industrial society as a Promethean departure from our natural limitations and its tragic obverse, which positions modernity as an example of a god that failed. Instead, it considers landscape from a vantage point wherein the distinction between nature and culture must be negotiated without the aid of an affirmative, messianic understanding of humanity's progress out of bondage and into mastery, but – equally – without the belief in a fixed and unchanging account of the natural world that conceives of it as an object that is unaffected by and indifferent to human beings.

This post-pastoral understanding of 'practically pre-industrial' can be used to understand a significant part of Hall's work. After all, her career as a novelist begins with the confrontation between industrial and pastoral landscapes in *Haweswater,* in which a representative from the Manchester Corporation is despatched to rural Westmorland to manage the relocation of Mardale farmers so that the valley where they live and work can be flooded using 'a flat arm of cement and brick [...] belonging to a colossal stone god' to form the Haweswater reservoir (Hall, 2002: 48). While a superficial reading of the novel might position it as a jeremiad against the dissolution of a 'perfect republic of shepherds and agriculturalists' at the behest of an industrial behemoth (Wordsworth cited in Purkis, 2014: 58), *Haweswater* is much more complex than this. The aim of Jack, the Promethean, to master nature is communicated through his desire to own a dead golden eagle; his remorse upon beholding his quarry, however, drives him into the fells to return the deceased raptor to its nest. Hall thus eschews heroic subjection of the landscape to possessive domination while ironizing a morbid conservationism that would preserve the landscape as a cold, dead fact. At the same time, she complicates any invitation the novel might be considered to issue to read Jack's fatal fall from the mountains he had sought to master as a manifestation of the landscape's ability to assert itself against those who would hubristically pit modernity against it. Despite Jack's personal undoing, *Haweswater* is emphatic in showing the completion of the reservoir; indeed, this is where the novel opens, with the flooding of Mardale. And just as the industrialist falls to his death while attempting to scale the landscape he desired first to instrumentalize and then to conserve, so his lover Janet – the daughter of a local farmer – is ultimately destroyed by the dam whose construction she wishes to allay. Thus, *Haweswater* refuses to adopt the simple pathos that might be expected of an historical novel lamenting the destruction of what, in *How to Paint a Dead Man,* are described as 'people's ideas about idylls and pleasure grounds [and] the myths of the sublime'. Instead, the final tone of the novel is ambivalent and reflective: we are addressed by a narrator who seeks to account for the story just related by picking through photographs, museum exhibitions and the tales recounted by former residents of Mardale. As this narrator tells us, 'in the valleys of Westmorland, strange fables and legends began to be told' (Hall, 2002: 258) in which the landscape becomes animistic, and an old oak tree is imbued with Janet's human consciousness. The locals 'recall a time when the tree was just a tree and Janet was just a girl' (Hall, 2002: 259), but the implication of Hall's debut, at its conclusion, is that we live beyond a moment when nature and culture can be kept separate.

From the outset of her career, then, Hall has sought to unsettle one of the most characteristic antinomies of modernity in her representation of landscape. If *Haweswater* complicates the nature/culture dichotomy at the heart of the pastoral by eliding the distinction between the industrial and the agrarian, *The Wolf Border*, published thirteen years later, performs a similar manoeuvre in relation to civilization and wilderness. Shortly after an epigraph translating the Finnish term that lends the novel its title – *susiraja*, 'the boundary between the capital region and the rest of the country', which 'suggests that everything outside the border is wilderness' (Hall, 2015: n.p.) – Hall immediately sets about examining how carefully crafted and meticulously governed the mythic, untamed landscapes of Lakeland are in fact:

> As a child, the territory seemed so wild that anything might be possible. The moors were endless, haunting; they hid everything and gave up secrets only intermittently – an orchid fluting in a bog, a flash of blue wing, some phantom, long-boned creature, caught for a moment against the horizon before disappearing. Only the ubiquitous sheep tamed the landscape. [Rachel] did not know it then, but in reality it was a kempt place, cultivated, even the high grassland covering the fells was manmade. Though it formed her notions of beauty, true wilderness lay elsewhere. (Hall, 2015: 29)

In what follows, *The Wolf Border* gradually comes to echo the conceptual elisions of *Haweswater* even as it reverses the polarities of the earlier novel. Whereas Jack comes to Westmorland in order to tame it, Rachel returns to the 'private Eden' (Hall, 2002: 32) of the Lake District in order to imbue it, once more, with wilderness. In both cases, the success of the hubristic projects in which these characters are engaged – the dam that would produce the Haweswater reservoir and the rewilding project that would see grey wolves roam the fells for the first time in half a millennium – exposes and complicates the brittle binaries that have structured popular perceptions of Lakeland since the industrial revolution. And between and among these two novels sits an entire corpus of writing – overwhelmingly set in and written about Cumbria and 'the North' – which, though created in the shadow of a Romantic inheritance that has produced an hypostatized, bucolic image of England's northern uplands, seeks to emphasize where the landscape exceeds the limits of this shadow.

If Hall's work is 'neo-Romantic', therefore, it is so in a highly qualified sense: that is, insofar as it hints at something akin to what Graham Huggan (2016: 159), describes as *'salvage geography'* (emphasis in original). In the work of the pre-eminent exponent of the New Nature Writing, Robert Macfarlane, salvage geography is 'an act of reclamation that recognizes wildness has been lost, but may yet have potential to re-seed itself; [... a]t the same time [...] in attaching memories to place, [it] also recognizes that place outstrips the capacities of human memory' (Huggan, 2016: 159). Yet Hall's work significantly exceeds the parameters of such a salvage geography in not only suggesting that the Cumbrian landscape outstrips the capacities of human memory but also by demonstrating scepticism with regard to whether human memory, or even human consciousness, can finally provide the means by which such a landscape might be made to cohere in the first place. Raymond Williams (1975/2016: 149) famously argues in *The Country and the City* that '[t]he very idea of landscape implies separation and observation', a process which divides subject from object and naturalizes the fraught relationship between both. And while, as Huggan suggests, the New Nature Writing seeks to produce a more complex account of this relationship, in the form that it so often takes it is not always clear that the dynamic Williams describes is being fundamentally disrupted.

'Salvage' is derived from the Latin *salvāre* ('to save'), but this root also yields 'salvation', which perhaps offers a clearer sense of what, finally, writers such as Macfarlane hope to locate. There is often a supernal, even quasi-mystical aspect to the New Nature Writing that positions 'nature' – however qualified – as a source of succour. Hall's novels and short stories are less reassuring insofar as they never straightforwardly emphasize the role of the naturalist-narrator in recovering or rebuilding an image of nature out of its ruins. Indeed, they more frequently refuse to do what a significant number of writers associated with the New Nature Writing ultimately seek to achieve: to re-enchant nature in the cold face of modernity.[1] Among Macfarlane's aims in *Landmarks* is to recover 'a kind of word magic, the power that certain terms possess to enchant our relations with nature and place' in order to locate opportunities for what he calls 're-wonderment' (Macfarlane, 2016: 3–4, 25). Yet, as closely attuned to the relationship between language and experience as Hall's work might be, the landscapes that it represents seem much less amenable to the kind of re-enchantment that Macfarlane describes. If the New Nature Writing seeks to perform its salvage geography by qualifying but ultimately preserving the coherence of the lyrical personae that it inherits from Romanticism, even as it reaches for a more complex relationship between those personae and the landscapes they describe, Hall's subjects are much less coherent. And if the note of reflexive ambivalence that Huggan hears in the narrators of the New Nature Writing produces landscapes that are a little more fragmented, a little less holistic, than those of their Romantic precursors, Hall's landscapes, which increasingly lack a unifying perspective that might make them legible, often end up seeming both impenetrable and yet curiously vital.

Against Cultural Geography

Another way of expressing this is to say that, while the personae adopted by writers such as Macfarlane might seek to adopt a more complex relationship with the landscapes they traverse and represent, they have still, to adapt Tim Ingold (2007: 5), 'contrived to dematerialize, or to sublimate into thought, the very medium in which the things in question' – that is, the actual stuff that constitutes the landscape – 'are [...] immersed'. The result of this kind of representational thinking is a relationship between subject and object that unavoidably renders the stuff of the landscape alive only insofar as it is endowed with significance using the conceptual and linguistic capacities of a human beholder. And the problem with this approach is that it overlooks the ways in which 'the very medium [... of] things' – their materiality – possesses a liveliness *prior* to its existence in representation and thereby deadens the very thing that it seeks to enchant. Hall's *oeuvre* achieves something quite different, emphasizing instead how landscapes outlast and are made more alive by the decentring of beholders who do not necessarily disappear but rather *become-object* through a material equation with the landscapes in which they are located. This is true even of Hall's most lyrical work, where the result is a very particular kind of post-pastoral narrative, articulated as a particularly enigmatic sort of tragedy. In true tragic form, the various 'ends' of *Haweswater* – Janet's, Jack's and ultimately Mardale's – are the novel's very conditions, insofar as Hall establishes the purpose of her narrative as being to explain how each came to disappear. Also in keeping with the generic expectations of tragedy, there are many ghosts that remain at its conclusion. But, far from offering closure, these ends afford the novel numerous endings which are, within the discourse of the narrative, staggered in such a way that they amount to no real ending at all, and in this sense the novel might be said to end unfinished. Instead of a complete landscape, the reader is left with the peculiar image of a tree – and, metonymically, an entire Westmorland valley – rendered newly and strangely animate by the very process that killed it: a landscape composed of rock, rain and now a great deal of brick and concrete which is vast, impassive, both emptied of and imbued with human consciousness, and – despite the many deaths that produced it – uncannily alive.

Such a construction of the Cumbrian landscape has significant implications for how we should understand the dialogue that Hall's work stages with its Romantic inheritance. But it also has wider ramifications for our understanding of the role that the concept of culture has played in producing the assumptions which shape contemporary nature writing and its reception. In describing her as a 'landscape artist', Walezak (2018: 2) suggests that Hall 'consistently deliberates Cumbria as a cultural landscape'. Yet I would suggest that the way in which Hall's work problematizes the relationship between nature and culture, subject and object, and persona and landscape, encourages us to revise our understanding of this deliberation, to the extent that Cumbria, in Hall's work, is ultimately not much of a *cultural* landscape at all. In an early contribution to the material turn, Sarah Whatmore challenges two conceptualizations of cultural landscape, the first of which treats it as something that is 'fashioned from a natural landscape by a cultural group' (Sauer cited in Whatmore, 2006: 602), the second as 'a cultural image, a pictorial way of representing [...] surroundings' (Davids and Cosgrove cited in Whatmore, 2006: 602). Whatmore challenges both, suggesting that they 'cast the making of landscapes (whether worked or represented) as an exclusively human achievement in which the stuff of the world is so much putty in our hands' (Whatmore, 2006: 603). She continues:

> [C]ultural geography's investments in questions of identity and culture have remained largely wedded to that most vociferously silent and self-evident subject of the social sciences, the 'in-here' of human being. So it is that recent contributions [to academic Geography] have sought to do (at least) three things. The first has been to re-animate the missing 'matter' of landscape, focusing attention on bodily involvements in the world in which landscapes are co-fabricated between more-than-human bodies and a lively earth. The second has been to interrogate 'the human' as no less a subject of ongoing co-fabrication than any other socio-material assemblage. The third [...] has been the redistribution of subjectivity as something that 'does not live inside, in the cellar of the soul, but outside in the dappled world'. (Whatmore, 2006: 603)[2]

We can conceive of Hall's evolving representation of Cumbria as a gradually increasing qualification of the descriptions of cultural geography offered by Whatmore and a growing manifestation within representation of the materialist preoccupations that are offered in the passage above. The earliest and most lyrical of her novels, *Haweswater* is also the most thorough in its investigation of Westmorland as a cultural landscape. Hall writes of Janet, who at various points in the novel functions as a synecdoche for Mardale more broadly, that '[t]he seasons of the farming community have structured her knowledge so that a margin of fell or common land does not exist without agricultural references' (Hall, 2002: 112). In other words, the cultural practices of the Westmorland farmers have played a critical role in shaping not just the landscape they inhabit but also the conceptual apparatus that they use to make sense of that landscape. To mobilize Whatmore's terminology, Janet is the foremost member of her cultural group and it is the close relationship between this cultural group and the landscape in which they live that allows Hall periodically to represent her pre-diluvian Westmorland setting in a pictorial idiom. From the vantage point of her classroom, for instance, Janet 'gaze[s] out of the smeared window panes to the fields and the fells beyond the school gates' (Hall, 2002: 17), in a passage that can easily be made sense of in terms of what Williams describes as 'separation and observation'.

Yet, even within her debut Hall begins to move away from this cultural understanding of landscape – away from the 'in-here' of subjectivity that lends much pastoral literature its lyrical personae – and towards a more complex position where the dichotomy between subject and object becomes indistinct, and the landscape less conceptually 'knowable'. The phytomorphic image that concludes *Haweswater* is where this aspect of the novel becomes most visible. The lyrical aspects of the text enabled by Janet's focalizing perspective are upset by a fabular conceit that sees this character fused uneasily with the landscape that she had previously helped the reader to make sense of. In keeping with the tricky temporality of the text, however, the displacement of the knowing subject is foreshadowed much earlier on. From the novel's opening pages, the fells are represented as somewhere the subject may easily encounter its existential limit and be rendered object. On their upper crags, snow forms 'unstable bridges over nothing but air' (Hall, 2002: 8); a little later, the annual melt is described as a cataract into the inhabited valleys below that is 'bitter, acid cold' and contains 'all the breaking soul of winter, thousands of dying flakes in one long, moving water-coffin' (Hall, 2002: 74). It is not obvious, in passages such as these, that the 'in-here' resides in the human and the 'out-there' in the landscape. Indeed, the two are frequently alloyed to a point of near indistinction: at another early point in the narrative, Janet's knowledge of the landscape is described as being 'as unconscious and simple as the mechanism of breathing' (Hall, 2002: 12), implying an emergent pre-conceptual or non-representational understanding of space. While Hall's debut does evidence an interest in the cultural geography of place, from its opening pages she offsets this geography by maintaining a focus on Janet's 'bodily involvement' with her home, which to her is 'a sacred place [...] a holy land', which 'reforge[s]' her each year: 'Her body chemistry alters as the terrain decomposes, turns, begins again' (Hall, 2002: 112). She may be among the last of Mardale's farmers, but throughout the text her characterization prefigures the arboreal transformation that takes place at the novel's conclusion, anticipating the 'valley of broken water [...] and living earth' (Hall, 2002: 236) that will remain upon her death, and through which her roots will grow.

Thus, in some respects *Haweswater* does indeed reflect the kind of geography Walezak writes of: one shaped by the social practices of the agricultural community whose inundation Hall describes, as well as the discursive practices that have produced the popular understanding of Lakeland evidenced in Jack's (ironically) Romantic fondness for hiking and climbing. However, the novel increasingly eschews the conceptualization of landscape that follows from such a geography. In fact, part of the point of the novel seems to be to narrate the displacement not just of the Mardale farmers but also the cultural geography of which they were guarantors, and to imagine another kind of geography that calls into question what Jane Bennett (2010: x) describes as 'the onto-theological binaries of life/matter, human/animal, will/determination, and organic/inorganic'. Indeed, rather than a salvage geography that seeks to rescue the discursive processes by which an inert landscape is leavened and made lively by the representational capacities of a linguistically-endowed and culturally-situated subject, we can perceive in Hall's work something closer to the vital materialism described by Ingold, Whatmore, Bennett and other thinkers associated with the material turn. Hall's preoccupation with the dissolution of the subject is not a manifestation of the morbidity of her work but, quite to the contrary, its vitalism. While her protagonists might frequently encounter – indeed, be drawn towards – their existential limits, this is less an example of tragedy, pessimism or even nihilism than what Grusin (2015: xi) characterizes as 'resistance to the privileged status of the autonomous male subject' and an attempt to complicate or even 'refus[e...] such fundamental logical oppositions as human/nonhuman and subject/object'. And far from producing deathly landscapes, the curious result is that – to adapt Bennett (2015: 223) – in Hall's novels and short stories 'fleshy, vegetal, mineral materials are encountered not as passive stuff awaiting animation by human or divine power, but as lively forces at work around and within us'. More pointedly, Hall's preoccupation with the dissolution of the self, the problematization and ultimate obliteration of the lyrical persona and, finally, the reduction of the subject to the status of one object among many others constitutes a gesture beyond cultural geography's 'signature concerns with the politics of representation and identity' (Whatmore, 2006: 600). Cottrell (2019: 680) claims that, over the course of her career, Hall has frequently sought to move beyond an understanding of politics as 'the intense inhabiting of identity'. I would go further: Hall's North is where identity is dissolved or undone, and what is left is the bare fact of a body in space.

Becoming-Object

A notable example of this aspect of Hall's work arrives at the very end of *Haweswater*, when Isaac, the son of Jack and Janet, drowns while diving in the eponymous reservoir: 'He was [...] dead. He was home' (Hall, 2002: 260). But while this might seem to position Cumbria as a morbid geography, the latter is also represented as vital and promissory – even amid human death. This is especially noticeable in the title story of Hall's first collection of short stories. The beginning of

'The Beautiful Indifference' sees the protagonist carefully attending to her presentation as she awaits her younger lover, who is travelling up from London to meet her. The story is saturated with self-destructive imagery: within two paragraphs the protagonist is wondering whether the mechanism that prevents her from opening her hotel room window more than two inches is 'really designed to stop suicides' (Hall, 2011: 41). Moreover, it becomes clear in retrospect that her ritual of self-care is being performed not just in anticipation of sexual pleasure but also of the self-annihilation that will attend pleasure. Tellingly, this anticipation is communicated by focusing on the tactile aspects of an object reduced to substance and affect: 'Lipstick never lasted long when they were together; he would always kiss her just after she had applied it, as if he liked the smearing, viscous sensation' (Hall, 2011: 41). Thus, just as the story's setting – York, a city that is initially described as possessing a 'tight northern gentility' (Hall, 2011: 42) – rapidly unhinges itself over the course of the first section of the story, so the protagonist's early decorum and carefully arranged attire fall away as the weekend becomes a place where 'the difference between pleasure and discomfort' is far from clear (Hall, 2011: 65). At the end of the story, the protagonist drives back to the Cumbrian fells and we leave her parked among the mountains, fantasizing about her own end and wondering, 'What would they say about her attire, if they found her in the bracken' there (Hall, 2011: 65). The dominant note is melancholy as the protagonist thinks of her father living alone among the ruins of a marriage which, it is implied, ended in his wife's suicide. Foreshadowed since the story's opening moments, it becomes clear in the concluding passages that this is something that might yet claim the life of his daughter: 'After she had left the train station she had bought three packets of painkillers, from different pharmacies. It had been easy. Her mother had been the same age' (Hall, 2011: 64). We leave the protagonist as she opens the car door, apparently intent on slipping into the inscrutable darkness of the Cumbrian fells to become a curiously attired cadaver.

Yet, while the ending of 'The Beautiful Indifference' might appear gloomy, there is a strange charge that resists any attempt to understand it as merely nihilistic. The drive back across the Pennines is marked by the emergence of Spring:

> On the moorland the bracken was beginning to regenerate. Tight green spirals were coming up through the sea of dead stalks. The curled fronds looked ovarian. Like the illustration of these organs they had shown her to explain. Now the word and the picture and the bracken were the same somehow. (Hall, 2011: 63)

This is an exercise in meticulous ambiguity wherein the relationships between birth and death, fecundity and sterility, are compelled into a state of indeterminacy. There is an implication that the protagonist's confrontation with her own mortality – the suicidal musings that pepper the story from its opening pages – are in response to an unexpected diagnosis, but the condition itself is conspicuously unprovided. The word in question is probably 'cancer', but it could be 'polycystic', presaging infertility, or even 'ectopic', indicating a birth anticipated but denied. In any event, Hall refuses to specify: earlier in the story the protagonist's lover enquires, in a different context, about her 'condition', only for her to reply, 'pathological loneliness' (Hall, 2011: 55). And the effect is to confuse life and death, mortality and vivacity in such a way that the one easily begins to look like the other. A friend has mocked this liaison with a younger man when the protagonist 'probably [doesn't] have long left' to 'defer' what is ruefully characterized as the 'sacrifice' of reproduction (Hall, 2011: 44). And, as if to mock this friend in turn, the one sex act in the story that is described to its conclusion culminates in the lover withdrawing before he ejaculates, his semen described as 'less thick' and, by implication, that much less (re)productive (Hall, 2011: 56).

Instead, 'The Beautiful Indifference' identifies the very immediate physicality of the relationship – rather than what, according to the friend, it ought to produce – as what is most promissory about it. This is also communicated by the fact that the protagonist finds her lover's work as a junior doctor fascinating, where her own as a writer of fiction is represented as tedious. Books are like 'oubliettes' (Hall, 2011: 47), the abstract world of representation lonely and carceral. During a public event the evening prior to the beginning of the narrative, she confessed to her readership that she would 'much rather be doing something else. Including blowing things up' (Hall, 2011: 47). Representation, it is implied, is a suspicious sort of work: rather than the meticulous labour of fictive world-building, this writer prefers to reduce things to 'the tactile world, atoms' (Hall, 2011: 47). She expresses more interest in a magazine article about 'psychology and kinetics' (Hall, 2011: 48) than she does in the novel through which she is currently struggling. And what is her relationship with the junior doctor if not a tactile world of atoms and kinetics, resulting in intense psychological experiences? It is his physicality, the physicality of his work and of what they do together, that most excites her. His appetite – sexual and gastronomic – pleases her to behold. Hall spends a full paragraph describing in visceral detail his dissection and consumption of 'dense tissue' and habit of licking the blood from his knife, which is, paradoxically, likened to 'television footage of big cats picking up their cubs, lifting the slack bodies harmlessly between their teeth' (Hall, 2011: 53–4). The landscape into which the protagonist disappears at the end of the story most closely captures the ambivalent relationship between vitality and mortality articulated here. It is in such a landscape that the self reaches its end, but it is also where the protagonist, in becoming bodily, will also become what she seems to desire most: not a subject but an object among objects; an assortment of atoms among a sea of others; matter in the midst of a landscape that is both material and alive. This is a beginning as much as an ending, a pregnant moment as much as one that marks a dissolution into nothingness. Indeed, it is not no-*thing* but some-*thing* that is the product of the protagonist's expiry as a subject: her existence as an object.

Yet there is a rub here that goes beyond the uneasy way in which female sexuality, objecthood and objectification are connected in this story. As Hall (2011: 65) writes in the final line of 'The Beautiful Indifference', opening the car door and disappearing into the fells is 'like opening a book'; in other words, entering the oubliette. There are two ways of interpreting this moment. On one view, the oubliette is, precisely, the decentring or even displacement of the subject. The word derives from the French *oublier* or 'to forget', two archaic forms of the latter meaning '[t]o lose remembrance of one's own station, position, or character' and '[t]o lose consciousness' (*OED Online*, 2019: n.p.). However, given that the metaphor of the oubliette is, earlier in the story, likened to books – and thus, as I have suggested, to the conceptual processes by which the liveliness of matter is captured in and by representation – the fact that the end of the protagonist's status as knowing subject is characterized as a kind of *mise en texte* appears to confront us with the limits of Hall's material imagination. After all, she is a writer: representation is what she does. Another way of framing this problem is to ask, if 'the word and the picture and the bracken [are] the same somehow', is what they have in common the fact that they are *products* of representation or that they possess a common material denominator that precedes their existence *in* representation? By way of moving towards my conclusion, I want now to consider the implications of Hall's material imagination for her aesthetics through a discussion of her representation of the animal in the BBC Short Story Prize-winning fabulation 'Mrs Fox', in which a fantastical vulpine transformation produces a body whose vitality invites but also exceeds conceptual explanation. What I want to suggest finally is that Hall's understanding of the creatureliness of the material body makes visible the tension between matter and representation in a way that foregrounds the possibilities of her material imagination within the confines of mimesis.

Creaturely Aesthetics

The transformation of Sophia in 'Mrs Fox' is a signal example of this tension. The relevant passage evidences major formal hallmarks of such scenes throughout literary history: a shift in tone towards the fantastic, a conspicuous increase in the use of abstract language, a demonstrative manipulation of narrative time and a culminating moment that asks to be read as revelation. Hence the focalizing perspective begins by noting mundanely that '[s]omething is wrong with her face' (Hall, 2018: 9) and initially the details of the transformation are communicated using simple descriptive sentences of comparable length. But as a 'trick of kiltering light' begins to affect the beholder's vision, Hall's grammar becomes more elastic, her clauses less complete and more abstract as they run on asyndetically, one after another, until a paragraph break pauses time and grants us a new, settled but altogether strange vision of a woman turned into a fox: 'She stops, within calling distance, were he not struck dumb. She looks over her shoulder. Topaz eyes glinting. Scorched face. Vixen' (Hall, 2018: 9). The ostentatious style of the preceding paragraph has been leading up to this moment, something communicated in the way that Hall's use of a repetitious consonance – 'running [...] running [...] running' as the 'reddening sun' transforms the 'red of her hair' into the 'red of her fur' – opens up onto an instructive assonance: in certain northern English dialects 'fur' and 'hair' would be a full rhyme. But, tellingly, the moment itself teeters on the edge of cliché: the male observer 'struck dumb' by the amorous, animalcular gaze of a woman looking over her shoulder with piercing eyes is, after all, the stock-in-trade of a visual economy in which female sexuality is frequently aestheticized using the metaphor of the vixen. In fact, what is 'wrong' about the transformation in this story is that its result is not – or not only – an abstraction, a figuration or a form of speech, but an actual fox. As Hall writes at the outset of this passage, Sophia's 'bones have been re-carved', and once '[a]ll the vestiges [are] shed' what remains is not just the overdetermined image of the vixen, but also a 'sudden, brazen *object*' (Hall, 2018: 9, emphasis added) whose insistent materiality the protagonist struggles to reckon with over the course of the rest of the story.

Thus, even as she makes a striking resource of expressive language in 'Mrs Fox', Hall seems to suggest that what such language produces is not just metaphor but matter. More radically, by emphasizing the materiality of the vixen, not only its figurative potential as metaphor, Hall inverts the commonplace attribution of vivacity and complexity to the mimetic capacity of language on the one hand and the inertness and passivity that, on the other, tend to be attributed to the sheerly material. Initially, the protagonist mourns Sophia: on the journey back to their house he 'bears her like a sacrifice, a forest Pietà' (Hall, 2018: 11). The implication is that she is deceased, reduced from being to flesh, life to cadaver, as in the numerous works within the stated genre of Christian art (foremost among them Michelangelo's *Pietà* of 1498–9). And the characterization of her body as being like that of Christ, cradled in his mother's arms after his crucifixion, lends an appropriate affective charge to the episode – pity – while promising that out of this death will emerge the new dematerialized life of the Spirit. Yet there is a keen irony here. Unlike Christ, whose body disappears in the midst of his resurrection and ascent to the immaterial realm of heaven, Sophia's new body remains stubbornly present. And though as she is carried home '[s]he is calm; she does not struggle' (Hall, 2018: 10), once there she is anything but inert. As soon as her bearer's grip weakens, 'she jumps, her back claws raking his forearm. She holds still a second or two, shakes, then goes into the kitchen, directly […] and jumps onto a chair next to the table' (Hall, 2018: 11). Hall thus offsets the 'confusion' and 'fugue' that follow immediately after the transformation of Sophia with the protagonist's 'acute discerning' of the 'spectacular evidence' that is the sheer material fact of the fox (Hall, 2018: 12). Unlike the polished marble figure of a pitiable, post-Passion Christ, moreover, this fox is anything but inert.

As the story develops, it maintains this characteristic tension between figure and matter, representation and reality, echoing the vixen-as-metaphor in drawing attention to Sophia's 'smoky, sexual' smell, '[t]he bend in her hind legs [… and] full, shapely thighs' while allowing these sexual metaphors to become entangled in and upset by the fox's material animality (Hall, 2018: 12). The most visceral example of this arrives when, searching for her one night, the protagonist 'treads in something slightly crusted and yielding' (Hall, 2018: 12). The detail is disgusting insofar as it refers to the product of the most private of bodily processes; at a more comical level, the scenario is also a spectacular transgression of the rules that attend such processes within even the most open and intimate domestic arrangements. More subtly, however, the conspicuously metonymic function of this detail also seems designed to upset any straightforward sense that the fox *stands* for something else. Here as elsewhere in this distinctly fabular narrative, Hall deploys what Roman Jakobson (1958: 92) famously identifies as the predominant method of 'the so-called "Realistic" trend' to undermine any reassuring reduction of the fox to metaphor.

And, as 'the grisly aroma of what he has trodden in rises to his nose' (Hall 2018: 12), she pushes her point home. The bathetic juxtaposition of astonishing, apparently magical transformation and the queasy, quotidian embarrassment that attends scraping excrement from one's foot is encapsulated in her telling choice of adjective. The aroma is 'grisly' not primarily in the *Oxford English Dictionary*'s sense of ß'[c]ausing horror, terror, or extreme fear', but rather in the dialectal sense – still common in northern England – of 'ugly' (*OED Online*, 2019: n.p.). And, as Gretchen E. Henderson suggests, one of the functions of ugliness is to adulterate or contaminate the aesthetic in a way that makes holistic understandings of beauty impossible:

> If we follow Aristotle's or [Leon Battista] Alberti's belief that a beautiful object bears coherence in totality (a sense of ideal form with a distinct boundary between itself and the world), then ugliness and its ilk carry something more ambiguous and less coherent, excessive or in a state of ruin. (Henderson, 2015: 10)

In this respect, the excrement in 'Mrs Fox' represents a material remainder that refuses to allow the protagonist to treat Sophia's transformation as the miraculous creation of a self-referential mimetic whole. It undermines the consolatory explanation that artifice would otherwise allow; it limits the protagonist's attempts to aestheticize his wife (as vixen, as *pietà*) and forces him instead to acknowledge the ways in which the excessiveness of matter undermines his attempts to use an existing conceptual apparatus to arrange his experiences within a representational whole.

A pithier way of expressing this is to say that, in 'Mrs Fox', the fox gives the lie to the vixen. It is the object that undermines the symbol, whose imperfection is, in turn, used to emphasize a material remainder, to remind us of the fact that matter will always exceed our attempt to capture it in language. Quoting Tom McCarthy in the course of critiquing his 2005 novel *Remainder*, Walter Benn Michaels writes:

> The attraction of the blank, of the sheerly material, is that it 'resists' our mappings, it doesn't allow us to 'impose' our 'readings of the land', and so, if you're a writer, it provides a model for 'the moment when

[…] language threatens (or promises) to become illegible'. For such a writer, it's not just that matter matters, it's that the matter that matters is language'. (Michaels, 2015: 77)

The last claim may be applicable to McCarthy's work, but not to Hall's, because while Hall's novels and short stories are certainly preoccupied with the 'sheerly material', they treat the latter as anything but 'blank'. What seems to be attractive about matter is, for Hall, its disobedience. And this disobedience – what Bennett (2010: 1) calls 'the negative power or recalcitrance of *things*' (emphasis added) – alerts us to an important characteristic of her work insofar as the relationship between the material and the conceptual is concerned: namely, its scepticism towards the transcendence of the former by the latter; that is, the idea that what we think of as material is anterior to and determined by the conceptual.[3]

Indeed, it is in relation to this story that we can apprehend most clearly how Hall's aesthetics displace the concept of the human by lending it an aspect of what Pieter Vermeulen (2015: 55) calls 'creatural life'. In a conceit that echoes a formal strategy frequently deployed by J. M. Coetzee (Vermeulen's subject), the narration of 'Mrs Fox' becomes more and more intensely bounded within the protagonist-focalizer's experience even as this character grows increasingly aware of his peripherality and even irrelevance. The result – one, I would suggest, common to much of Hall's work – is to expose to the story's readers that 'it is a crucial aspect of their condition that they remain riveted to cultural forms that can no longer defend them' from '*ontological vulnerability*' (Vermeulen, 2015: 55, 56, emphasis in original). The cultural form that interests Vermeulen is the novel, but I would suggest that for Hall it is, more broadly, the representational means by which we make sense of the material configuration of our bodies and the spaces in which they are located. Because, as I have suggested over the course of this chapter, for Hall it is not only the type of life we label 'sentient' that deserves to be described using Bennett's (2010: xi) fabulous phrase 'quirky stuff'. In fact, what is vital about the animal in 'Mrs Fox' is not so much the fact that it *is* alive but rather that it is both adamantly material and comically indifferent to the protagonist's attempts to make sense of it. And herein lies the basis for understanding how Hall's vitalism far exceeds the narrow confines of 'life' and arises wherever matter manages to exceed conceptual explanation and resist the deadening tendency of representation to capture, clarify and categorize.

The final location of some remainder that is located *in extremis* and is vital, extant, *there*, which attests to our finitude and our 'ending unfinished' is repeated across Hall's work: indeed, as I have suggested, it is written into the very landscape of her fiction. It is manifested in the titular creature of 'Mrs Fox', the cadaver that outlasts 'The Beautiful Indifference' and the oak tree which, at the conclusion of *Haweswater*, renders Mardale both vital and haunted, alive in the very midst of its desolation. In *The Wolf Border* it can be seen in Rachel's son, who 'draws the eye, for no reason, like a newly unwrapped gift' (Hall, 2015: 259). As so often in Hall's work it is manifested in animals: in the wolves that slip out of their enclosure at the end of *The Wolf Border* but also, in 'Bees', in the red fox – another fox, another 'unapologetic [...] little hunter' (Hall, 2011: 83). And it is there in *How to Paint a Dead Man* when Susan discovers that '[her] body will keep explaining to [her] how it all works, this original experiment, this lifelong gift' (Hall, 2009: 285). But it is perhaps most readily perceptible in that most common substance, blood: that symbol of vitality which is not itself alive, which stubbornly confronts us with both our reddish anatomy and our finitude. In Hall's work the key images are often sanguinary. This much can be seen in a notable section heading of *The Wolf Border*, where Hall (2015: 189) suggests that 'we are all red on the inside'. Blood is the very stuff of life: a recent 'biography' of the substance (Hill, 2013) makes clear the popular resonance of this truism. And, etymologically, it is the Proto-Celtic word for this substance – *īsarnom* – that lends us, via the Old English *īsern* and Middle English *iren* a byword for all that is *there*, all that will remain despite our attempts to explain it. As Hall (2015: 79) states in another chapter heading from the same novel, 'everything tends towards iron'.

Acknowledgement

I would like to thank my colleague Benjamin Garlick, who played a significant role in the production of this chapter by directing me to the theoretical and critical literature on the material turn.

Notes

1. This aspect of the NNW is evidenced in the British subtitle of George Monbiot's *Feral: Searching for Enchantment on the Frontiers of Rewilding* (2013; in its paperback reissue subtitled, more soberly, *Rewilding the Land, Sea and Human Life*).
2. Whatmore is quoting Bruno Latour's (2002) essay 'Body, Cyborgs and the Politics of Incarnation' at the end of this passage.
3. In this respect, it evidences a suspicion of one of the most fundamental metaphysical dualisms of modern Western philosophy, between thought or idea (the Cartesian *res cogitans*) on the one hand and, on the other, matter or body (*res extensa*). Discussing Hall's 2004 novel *The Electric Michelangelo*, Ashley Orr (2017: 108) argues that 'Hall's depiction of bodies, and, chiefly, freak or non-normative bodies, is far more reflective of the fluid, unbounded body of the Middle Ages than the restricted body of modernity'. On the basis of what I have argued in relation to 'Mrs Fox', we might add animal bodies to Orr's list.

Works Cited

Bennett, J. (2010) *Vibrant Matter: A Political Ecology of Things*. Durham, NC: Duke University Press.

Bennett, J. (2015) 'Systems and Things: On Vital Materialism and Object-Oriented Philosophy', in R. Grusin (ed.) *The Non-Human Turn*, pp. 223–39. Minneapolis: University of Minnesota Press.

Cottrell, A. (2019) 'The Power of Love: From Feminist Utopia to the Politics of Imperceptibility in Sarah Hall's Fiction', *Textual Practice* 33(4): 679–93, DOI: 10.1080/0950236X.2017.1371218

Davidson, P. (2005) *The Idea of North*. London: Reaktion Books.

Gifford, T. (1999) *Pastoral*. London: Routledge.

Grusin, R. (2015) Introduction, In: Grusin, R. (ed.), *The Nonhuman Turn*. Minneapolis: Minnesota University Press.

Hall, S and Hobbs, P. (2017) 'Introduction', in S. Hall and P. Hobbs (eds) *Sex and Death*, pp. 1–3. London: Faber.
Hall, S. (2002) *Haweswater*. London: Faber.
Hall, S. (2009) *How to Paint a Dead Man*. London: Faber.
Hall, S. (2011) *The Beautiful Indifference*. London: Faber.
Hall, S. (2015) *The Wolf Border*. London: Faber.
Hall, S. (2018) *Madam Zero*. London: Faber.
Henderson, G. (2015) *Ugliness: A Cultural History*. London: Reaktion Books.
Hill, L. (2013) *Blood: A Biography of the Stuff of Life*. London: Oneworld.
Huggan G. (2016) 'Back to the Future: The "New Nature Writing", Ecological Boredom, and the Recall of the Wild', *Prose Studies* 38(2): 152–71, DOI: 10.1080/01440357.2016.1195902
Ingold, T. (2007) 'Materials Against Materiality', *Archaeological Dialogues* 14(1):1–16.
Jakobson, R. (1958) *Fundamentals of Language*. The Hague: Mouton.
Latour, B. (2002) 'Body, Cyborgs and the Politics of Incarnation', Sweeney, S. and Hodder, I. (eds) *The Body*. Cambridge: Cambridge University Press.
Lilley, D. (2016) 'Unsettling Environments: New Pastorals in Kazuo Ishiguro's *Never Let Me Go* and Sarah Hall's *The Carhullan Army*.' *Green Letters* 20(1): 60–71, DOI: 10.1080/14688417.2015.1123103
Macfarlane, R. (2016) *Landmarks*. London: Penguin.
Michaels, W. (2015) *The Beauty of a Social Problem: Photography, Autonomy, Economy*. Chicago: University of Chicago Press.
Monbiot, G. (2013) *Feral: Searching for Enchantment on the Frontiers of Rewilding*. London: Penguin.
Orr, A. (2017) 'Inked In: The Feminist Politics of Tattooing in Sarah Hall's *The Electric Michelangelo*', *Neo-Victorian Studies* 9(2): 97–125.
OED Online (2019) Oxford University Press, December.
Purkis, J. (2014) *A Preface to Wordsworth: Revised Edition*. London: Routledge.
Thrift, N. (2008) *Non-Representational Theory: Space, Politics, Affect*. London: Routledge.
Vermeulen, P. (2015) *Contemporary Literature and the End of the Novel: Creature, Affect, Form*. London: Palgrave Macmillan.
Walezak, E. (2018) 'Landscape and Identity: Utopian/Dystopian Cumbria in Sarah Hall's The Carhullan Army', *Critique: Studies in Contemporary Fiction* 60(1): 67–74, DOI: 10.1080/00111619.2018.1479242

Whatmore, S. (2006) 'Materialist Returns: Practising Cultural Geography in and for a More-Than-Human World', *Cultural Geographies* 13: 600–9.
Williams, R. (1975/2016) *The Country and the City*. London: Vintage.
Wilson, E. (1999) 'Feminist Science Studies', *Australian Feminist Studies* 14(29): 7–18.

NOTES ON CONTRIBUTORS

Chloé Ashbridge is a Lecturer in Modern and Contemporary Literature at Newcastle University, having completed her PhD at the University of Nottingham in 2021. Her research primarily concerns the interdependence of British literary culture and politics, with a particular emphasis on representations of Northern England. She is currently writing her first monograph, *Rewriting the North: Contemporary British Fiction and the Politics of Devolution* (Routledge, 2023), which examines the extent to which twenty-first-century fiction about the English North imagines democratic alternatives to the centralised British state form. Additional publications include a forthcoming book chapter on the millennial novel and neoliberal culture in *Locating Classed Subjectivities* (Routledge, 2022), and an article on Brexit fiction in the *Open Library of Humanities* (2020).

Alexander Beaumont is Senior Lecturer in Literature and Politics at York St John University. He is the author of *Contemporary British Fiction and the Cultural Politics of Disenfranchisement* (2015) as well as essays and book chapters on a wide range of postwar and contemporary British writers.

Elke D'hoker is a Professor of English Literature at the University of Leuven. She has published widely on contemporary British and Irish fiction, with a focus on the genre of the short story. Her most recent monograph is *Irish Women Writers and the Modern Short Story* (2016).

Notes on Contributors

Melanie Ebdon is a Senior Lecturer in Literary Studies at Staffordshire University. Her research interests are in the contemporary novel, with emphasis on ecocriticism and the posthuman. Her teaching at undergraduate and postgraduate levels covers these areas as well as postcolonial studies, magical realism and Gothic fiction.

Francesca Pierini is Adjunct Lecturer in English at University of Basel. Forthcoming publications include 'Michel Foucault and Edward Said: The Knowledge of Power and the Foundation of Colonial Discourse Analysis' (J.Vrin); 'Roma Spelled Backwards: Love and Heterotopic Space in Contemporary Romance Novels Set in Italy'.

Natalie Riley is a doctoral candidate and postgraduate organizer of the Institute for Medical Humanities Network at Durham University. Funded by the Wellcome Trust, her project explores the mind sciences and the contemporary novel. She has publications forthcoming in the *Journal of Literature and Science* and *BMJ: Medical Humanities*.

Pieter Vermeulen is an associate professor of American and Comparative Literature at the University of Leuven. He is the author of *Romanticism After the Holocaust* (2010), *Contemporary Literature and the End of the Novel: Creature, Affect, Form* (2015), and *Literature and the Anthropocene* (2020).

Emilie Walezak is a Professor of contemporary British literature at Université de Nantes. A specialist of contemporary British women's writing, she has devoted several articles to the works of Angela Carter, A. S. Byatt, Sarah Hall, Rose Tremain and Jeanette Winterson. She is the author of *Rose Tremain: A Critical Introduction* (2017).

Index

allegory 23, 59, 129, 141, 167
ambiguity 20, 105, 142, 210
Anthropocene 22, 35, 39, 74, 110, 119
Aristotle 56, 66, 74, 215
  'Great Chain of Being' 56
  'Scale of Nature' 57
  zoē 66, 73
Atwood, Margaret
  Handmaid's Tale, The 13
  Maddaddam 36
autodiegetic narration 13
Barker, Pat 12
Barth, John
  'The Literature of Exhaustion' 38, 53
BBC National Short Story Award 18–19, 167
biological materialism 89
biology 40, 78, 85, 89, 92–96, 169
Boxall, Peter 78
Bracke, Astrid
  Climate Crisis and the 21st-Century British Novel 26, 51, 53
British Antarctic Survey 33
Byatt, A. S. 78
Carter, Angela 20, 58, 75

Cencrastus 129
Christian, Barbara 34
Clancy, Kate 18
cli-fi 31, 36, 52n.1
Coetzee, J. M. 216
Coleridge, Samuel Taylor 49
Copernicus 35
Cornwall 136
Cumbria 9, 15, 24, 29, 98, 121–122, 125, 127, 132–134, 136, 138, 149–153, 158–159, 162–163, 166, 168–171, 198–199, 202, 205, 208, 219
Dainotto, Robert M. 174–175, 191–192
  Europe (In Theory) 174
Darwin, Charles 35, 97
Dawkins, Richard 78, 97
  Selfish Gene, The 78, 97
death 18, 27, 65, 74, 77, 88, 90, 96, 98, 219
deconstructing individualism 39
deforestation 51
'dignity of labour' 11
doppelgänger 182
dystopia 9, 14–15, 71, 103, 129, 134, 149, 153, 155, 161

Eagleton, Terry 53
ecocentrism 33–39
ecocriticism 22, 35, 67
ecofeminism 150–151, 157, 161, 163, 168–169
ecological disaster 55
ecology 31, 37, 43, 117, 135, 155
economy 112, 114–115, 169, 213
ecosophy 34, 37, 39
ecosystemic health 38
Edge Hill University Short Story Prize 18
egalitarian counterculture 13
embodiment 23–24
'end of history' 12, 14
England 8–10, 23–24, 105, 117, 121–129, 131, 133–138, 140–142, 144–148, 149, 152–154, 156, 167, 191, 196, 198, 202, 215, 221
Englishness 24, 124, 130–131, 134–135, 145–148
Enlightenment 175
Feder, Helena
  Oxford Handbook of Ecocriticism, The 38, 53
Fellini, Federico
  I Vitelloni 180
feminism 7, 9, 20, 24, 26, 34, 122, 150–151, 154–159, 164, 168–169, 197
First World War 102, 125, 165
Foucault, Michel 114, 184, 188, 191
Garnett, David
  Lady into Fox 22, 57–63, 74
Generation X 33
Guardian 18, 26–28, 148, 170
Hall, Sarah

awards
  BBC Short Story Award 17–19
fiction
  Carhullan Army, The 5, 7, 9, 13–14, 24, 27–29, 31–32, 37, 42, 53, 55, 97–98, 103, 105, 107, 119, 121–122, 124, 126, 131, 133–134, 142, 147, 149, 153–155, 159–160, 162–164, 170, 219
  Daughters of the North 13
  Electric Michelangelo, The 5, 7, 11–14, 20, 27–28, 43, 48–49, 53, 55, 101–103, 119, 218–219
  Haweswater 5, 7–10, 12–13, 24, 27, 31, 38, 44–45, 47, 49, 53, 55, 97, 99–104, 107–109, 116–117, 119, 121, 124–127, 131, 140, 147, 149, 152, 154–155, 158, 160, 162–163, 165, 170, 200–202, 204, 206–208, 217, 219
  How to Paint a Dead Man 5, 7, 15–16, 23–24, 27, 38–39, 42, 44–45, 49, 51, 53, 77–98, 79–80, 89–90, 92–93, 96, 98, 102–104, 119, 173–174, 176, 188–189, 192, 198, 200, 217, 219
  Wolf Border, The 5, 7, 16–17, 23, 27, 29, 37, 44, 46, 50–51, 53, 55, 77, 79, 88–89, 92–93, 95–96, 98, 100–102, 104–105, 107,

Index

109, 111, 113, 115–119, 122, 124, 127–131, 133–142, 144–145, 147, 149, 153, 155–156, 159–160, 162–163, 166–167, 169–170, 198–199, 201, 217, 219
short fiction
'The Agency' 70–71
Beautiful Indifference, The 17, 20, 64, 68, 70, 209–211, 217
'Bees' 55–76, 63–76, 217–220
'Butcher's Perfume' 17, 20, 49–50, 63, 65, 68, 71
'Goodnight Nobody' 18, 64, 72
'The Grotesques' 19
'Later, His Ghost' 19, 21, 50–51, 66, 72–73
'Live That You May Live' 19
'Luxury Hour' 18, 33
'M' 19
Madame Zero 5, 18, 26–27, 31, 54, 56–57, 64, 69, 74
'Mrs Fox' 7, 17–18, 21–22, 31, 37, 45, 55–56, 58–60, 62–64, 66, 69–72, 167, 212–213, 215–218
'The Nightlong River' 64, 68, 71–72
'Orton' 19
'She Murdered Mortal He' 17, 64–65, 68
'Sudden Traveller' 19, 21
Sudden Traveller 19, 21
'Theatre Six' 18
'Vutjärvi' 18
'Who Pays' 19

'Wilderness' 21
with Peter Hobbs
Sex & Death 18, 27–30, 65–76, 74–76, 77–98, 90–98, 98
Hegel 175
Herman, David 56, 66
heterogeneity 57
historical fiction 10, 14
history 1, 10–14, 19, 31, 34, 39, 42, 46, 146, 150, 164–165, 167, 169, 175, 188, 191–192, 195, 212
Holyrood 130
hooks, bell 34
humanism 56, 65
Hunter, Megan 36
hybridity 40, 57, 73
idealism 40, 45, 144
individualism 22, 39–42, 44, 52
industrialism 31
infidelity 41
intertextuality 81, 128–129
Italy viii, 15, 39, 173–176, 178, 183, 186, 188–192, 222
Johnson, Daisy
Fen 21
Kafka, Franz
'In the Penal Colony' 13
Metamorphosis 57
Kay, Jackie 20
Kennedy, A. L. 20
Lake District 9, 25, 32, 109, 158, 162, 164, 169, 196, 199, 202
Lanchester, John
Capital 15
Land Reform Act 154
landscape 8–9, 17, 25, 39, 43, 81,

225

83, 88, 103–104, 108, 117, 124–125, 132–134, 138–140, 142, 144, 150–151, 157–166, 168–169, 185, 196–202, 204–207, 211, 217
Latour, Bruno
  'Body, Cyborgs and the Politics of Incarnation' 218–219
law 116, 125, 152, 154–155, 169
Lawrence, D. H. 20
Lea, Daniel 25, 32, 41, 55, 79, 126, 166
Lefebvre, Henri 24, 150–151, 156–157, 160, 162–164, 170
Lessing, Doris 20
Leuven 2, 8
lyricism 25, 83, 191, 203–204, 206, 208
Macfarlane, Robert 202–203, 219
  Landmarks 203, 219
magical realism 37
Margin Call (film) 112
Marxism 150–151, 157
material imagination 196–197, 212
materialism 20
  of the body 31–32
material process 13
McCarthy, Cormac
  Road, The 36, 50
McCarthy, Tom vi, 6, 25n.1, 27, 32, 215
  Remainder 215
McEwan, Ian 78
McGregor, Jon 6, 21, 25, 32, 36
  This Isn't The Sort of Thing That Happens to Someone Like You 21
Mediaeval literature 57
memory
  cultural 36, 163
  genotypic 36–37, 39, 41, 52
  personal 36
metafiction 20
metamorphosis 22, 31, 57–61
  human–animal 63
metanarratives 34
metonymical linking 63
minimalism 20
Mitchell, David 15, 36
  Cloud Atlas 15
Modern Fiction Studies 33, 54
modernity 10, 12
  positivistic cultural idealism of 40
Monbiot, George
  Feral: Searching for Enchantment on the Frontiers of Rewilding 148, 218–219
Morandi, Giorgio 15
Morton, Timothy
  Hyperobjects: Philosophy and Ecology after the End of the World 34, 54
motherhood 20, 23, 44, 46–47, 58, 87, 92–94, 96, 102, 105, 157
Mozley, Fiona 36
Nairn, Tom
  Break-Up of Britain, The 122, 148
National Health Service (NHS) 105, 111–112
natural selection 78, 85, 93
nature 21–24, 31–36, 38–44, 48–49, 56, 58–59, 61,

65, 77, 79–81, 83, 88, 91,
  95–96, 99–100, 102–104,
  106–113, 115–116, 131–
  132, 144, 151, 156–158,
  160–161, 175, 186, 189,
  195, 197–201, 203, 205
neo-Darwinism 78, 85, 94
neoliberalism 23, 102, 112–116
neo-materialist 56, 65
neo-Romantic 196, 198, 202
New Edinburgh Review 129
New Statesman 18
Nietzsche, Friedrich 22–23, 55,
  55–76, 57, 67–68, 70–75,
  192
  freedom as responsibility 70
  gift-giving 23, 57, 70–73
  Thus Spake Zarathustra 67,
    70, 75
  Übermensch 67, 70
Norris, Christopher 53
O'Hagan, Andrew 25n.1, 32
othering 61
Ovid
  Metamorphoses 57
pandemic 153
parody 20
pastoral 9, 24–25, 32, 36, 104,
  124, 130–137, 142–145,
  150, 157, 159–160, 163,
  165, 196, 198–201, 204,
  206
patriarchal
  authority 62
  worldview 63
personal
  memory 36
Piaget, Jean 177, 183–184, 186,
  191
Pick, Anat 66

politics 8, 46, 124, 129–130,
  133–134, 137, 139, 145,
  151–152, 160, 208
polyphonic form 15
posthumanism 22, 57, 65, 73, 85
posthumanist 38, 56, 65, 67
postmillennial fiction 51
postmodernism 6, 15, 32–34,
  38–39, 40, 43, 49, 52–54,
  57, 79
postmodernity
  capitalist logic of 40
post-pastoral 24–25, 131–136,
  142, 144, 150, 157,
  159–160, 163, 165, 196,
  199–200, 204
pregnancy 11, 41–42, 42, 44,
  46–48, 50, 58, 69, 72, 87,
  92, 111, 143, 154–155,
  155, 160–161, 168–169,
  183, 211
psychological realism 21
radicalism 14
Radical Scotland 129
reproduction 88
rewilding 7, 24, 88, 112, 115,
  127, 129, 131, 134–135,
  137–142, 144, 202
romance 10, 45, 183
Romantic poetry 32
Scotland 100, 116–117, 122–123,
  128–130, 136, 141, 145–
  146, 148, 153–154, 160
Second World War 39, 43, 109
self
  animal 17, 44, 46, 48
  authentic 43
  inauthentic 43
  selfhood 37, 42

sensuality 60, 132, 163
Serres, Michel
Incandescent, The 36
sex 16, 44–47, 70, 77–78, 89–92, 143, 156–158, 164, 167, 184, 210
Shakespeare, William
Tempest, The 50, 72
short fiction 2, 6–8, 15–22, 31, 33, 45, 50, 53, 56–57, 65, 73, 77, 167
Simpson, Helen 20
Smith, Ali 15, 20, 25, 32
Hotel World 15 25n.1
Smith, Zadie 6, 15, 20, 28, 78
social constructedness 20
sociology 169
Soper, Kate
What is Nature? 35, 54
Spanos, William 181, 193
spatialization 24
speculative fiction 14, 149
suicide 210
Sunday Times EFG Private Bank Short Story Award 18
Swift, Graham 78
tableau vivant 181
tattoos 12, 43, 101
techno-scientific world 52
transgender age 47
trans-species relationality 56
USA 43, 100–101, 103, 118
Vice 7, 10, 18, 29, 81, 98
victimhood 62
Waugh, Patricia 53
Westall, Claire
and Gardiner, Michael
Literature of an Independent

England 123, 148
Wheeler, Wendy 53
White, Hayden
Tropics of Discourse 177, 193
Whyte, Christopher 129
Williams, Eley
Attrib. and Other Stories 21
Wilson, E. O. 78
Winterson, Jeanette 13, 78
Written on the Body 13
Wolfe, Cary 66
Wolf of Wall Street, The (film) 112
Wood, Lucy
Sing of the Shore, The 21
Wordsworth, William 162, 165
Yellowstone National Park 112

www.ingramcontent.com/pod-product-compliance
Lightning Source LLC
Chambersburg PA
CBHW051611230426
43668CB00013B/2069